Blended Learning in English Language Teaching: Course Design and Implementation

Edited by Brian Tomlinson and Claire Whittaker

ISBN 978-0-86355-706-4

© **British Council 2013** Brand and Design/C526
10 Spring Gardens
London SW1A 2BN, UK

www.britishcouncil.org

Contents

Foreword

John Knagg OBE

In recent years it has become the norm for publishers to include technology-mediated elements alongside traditional printed materials in their publications. At institutional level teachers increasingly include technology-mediated learning in their courses. Yet there has been relatively little discussion and writing about the principles that should be applied in blending elements which use technology with more traditional face-to-face teaching in the same course. This volume is a contribution to such a discussion.

While many of the principles will be applicable to wider educational contexts, this publication is rooted in the world of English Language Teaching (ELT). It is centred on the description of 20 real case studies from around the world in the areas of English for Academic Purposes (EAP), English for Specific Purposes (ESP), teacher education and general English as a Foreign Language teaching. These case studies are prefaced, interspersed, and followed by exploration of the concepts of blending and interpretation, and discussion of the application of the concepts in the case studies. We hope that this approach will make the book practically useful as a self-study guide to the area for educationalists, and also be a source of inspiration for students on teacher training and academic courses in the areas of education, language teaching, and applied linguistics.

The genesis of this book was an original idea by Claire Whittaker to build on her practical and academic work in blended learning in ELT and to generate principles that would be of real practical help to course designers, which in turn would lead to more effective learning and satisfied students. Brian Tomlinson has edited the papers and added his own commentaries to make the final product a true collaboration between the two editors and the authors of the case studies. The British Council thanks them all, and hopes that you find the book both useful and enjoyable.

John Knagg OBE
Head Research and Consultancy,
English and Examinations, British Council

Acknowledgements

We would like to thank the British Council for inviting us to edit this volume and in particular Adrian Odell for being informative, patient and supportive throughout the process of its development. We would also like to thank Melissa Cudmore at the British Council for encouraging Claire to submit the proposal for this publication back in April 2011, and John Knagg who drove the process forward. Thanks also go to John for his advice and support along the way.

We would like to express our gratitude to all the authors of chapters in this volume for their hard work, their willingness to consider constructive criticism and their speed in completing revisions.

Brian Tomlinson and Claire Whittaker

Preface

Claire Whittaker

When I took up the post of Training and Systems Manager with the British Council in Bosnia and Herzegovina in 2003, little did I know that it would result in the proposal for this publication, or better still that the proposal would be accepted. The rest, as they say, is history. Prior to this post my experience of using computers in English Language Teaching (ELT) had been somewhat limited. I had first used them as a teacher in 1997 when I had access to a computer room with an internet connection and a limited number of CD-ROMs. I used them for extension activities to complement my face-to-face sessions by providing the students with additional controlled practice of the grammar or vocabulary that had just been presented.

This experience piqued my interest in using computers for language teaching and learning and so I read articles and books on computer-assisted language learning (CALL) in an attempt to find practical suggestions for their successful integration and usage. I also attended courses on information and communications technology (ICT) in ELT, as it was then referred to, in my quest for knowledge. This interest and limited amount of experience and knowledge did not, however, adequately prepare me for my role as Training and Systems Manager in which I 'inherited' a blended learning course that was being used to teach English to military personnel in the armed forces of Bosnia and Herzegovina. It was also the first time that I had heard the term 'blended learning' and I have to say, initially, I was sceptical about its longevity; how wrong I was.

One of my first tasks in the role was to carry out a study into delivery of the English language in the 13 geographically spread language centres, to become familiar with their working practices. This highlighted the numerous significant inconsistencies in the language delivery between them, for example the length of courses, the timetables and syllabi. I felt that we needed to standardise the language delivery, not only to be able to manage the system more effectively, but also to provide each student with comparable learning opportunities. At this stage I was unconcerned by the fact that these courses employed a blended learning approach rather than a traditional face-to-face approach. Nor did I realise what it entailed or appreciate its potential. My outlook was soon to change though, once I began to understand the complexities of designing, or in my case redesigning, a blended learning course.

Only once the course content and length had been standardised did I begin to question the blend itself and to consider the design, not only at lesson level but also at course level, for the first time. Unwittingly this resulted in what was to become a three-year iterative redesign process. Throughout this time I continued to read articles and books on what was now largely being termed blended learning, but was frustrated by the lack of advice on the principles and practicalities of blended learning course design (above lesson level) and descriptions or studies of blends in ELT contexts.

To address this deficit I proposed this publication so that ELT practitioners could formally share descriptions of their blends from a range of ELT courses (English for Academic Purposes, English for Specific Purposes, teacher training, and general English) and contexts, which most likely had been designed in relative isolation. It is hoped that these blends can be replicated or adapted by other practitioners to suit their particular teaching and learning contexts. In addition, the guiding principles and practical considerations that shaped the blends will hopefully help practitioners achieve a principled approach to blended learning course design in their contexts.

Introduction

Claire Whittaker

Introduction

This introductory chapter will provide an overview of blended learning by considering where the term originated and by seeking to define what it means in corporate training, higher education and English Language Teaching (ELT). It will also establish why these three sectors employ a blended learning approach, outline a number of the models they use for blending, and consider the ways in which blended learning is effective. It will conclude with a summary of why getting the blend right is important, whilst acknowledging that this is not an easy task and that further research on blended learning is required in ELT contexts.

Blended learning – a definition

The term blended learning originated in the business world in connection with corporate training (Sharma and Barrett, 2007), then was employed in higher education (MacDonald, 2006) and lastly it appeared in language teaching and learning. It is difficult to say exactly when the term became commonplace in ELT although I suggest that it coincided with the publication of Sharma and Barrett's book *Blended Learning* in 2007. Although I had first heard the term in late 2003, the publication of this book cemented its place in ELT in my mind.

There is some debate as to whether it was simply the term that was coined in corporate training, rather than the actual approach to teaching and/or learning, with Oliver and Trigwell (2005) arguing that it was simply the term. Masie, in Bonk and Graham (2006: 22), appears to agree with this by boldly stating that 'all learning is blended learning'. In the same article, Masie (2006: 22) goes on to state that '...blended learning has always been a major part of the landscape of training, learning and instruction' and encourages us to think back to our college days when the pedagogical approach involved a number of different teaching strategies. Personally I feel that the adoption of the term symbolises a change in what is being blended nowadays, as it signifies the inclusion of computer technology providing online or offline activities and materials in the mix, rather than implying this is a wholly new approach to teaching and learning.

Despite its widespread use in corporate training, higher education and latterly the field of ELT, many claim that the term blended learning is difficult to define (Kerres and de Witt, 2003; Oliver and Trigwell, 2005; Sharpe et al. 2006; MacDonald, 2006; Sharma and Barrett, 2007), the difficulty arising because consensus has not been reached on one definitive definition. Furthermore, the term itself has not been fully adopted in these three settings, where it is at times referred to as 'hybrid or mixed learning' (Stracke, 2007: 57); 'e-learning' (Shepard, 2005) or 'b-learning' (Banados, 2006: 534). Smith and Kurthen (2007) in Gruba and Hinkelman (2012: 4) attempt to differentiate some of these terms by using percentages (see Table 1).

Table 1: Taxonomy of terms related to blended learning (Smith and Kurthen 2007, in Gruba and Hinkelman 2012: 4)

Term	Definition
Web-enhanced	Subjects that make use of a minimal amount of online materials, such as posting a syllabus and course announcements.
Blended	Subjects that utilise some significant online activities in otherwise face-to-face learning, but less than 45 per cent.
Hybrid	Subjects in which online activities replace 45–80 per cent of face-to-face class meetings.
Fully online	Subjects in which 80 per cent or more of learning materials are conducted online.

In relation to ELT, Dudeney and Hockly (2007) also use percentages to differentiate between online courses, blended language learning courses, and face-to-face language learning courses with additional online materials (for more information see section below entitled 'ELT blends'). Despite these perceived differences I would argue that many of the terms are synonymous and that in ELT 'blended learning' is the term most commonly used to refer to any combination of face-to-face teaching with computer technology (online and offline activities/materials).

From a corporate perspective, Singh and Reed (2001: 1) describe blended learning as being 'a learning program where more than one delivery mode is being used with the objective of optimizing the learning outcome and cost of program delivery'. They do not expand on what the delivery modes are in their definition, yet a more explicit definition from Valiathan (2002: 1) suggests they may include 'face-to-face classrooms, live e-learning, and self-paced learning'. Reid-Young (n.d.) also provides us with a set of delivery modes which differ slightly from Valiathan's (2002) and 'may range from classroom sessions to mentoring arrangements or the support of a subject matter expert in the same office or area.'

With reference to blended learning in higher education, it has been defined as: 'a combination of technology and classroom instruction in a flexible approach to learning that recognises the benefits of delivering some training and assessment online but also uses other modes to make up a complete training programme which can improve learning outcomes and/or save costs' (Banados, 2006: 534).

Here the lead modes are identified as technology and classroom instruction, although interestingly the 'other modes' are not specified. This reference to 'other modes' is of personal interest as the blend I helped redesign had three modes, face-to-face, computer, and self-study that took place in self-access centres situated in the same building as the classrooms and computer rooms, which in my opinion is atypical of most blends described in ELT. Similar definitions to Banados's (2006) are given by de Gregorio-Godeo (2005) and MacDonald (2006).

Unlike the definitions found for blended learning in corporate training and higher education those provided in relation to language teaching and learning seem rather succinct. Neumeier, for example, describes blended learning in relation to her study as being 'a combination of face-to-face (FtF) and computer assisted learning (CAL) in a single teaching and learning environment' (2005: 164). Stracke (2007: 57) offers an almost identical definition in her study into why learners leave blended learning courses (for further details on this study see section below entitled 'Why a good blend is important'): 'blended language learning (BLL) – a particular learning and teaching environment, that combines face-to-face (f2f) and computer assisted language learning (CALL). In this instance, the "blend" consisted of learners' independent self-study phases at a computer, with a CD-ROM, and traditional f2f classroom learning.'

Dudeney and Hockly (2007) and Sharma and Barrett (2007), who to ELT practitioners are probably the most widely recognised authors on the topic, provide remarkably similar definitions to Neumeier (2005) and Stracke (2007) with the only slight difference concerning the reference to the CAL(L) mode. Sharma and Barrett (2007: 7) substitute it with 'technology': 'Blended learning refers to a language course which combines a face-to-face (F2F) classroom component with an appropriate use of technology. The term technology covers a wide range of recent technologies, such as the Internet, CD-ROMs and interactive whiteboards'. Dudeney and Hockly (2007: 137) also avoid using the term CAL(L) and substitute it with 'online' delivery instead: '[Blended learning] is a mixture of online and face-to-face course delivery'. However, they go on to widen this description by stating that 'in some situations the digital element is done offline with a CD-ROM'.

Why employ a blended learning approach?

According to Dewar and Whittington (2004) differences have been identified as to why the corporate sector and academic sector introduced blended learning solutions. For the corporate sector the results from an online survey reported by Sparrow in Dewar and Whittington (2004: 5) list the following reasons: ability to match learning styles (80 per cent); individually tailored solutions (70 per cent); improve the learning rate (62 per cent); exploit the investments they have already made in re-usable training resources (59 per cent); shortage of time to use purely classroom events (57 per cent). They do not elaborate on the content of this list, nor provide evidence that any of the reasons given are actually valid and not purely assumptions, for example. improving the learning rate.

There are commonalities between the above list and that of Singh and Reed (2001). They identified four benefits to using a blended learning solution a couple of years before the above study was conducted, which were: improved learning effectiveness; extending the reach; optimising development cost and time; optimising business results (reduces travel costs and learning objectives are obtained quicker). Sharma and Barrett (2007) also refer to the cost-saving element of blended learning with reference to the business world, as work time is not sacrificed for training and furthermore travel costs are negated. In addition to cost savings they also emphasise the 'convenience' of blended learning courses as students can study when they want, at the speed they want. It would appear that cost saving was an important driver for change in the move towards blended learning in the business world and we will see the same is also true in the academic sector.

With regard to the academic sector both Dewar and Whittington (2004) and Graham (2004) cite Osguthorpe and Graham's (2003) six suggested reasons: pedagogical richness; access to knowledge; social interaction; personal agency (i.e. learner control and choice); cost effectiveness; and ease of revision. Interestingly the term 'pedagogical richness' is used rather than 'pedagogical effectiveness'. Presumably what is meant by the phrase is the variety of different pedagogical approaches that can be incorporated in a blend, rather than if they are effective or not. Marsh et al. (2003) also mention the use of a blended learning solution to reduce costs in higher education, as well as improving the teaching of large groups. Likewise, MacDonald (2006: 22) refers to ever expanding classroom numbers as well as 'changes in student demography ...a growth in part-time study' as reasons for incorporating 'online media'. Sharpe et al. (2006) found from their review of blended e-learning in the tertiary sector that 'although the rationales for blended e-learning were highly contextualised and specific to each institution they included: flexibility of provision, supporting diversity, enhancing the campus experience, operating in a global context and efficiency'. Nicolson et al. (2011) reiterate Sharpe et al.'s (2006) findings regarding flexibility as they claim that, in a UK context in particular, there is a demand for flexible learning opportunities that has been driven by social, cultural, economic and political changes.

Graham (2004: 7) and Graham et al., as quoted in Stracke (2007: 59), have condensed these lists down to three main reasons in higher education which are: improved pedagogy; increased access/flexibility; and increased cost effectiveness. Improved pedagogy is often cited as a reason for implementing a blended learning approach yet most authors do not expand on the subject. Indeed the phrase 'pedagogy before technology' (Beetham and Sharpe, 2007: 3) has been used by some reflective practitioners to stress the need to adopt technology for pedagogical reasons and because it adds value to the teaching rather than simply as an add-on.

Improved pedagogy is also claimed with reference to blended learning in ELT although once again little appears to have been written on the subject apart from such general statements as: 'blended learning seeks to combine the best of the taught element of a course with the benefits of technology, so that, the argument goes, better learning outcomes can be achieved' (Sharma, 2007). In a different publication Sharma and Barrett (2007: 7) are slightly more explicit and say 'we will assume that you have decided to incorporate technology into a language course for a pedagogical reason, and by doing so, you are adding value to the teaching'. Sharma and Barrett (2007) also believe that cost, convenience and being able to work in your own time and at your own pace, the reasons they cite for blended learning being employed in the business world, are also applicable to language teaching. Based on my experience I have to question Sharma and Barrett's (2007) belief that cost effectiveness is a valid reason for employing blended learning in ELT because the initial financial outlay for hardware and software is usually prohibitively expensive, without counting the ongoing maintenance, replacement and upgrading costs. Admittedly though, this will depend on the design of the blend and context as learners may be expected to use their own computers rather than having them provided.

Interestingly, in a later publication Hockly (2011: 58) does not repeat the reasons given by Sharma and Barrett (2007) for employing blended learning in ELT but provides us with three additional ones:

- Learners' expectations – learners nowadays expect technology to be integrated into their language classes, (although I believe this to be highly context dependent).

- Flexibility – learners expect to be able to fit learning into their busy lives, especially professional adults and university students.

- Ministry of Education (or similar) directives – in some contexts teachers are expected to offer blended learning options.

Different blends

Once the initial decision has been taken to employ a blended learning approach then the next stage is to determine the blend itself and according to Reid-Young (n.d.) and with reference to the business world there are a multitude of models to choose from. Ultimately this means that there is '...no single optimal mix. What configuration is best can only be determined relative to whatever goals and constraints are presented in a given situation' (Shaw and Igneri, 2006: 3). Graham (2004) also makes this point, stressing the 'infinite' number of design solutions and their context dependency. This latter point is particularly important as to my mind the context is all, and a thorough analysis of it is vital, as is identifying your drivers for change before developing a blend.

This variety of options can both pose problems and provide opportunities for course designers. Rossett et al. (2003) exemplify this by quoting part of a conversation overheard at a conference in which a delegate, who accepts blended learning as a concept, questions *what* to blend and *how* to blend. The authors offer three guidelines to consider for achieving successfully blended combinations: stability and urgency (how long will the course content be valid for and how long do the course planners have to develop the course?); touches and cost (are face-to-face sessions necessary or will technology alone be sufficient and how much are people or organisations willing to invest in terms of time and money?); learning resources and experience (will the learning resources endure the test of time or will they quickly become redundant and how will the learners work, e.g. alone, at home, at work?).

Valiathan (2002) identifies three models, as opposed to guidelines, that have emerged from the business world namely: skills-driven, attitude-driven and competency-driven learning. Reid-Young (n.d) provides us with three more 'typical' examples: course model, reference-based learning and pre-assessment model. There is no apparent overlap between the models, and as with the guidelines they do not appear to have an immediate bearing on language learning and teaching.

Dewar and Whittington (2004) reviewed Valiathan's (2002) model along with two others in their literature review, but ultimately preferred Hocutt's (2001) ideas on blended learning. Rather than identifying the individual components of a blended learning model, Hocutt (2001) takes a different perspective and proposes four ways in which the components should interact with each other. Dewar and Whittington (2004: 10) list these as:

1. blended learning components have a mutual awareness of each other

2. components are consistent in language, style and technique

3. components need to be appropriately redundant; (which I interpret to mean they can be optional or compulsory)

4. components have to seamlessly transition from one component to another.

Graham (2004), like Reid-Young (n.d.) above, also refers to 'course level' blending, (in addition to activity level, programme level and institutional level), claiming it to be one of the most frequently used. However, the definition given is slightly different to that of Reid-Young (n.d.) in that it 'entails a combination of distinct F2F and CM [computer-mediated] activities'. Reid-Young suggests that the students only meet for face-to-face sessions if it is possible. Both authors though credit it with being commonly used in universities. According to Graham's (2004) definition of a 'course model' this would appear to me to be the most commonly used model in ELT too.

There are six major issues that Graham (2004) believes a course designer should consider prior to designing a blended learning course:

1. The role of live interaction – how necessary is the face-to-face component of the course? Certainly in ELT it would seem fair to say students place a great deal of emphasis on this element of the course and that it is vital.

2. The role of learner choice and self-regulation – how much guidance should the students be given when it comes to choosing the type of blended learning course they participate in, in particular in relation to university courses?

3. Models for support and training – how to support and train the instructors and students in a blended learning environment plus provide technological support.

4. Finding balance between innovation and production – and how to do so in a cost effective way.

5. Cultural adaptation – should the materials be adapted to suit local audiences?

6. Dealing with the digital divide – can affordable blended learning models be developed to accommodate those at the bottom of the socio-economic spectrum?

ELT blends

With reference to ELT, Sharma (2007) suggests 'for blended learning to be effective the two component parts should be integrated with the technology complementing and not replacing the efforts of the teacher'. In the same article Sharma (2007) provides us with five practical examples of how to follow the guidelines at lesson level:

1. A teacher prepares their students for giving a presentation firstly by discussing the topic, then by allowing them to practise fixed phrases using a CD-ROM, then by watching a video on presentations, before finally they prepare and deliver their own.

2. Using a class wiki (a website on which the pages can be edited by the users, e.g. Wikipedia).

3. Creating a podcast (a computer audio file).

4. Downloading Moodle software (a platform) to support a virtual learning environment (VLE).

5. Setting up a blog (an online diary).

To achieve a 'principled approach' to blended learning Sharma and Barrett (2007: 13–14) suggest the following four guiding principles:

1. Firstly, they advise you to 'separate the role of the teacher and the role of technology' as the roles are not interchangeable, but they are complementary.

2. Secondly, 'teach in a principled way' using means that best suit the learners' needs, i.e. pedagogically driven.

3. Thirdly, 'use technology to complement and enhance F2F teaching' meaning that the two modes should complement each other, and which seems to suggest that face-to-face is exclusively the lead mode.

4. Lastly, 'It's not so much the program, more what you do with it' (Jones, 1986). To illustrate this final statement three examples of how to use a CD-ROM are given, from an individual using it alone at home, to follow up practice in self-study or at home after a class, to actually using it in class as part of a presentation.

Dudeney and Hockly (2007: 138–139) refer to a blended learning course where 75 per cent is delivered online and 25 per cent face-to-face in their list of three possible course designs for online learning in language learning environments:

- A 100 per cent online language learning course, where the course is not unlike a coursebook online.

- A blended language learning course, where 75 per cent is delivered online and 25 per cent face-to-face.

- A face-to-face language learning course with additional online materials, where online tools are used to support and extend face-to-face lessons.

Personally, I question how helpful it is to define the terms using percentages as I believe these figures can vary widely from those given yet still the course could be defined as a blended learning course. Moreover, I would refer to their third example as a blended learning course too, with the difference being that the face-to-face mode is the lead mode in that blend. This, it could be argued, highlights the difficulty of defining blended learning that was referred to earlier in this chapter. Prior to designing the three online learning courses listed above Dudeney and Hockly (2007) recommend that the designer answers a series of questions which operate rather like a checklist. These are categorised under five headings: delivery mode, task design and materials, learners, teachers/tutors, assessment and evaluation.

Banados (2006) provides us with an extremely informative study into a working model of blended learning used to teach English in the Universidad de Concepción (UdeC), Chile, which considers the design at course level rather than lesson level. The course is comprised of four elements, which are:

a. Learners' independent work on a dedicated platform with the UdeC English Online software.

b. Face-to-face English as a foreign language (EFL) classes led by teachers who are also students' online tutors.

c. Online monitoring carried out by these teachers.

d. Weekly conversation classes with native speakers of English.

Unfortunately the study does not specify how these elements are integrated, or the percentage of time spent on each. It does, however, detail the three factors that were taken into consideration prior to designing the course which were: the fact that students prefer face-to-face classes to online learning; the programme's focus was to teach listening and speaking; and that in addition to English, students needed to learn ICT.

Is blended learning effective?

Two of the reasons for employing a blended approach that are given above are improved learning effectiveness and cost effectiveness, but how effective really is blended learning? And in what ways is it effective? According to Dewar and Whittington (2004: 5) there is a good deal less literature on the effectiveness of blended learning than there is defining it and suggesting how to implement it. They state that 'There is some anecdotal evidence about how well participants liked blended learning and many articles outlining the costs saving associated with integrating technology. There is also a growing literature base about the learning outcomes achieved through using various types of technology. The biggest challenge is finding studies that specifically address blended learning, as opposed to the use of technology alone.'

In the context of higher education, Dziuban et al. (2004: 5) found that their blended learning courses had 'the potential to increase student learning outcomes while lowering attrition rates in comparison with equivalent fully online courses' and that blended learning results 'in success and attrition rates [were] comparable to the face-to-face modality for all ethnicities.' A study conducted by Harker and Koutsantoni (2005: 197) also found that 'the blended learning mode was much more effective in student retention' than the distance learning mode on their English for Academic Purposes (EAP) programme, 'whilst students' achievement levels were similar in both groups' as were their satisfaction rates.

A number of studies investigate learners' attitudes towards blended learning. Leakey and Ranchoux (2006: 367) found that 'the students in large measure found the blended CALL experience a positive and motivating one and tended towards preferring [this approach] to the traditional classroom based learning.' Brett's (1996) results showed 'strongly favourable attitudes; that learners believed they could learn effectively from multimedia and that it delivered a high quality independent learning experience.' Lin (2003: 1) also found that the majority of Taiwanese EFL learners 'had a positive attitude towards the use of multimedia resources in their language programme, appreciating, in particular, opportunities to practice and extend their language abilities by surfing the internet, to take laboratory-based listening tests via a test analyzer, and to record and save their own writing and to make use of multimedia resources for developing their reading skills'.

In response to the question 'Is the TELL [technology-enhanced language learning] course an effective curricular design for achieving second language development?' Adair-Hauck et al. (1999: 293) found that 'after carefully monitoring and assessing language skills in listening, speaking, writing and cultural knowledge, we recognise that the TELL course was indeed effective in helping our students learn French. Its strength in this particular instructional context appeared to be in writing and its weakness in speaking.' Contrary to their findings regarding speaking, Banados's (2006: 542–543) results indicated 'a remarkable improvement in speaking skills' in addition to 'important improvements in all the skills, especially in listening, pronunciation, vocabulary and grammar' in a study carried out with students on an English programme in a Chilean University.

Little more appears to have been published on the effectiveness of blended learning since Dewar and Whittington (2004) noted the lack of literature on the subject. A number of studies have been conducted on learners' attitudes, concluding that they are positive towards the integration of CALL or multimedia. At tertiary level evidence indicates that blended learning may improve student retention rates. However, there is little evidence available to suggest that blended learning is pedagogically effective even though 'improved pedagogy' is often cited as a reason for blending. This leaves me questioning if this is a primary consideration for many of the educational providers for adopting a blended approach especially at tertiary level and maybe increasingly so in the EFL sector, or if flexibility and cost, to provide a competitive edge in a global market, are the real drivers for change.

Clearly more studies to investigate the pedagogical effectiveness of blended learning in ELT are required that provide us with empirical rather than impressionistic evidence in its favour. However, Salaberry (2001: 52) cautions that 'a healthy dose of scepticism about the pedagogical effectiveness of many current technological tools appears to be well justified if one considers the perhaps overly enthusiastic reaction to previous technological breakthroughs' such as language labs, cassette recorders, and computer-assisted instruction.

Why a good blend is important

Getting the blend right is important as ultimately it can affect student retention, as Stracke's (2007) study revealed. The results indicated that students left the blended learning course they were attending for three main reasons:

- 'a perceived lack of support and connection/complementarity between the f2f and computer-assisted components of the "blend"
- a perceived lack of usage of the paper medium for reading and writing
- and the rejection of the computer as a medium of language learning' (Stracke, 2007: 57).

Two out of the three of these reasons Stracke (2007) gives are referred to in other articles on blended learning. The 'complementarity' aspect is one that Sharma and Barrett (2007) emphasise as being important in their guidelines and principles for blended learning. It certainly heavily influenced the design of my blend (see Chapter 16), resulting in the content of the three modes being linked to a relatively high degree either by grammar, vocabulary or topic. Also Banados (2006) found that students preferred face-to-face to online learning, so designed her course accordingly. This was also true in my context which meant that the face-to-face mode was the 'lead' mode in the blend. This would seem to indicate that getting the balance right in terms of the percentage of time spent on each of the modes, and the way they are integrated, is significant.

Regardless of the variety of suggested models, guidelines and frameworks authors seem to be united in the belief that 'determining the right blend isn't easy or to be taken lightly' (Hofmann, 2001: 3). This is a sentiment shared by both Sharma (2007) and Neumeier (2005). There are also words of warning from Sharma and Barrett (2007: 8) that 'a blended learning course run without a principled approach may be seen as an "eclectic" blending together of course components, and can end up as rather a mish-mash ... learners may suffer "the worst of both worlds"'. Graham (2004) also notes that a blended learning course can also be comprised of the least effective modes just as easily as the most effective modes, although this is rarely acknowledged.

Studies conducted into how best to integrate technology into the curriculum appear to confirm the viewpoints in the preceding paragraph. For example Gillespie and McKee's (1999: 452) study concluded that 'CALL – and other technology – should not be brought in piecemeal, but be part of a structured learning environment'. A similar study conducted by Adair-Hauck et al. (1999: 269) also proposed that their results 'may be interpreted that it is both feasible and desirable to integrate in principled ways TELL activities into the language learning curriculum'.

Later studies continue to reach the same conclusion. Yang (2001: 91) summarised a study into web-based research projects at university level by observing that 'computer learning networks have the potential to empower students in well-designed learning environments'. The implication being that 'effective implementation of technology is not accomplished just as an 'add-on' to existing tools, it must be synergised into the language learning environment with the support of surrounding educational systems' (Yang, 2001: 92). Articles by Lin (2003) and Fujieda and Matsuura (2005) also reiterate the importance of integration and Sharpe and Oliver (2007: 49) warn against treating technology as a 'bolt-on'.

However, 'there is, of course, no single perfect blend – the concept is grounded on the notion of flexibility' (Lamping, 2004: 7) and must surely be largely context dependent. Furthermore, developing a blend is an iterative process according to Beetham and Sharpe (2007: 8) who believe that 'effective designs will evolve only through cycles of practice, evaluation and reflection'. Rossett et al. stress that 'there's no cookbook for blends' (2003: 1) and state, with reference to the business world, that 'the topic cries out for empirical research'. In relation to ELT Neumeier (2005: 176) supports this statement and emphasises that 'further research is needed in order to enhance the quality of blended learning environments'. Westbrook (2008: 14) concurs, as to his mind most of the research on blended learning has been carried out in the tertiary sector and therefore there is a 'huge deficit in terms of research on using blended learning by individuals or small language schools'. It is therefore envisaged that the case studies in this publication will inform professional practice and enhance the theory of blended learning course design in ELT by adding to the rather limited current knowledge base.

References

Adair-Hauck, B Willingham-McLain, L and Earnest Youngs, B (1999) Evaluating the integration of technology and second language learning. *CALICO Journal* 17/2: 269–306.

Banados, E (2006) A blended-learning pedagogical model for teaching and learning EFL successfully through an online interactive multimedia environment. *CALICO Journal* 23/3: 533–550.

Beetham, H and Sharpe, R (2007) 'An introduction to rethinking pedagogy for a digital age', in Beetham, H and Sharpe, R (eds) *Rethinking Pedagogy for a Digital Age*. Abingdon, Oxon: Routledge, 1–10.

Brett, P (1996) Using multimedia: an investigation of learners' attitudes. *Computer Assisted Language Learning* 9/2–3: 191–212.

de Gregorio-Godeo, E (2005) *Blended Learning as a Resource for Integrating Self-Access and Traditional Face-to-Face Tuition in EFL Tertiary Education.* Available online at http://citeseerx.ist.psu.edu/viewdoc/download?doi=10.1.1.122.8123&rep=rep1&type=pdf

Dewar, T and Whittington, D (2004) *Calliope Learning: Blended Learning Research Report.* Available online at www.calliopelearning.com/wp-content/uploads/2012/08/blended.pdf

Dudeney, G and Hockly, N (2007) *How to... Teach English with Technology*. Harlow: Pearson Education Limited.

Dzuiban, CD, Hartman, JL and Moskal, PD (2004) *Blended Learning.* Available online at http://net.educause.edu/ir/library/pdf/erb0407.pdf

Fujieda, M and Matsuura, H (2005) *Japanese EFL Learners' Attitudes toward CALL.* Available online at www.econ.fukushima-u.ac.jp/~matsuura/lla.html

Gillespie, J and McKee, J (1999) Does it fit and does it make any difference? Integrating CALL into the Curriculum. *Computer Assisted Language Learning* 12/5: 441–455.

Graham, C (2004) *Blended Learning Systems: Definition, Current Trends, and Future Directions.* Available online at www.publicationshare.com

Gruba, P and Hinkelman, J (2012) *Blended Technologies in Second Language Classrooms*. Basingstoke: Palgrave Macmillan.

Harker, M and Koutsantoni, D (2005) Can it be as effective? Distance versus blended learning in a web-based EAP programme. *ReCALL* 17/2: 197–216.

Hockly, N (2011) Five things you always wanted to know about blended learning (but were afraid to ask). *English Teaching Professional* 75: 58.

Hocutt, R (2001) The Second e-Learning Wave. *Training Magazine* 38/9: 96.

Hofmann, J (2001) *Blended Learning Case Study.* Available online at www.pttmedia.com/newmedia_knowhow/KnowHow_Design/Instructional%20Design/iLive/Blended%20Learning%20Case%20Study.htm

Jones, C (1986) It's not so much the program, more what you do with it: the importance of methodology in CALL. *System* 14/2: 171–178.

Kerres, M and de Witt, C (2003) A didactical framework for the design of blended learning arrangements. *Journal of Educational Media* 28/2–3: 101–113.

Lamping, A (2004) *Blended Language Learning.* Available online at www.bbc.co.uk/languages/tutors/blended_learning/blended_learning_report.pdf

Leakey, J and Ranchoux, A (2006) BLINGUA. A blended language learning approach for CALL. *Computer Assisted Language Learning* 19/4: 357–372.

Lin, A (2003) An initial study on EFL Learners' attitudes towards multimedia application in language learning. *Teaching English with Technology* 3/2. Available online at www.tewtjournal.org/VOL%203/ISSUE%202/01_ANINITIALSTUDY.pdf

MacDonald, J (2006) *Blended Learning and Online Tutoring.* Aldershot, Hampshire: Gower.

Marsh, GE, McFadden, AC and Price, BJ (2003) *Blended Instruction: Adapting Conventional Instruction for Large Classes.* Available online at www.westga.edu/~distance/ojdla/winter64/marsh64.htm

Masie, E (2006) 'The blended learning imperative', in Bonk, C and Graham, C (eds) *Handbook of blended learning: Global perspectives, local designs.* San Francisco, CA: Pfeiffer Publishing, 22–26.

Neumeier, P (2005) A closer look at blended learning – parameters for designing a blended learning environment for language teaching and learning. *ReCALL* 17/2: 163–178.

Nicolson, M, Murphy, L and Southgate, M (eds) (2011) *Language Teaching in Blended Contexts.* Edinburgh: Dunedin Academic Press.

Oliver, M and Trigwell, K (2005) Can 'blended learning' be redeemed? *E-Learning* 2/1: 17–26.

Osguthorpe, RT and Graham, CR (2003) Blended learning systems: Definitions and directions. *Quarterly Review of Distance Learning* 4/3: 227–234.

Reid-Young, A (n.d.) *The Key to E-learning is B-learning.* Available online at www.hci.au/hcisite5/library/materials/B-learning.htm

Rossett, A, Douglis, F and Frazee, RV (2003) *Strategies for Building Blended Learning*. Available online at https://files.pbworks.com/download/P3s9Jzj67I/ablendedmaricopa/1240589/Strategies%20Building%20Blended%20Learning.pdf

Salaberry, MF (2001) The use of technology for second language learning and teaching: a retrospective. *The Modern Language Journal* 85: 39–56.

Sharma, P and Barrett, B (2007) *Blended Learning*. Oxford: Macmillan.

Sharma, P (2007) Try a blend that creates a new class of learning. *Guardian Weekly* (16 February 2007).

Sharpe, R, Benfield, G, Roberts, G and Francis, R (2006) *The Undergraduate Experience of Blended E-learning: a Review of UK Literature and Practice*. Available online at www.heacademy.ac.uk/assets/documents/research/literature_reviews/blended_elearning_exec_summary_1.pdf

Sharpe, R and Oliver, M (2007) 'Designing courses for e-learning', in Beetham, H and Sharpe, R (eds) *Rethinking Pedagogy for a Digital Age*. Abingdon, Oxon: Routledge, 41–51.

Shaw, S and Igneri, N (2006) *Effectively Implementing a Blended Learning Approach*. Available online at http://wvuheducation.com/LinkClick.aspx?fileticket=7Hhk4Bw4lyg%3D&tabid=148

Shepard, J (2005) An e-recipe for success. *EL Gazette* 312, December: 5.

Singh, H and Reed, C (2001) *A White Paper: Achieving Success with Blended Learning*. Available online at www.p2partners.co.uk

Stracke, E (2007) A road to understanding: A qualitative study into why learners drop out of a blended language learning (BLL) environment. *ReCALL* 19/1: 57–78.

Valiathan, P (2002) *Blended Learning Models*. Available online at www.purnima-valiathan.com/readings/Blended-Learning-Models-2002-ASTD.pdf

Westbrook, K (2008) The beginning of the end for blended learning? *IATEFL CALL Review*, Summer: 12–15.

Yang, SC (2001) Integrating computer-mediated tools into the language curriculum. *Journal of Computer Assisted Learning* 17: 85–93.

Part 1 – English for Academic Purposes

1

A collaborative online reading and research project

Jody Gilbert

Introduction

In general English for Academic Purposes (EAP) programmes, the overarching goal is to prepare non-native speaker students for the language demands and cross-cultural challenges of typical undergraduate coursework in English-medium post-secondary institutions. Today, this coursework includes an expectation that faculty and students will use a variety of technologies to support teaching and learning, including internet-based research sources.

This paper describes the conception and implementation of an EAP reading project designed to help students develop effective online reading and research skills. In addition to providing opportunities to practise traditional reading skills such as skimming, scanning, and critical reading, the project aims to help learners gain autonomous strategies for evaluating the credibility of online information. A student-centred, experiential learning approach to instruction framed the design. This required students to do most of the project work online, and involved a blend of face-to-face activity in computer labs along with out-of-class online collaboration.

Teaching context

The University of Lethbridge in Alberta, Canada, operates a small EAP programme for undergraduate-bound students who have not yet met the English language proficiency requirement for undergraduate admission. Completion of the Advanced level of the University's EAP programme is one option for satisfying this requirement.

The EAP programme has a modular structure consisting of four courses at three levels. Each course (Grammar, Reading, Writing, Communication) is normally taught by a different instructor, for five classroom hours each week. EAP semesters run three times per year, for 13 weeks, with class sizes generally ranging between ten and 18 students. Historically, the majority of students come from China, Korea, and Japan.

All EAP classrooms have networked computers and data projectors. The majority of students have their own laptop computers with wireless internet access. There is also excellent access to computer labs and networked computer stations throughout the campus. Hardware in the labs is updated annually, and all labs have data projectors and whiteboards. The university supports Moodle as its official online course management system.

Advanced level students are expected to demonstrate a high degree of autonomy when undertaking key tasks such as writing research papers and delivering presentations. In many of these assignments, students use internet-based information for content. My personal observations and evaluations of student work led me to research use of the internet by English as a Second Language (ESL) students, both in general and in my immediate teaching context.

Students in the Advanced Writing course often include internet-based references in their work. Sometimes this information is taken from religiously biased, commercial, or politically motivated websites, where more objective or neutral evidence was required for the assignment. In one instance, I observed a student who was searching for information on the website http://worldhealthorganization.com. The student believed that she was viewing the official World Health Organization website (http://who.int/en). She remarked that she had spent around 15 minutes exploring this commercial site before I approached her.

Teaching English for speakers of other languages (TESOL) researchers also recognise that students may require specific guidance on appropriate use of internet-based information to support academic study. For example, Hedge (2000: 215) remarks that problems are 'increasingly noticed by teachers as students access information on the internet' and that 'there are no gatekeepers here [on the internet] and users may need to evaluate information carefully'. Jarvis (2009: 51) questions whether EAP students are able to make appropriate and effective use of internet resources in their academic work. He writes, 'The notion of equipping learners for academic study raises specific challenges of e-literacy skills for non-native speakers (NNS) of English and it is by no means clear whether EAP providers are rising to this challenge'. Based on this evidence, I determined that my Advanced level students needed further guidance and preparation if they were to make properly informed decisions about the credibility and applicability of information they were finding on internet web pages. In response, I created the 'Online Reading and Research' project in the Advanced Reading course.

The Advanced Reading course curriculum is based on a core ESL reading text which is used for the length of the course, but the course instructor is free to choose further readings and activities to supplement the text. Key tasks and skills in the course include summarising, critical reading, reading strategies, and reading response. The activities in the project were created with these learning goals in mind.

Design and rationale

The design of the project was underpinned by the notion that the critical literacy and language skills which support effective online reading and research are probably best developed through student-centred experiential learning.

Experiential learning allows students to explore ideas from their own perspectives, building individual understanding of new ideas and information based on previous experience and knowledge. Many learning theorists reason that the current information-driven environment demands a student-centred, relevant, and engaging approach to teaching, wherein students are equipped with the dynamic skills and autonomous strategies for managing information in an increasingly complex and rapidly changing society.

Based on their study, Levine et al. (2000) conclude that an online networked reading environment can provide opportunities for authentic reading experiences, and is conducive to the development of critical reading skills. Slaouti (2002: 119) stresses the need for EAP learners to 'experience the texts that websites provide as part of a strategy to develop real world skills'. In order to build awareness and develop critical literacy skills for reading and researching online, a number of authors recommend having students work through web evaluation experiences (see Gardner et al. 1999; Kasper, 2000; Stapleton, 2005). Slaouti (2002) and Jones (1996, cited in Slaouti, 2002) recommend a constructivist, learner-centred pedagogical approach to developing critical literacy skills in learners, which can prepare them to work more effectively with constantly changing technology.

Miller et al. (2012: 184) note that a project-based learning approach '...lends itself to the use of new technologies because students can be encouraged to draw on a range of technological tools in order to research, present and share their projects'. My strong belief in the potential benefits of integrating technology into the project, and confidence with the technical aspects of campus resources (networked computer labs, data projectors, Moodle) led to a blended learning design. As determined by the pedagogical aims, the project necessarily involved student use of the internet to search for, read, and evaluate web-based information. In addition, the project required groups to post their initial summaries and evaluations on the Moodle forum. According to Garrison and Vaughan (2008: 24), such asynchronous text-based environments can decrease cognitive load and '...would appear to offer students a considerable advantage in processing information and constructing meaning'.

Moodle was already established as an online learning space in the course, serving administrative functions such as scheduling and posting of course grades, and hosting a variety of learning activities including links to interactive reading skill exercises and course vocabulary learning resources materials. The availability of well-equipped computer labs meant that induction and other initial online work could occur in a face-to-face setting during regular classroom hours. Groups could then do the project work outside of regular class time by using the online Moodle forums, which allowed students the flexibility to choose when and where they would contribute to their group project.

The project: preparation and induction

At the beginning of the Advanced Reading course, the class met face-to-face in the computer lab to take part in general induction activities on the Moodle website, such as navigating the site, accessing site resources, creating forum posts, and hyperlinking in forum posts. Students then regularly used the Moodle site to access course resources and activities. Specific preparation for the Collaborative Online Reading and Research Project occurred in the third and fourth week of the course and required a total of around five hours of computer lab class time.

Preliminary student-led discussions took place around the students' perceived benefits and pitfalls of internet use for research purposes, experiences and the nature of internet searches and reading online, and topics of interest for researching online. Groups of three students were formed based on shared research interests. When the online work began, carefully structured guidance was provided. Links to website evaluation guides were posted on Moodle, including the local University of Lethbridge Library (http://libguides.uleth.ca/content.php?pid=314580&sid=2576367), University of Alberta (www.library.ualberta.ca/instruction/science/evalweb.pdf), and University of California at Berkley (www.lib.berkeley.edu/TeachingLib/Guides/Internet/Evaluate.html) websites. The guides and checklists were reviewed with the class and groups used them to evaluate several web pages on the topics of 'immigration' and 'Martin Luther King.' The web pages were pre-selected to provide experiences with both reliable and unreliable information sources, and groups were asked to rate the information on each webpage as *unreliable, reliable,* or *highly reliable*, using the web evaluation tools provided earlier. Following this exercise, a class discussion allowed learners to reflect on and share their experiences. Next, each group developed research questions based on their shared interests, and conducted an internet search for one article related to their topic. Requirements for the project were introduced at the end of this session.

Transition to online collaboration

Groups transitioned to online work, and no further official classroom time for the project was scheduled. However, I did provide regular opportunities for students to ask questions or voice any concerns about the project. Each group was required to post brief summaries of around 150 words and critical webpage evaluations of eight different information sources on the web, related to the group topic/research questions. Groups were encouraged to complete full evaluation posts of any *unreliable* web pages they encountered, since it is in the process of doing so that they were most likely to develop the critical literacy skills needed to evaluate internet-based information sources. The minimum length of each sourced article was 1,000 words. Groups posted their summary evaluation submissions on the Moodle course forum, and included hyperlinks to the web pages they summarised and evaluated in each post. This allowed for quick user access to the web pages under scrutiny.

The first post was considered a 'practice post' and groups received extensive, detailed feedback from me in the form of a public reply on the forum. All class participants were able to see the work of other groups as it was posted and review my feedback posts on the work as well. Students were encouraged to post further comments or questions if desired.

Over the next five weeks, groups posted the remaining seven summary evaluations on the Moodle forum but received private feedback from me. At the end of the semester, each group delivered a ten to fifteen minute presentation, bringing the online phase of the project back into the classroom. The presentation included a step-by-step analysis of two of each group's evaluated web pages as they were displayed on-screen for the class, and a reflection on research activities, web page evaluation strategies, and collaborative processes involved in the project. A question and answer session followed each presentation.

Discussion

Internet searches and the summary and evaluation of web pages were the main tasks for this project. Feedback indicated that participants saw the online forums as a logical option for collaboration, and the transition to online work went smoothly. The content of the web page evaluation posts revealed that the students were focusing on relevant webpage features to judge reliability. I have used the project in other semesters with some slight modifications based on this feedback, and seen similar results. The blended design contributed to a positive and meaningful learning experience for the participants, and several students commented that assessing web pages for credibility was a new activity for them and they found the project useful:

> ...it was a good experience to learn how to evaluate web page. Before we learn it, I have never thought about the credibility of web pages. ...For our future study, evaluation is essential. Now, I always think and evaluate web pages before click them.

> Studying web sites evaluation and practising critical thinking was very useful and interesting.

> You gave us a chance to think critically and we achieved it unconsciously.

One student commented that her understanding began to change as she realised the relevance and importance of evaluating web-based information:

> Actually, at the beginning I did not know why I was doing the project. However, as the time went by and I started my research paper, I realized how important the skills of determining whether the website I am looking at is credible. The time spent for this project was absolutely worthwhile, for I was able to recognize whether a website can be used for my research paper almost at first look. I am pretty sure that I have gained a good strategy of finding reliable sources on the web.

Open classroom discussions and careful learner preparation in key aspects of the project probably provided motivation and contributed to the project's success. These aspects include induction, relevance of the learning aims, and the rationale for using online forums in the project.

A 'dry run' of the project tasks in a face-to-face setting was essential. For second language learners working online, a lack of confidence in language skills can be exacerbated by limited experience with technology, and this in turn can decrease motivation. Experts caution against introducing technology to the learning environment too quickly, and recommend sufficient scaffolding and close monitoring of student activity as technology is integrated into classroom activities (Ramachandran, 2004; Luzón-Marco, 2010). Coming into the project, students were already familiar with navigation and features of the Moodle course site. The project design included opportunity for participants to work together on structured tasks in a face-to-face setting before transitioning to online collaboration. Networked computer labs with data projectors provide the best support for this, as students can follow the teacher-demonstrated tasks on-screen and immediately attempt the tasks on their own computers.

The face-to-face induction sessions provided insight into the kinds of difficulties students might experience while working on the project tasks during the online phase. For example, students can find it challenging to deal with the overwhelming volume of information that is returned when conducting web searches, and an induction period provides opportunities to discuss effective search strategies before students tackle web searches on their own. In this project, I initially provided links to several different web page evaluation templates and asked students to choose the resource that they preferred. However, most students found the choice difficult, and wanted a recommendation instead. In my second experience with the project, I provided more guidance and structure here, making students aware of the different guides available, but recommending the *UC Berkley* site in particular, based on positive student feedback.

Another motivator for students was probably my effort to make clear links between the blended activities and learning aims, and the students' perceived relevance of those aims. An informal discussion at the start of the project revealed, as expected, that all students in the class regularly searched the internet for information to support their study. However, relatively few students reported that they normally questioned the credibility of the information on the internet. Some were quite surprised to be 'tricked' by the unreliable sites in the preparation tasks, and I believe this experience generated interest and motivation to learn.

The online user interface for collaboration was not complex, and user issues were minimal. There were no connectivity issues, or technical difficulties with Moodle. Some groups turned to additional technologies to facilitate collaboration, and reported using Skype, MSN, and web-based document storage in their work. Students cited collaborative challenges, including the sharing of workloads and group dynamics, but no students attributed these difficulties to the online mode of work. There were also no concerns about the time required to complete the project, even with the study load of three other Advanced level EAP courses.

The online phase of the project allowed group members flexibility in time and place of their work. Most importantly, the forums appeared to facilitate learning in important ways, although they were used mainly to display and share student work rather than as interactive discussion boards. The Moodle forums provided public evidence of the project work and teacher feedback, documenting individual and group learning as the projects developed. In turn, students had opportunities to learn from the work of their classmates. Several students commented that seeing the work of other groups on the forums motivated them to work harder to improve their own work. For example, one student wrote:

> ...I think model [sic] was good. We can see other groups' work. It motivated us to work harder than them. Furthermore, you can check everyone's work at the same time which was very convenient.

Conclusion

Students received course credit for their work in the Online Reading and Research project, based on a topic proposal and the summary evaluation posts. This no doubt contributed to their motivation to work online, but the class discussions and student feedback also indicated that students perceived immediate practical value and relevance in the project and the use of the Moodle forums to facilitate the group work.

For this particular EAP project, the use of technology is inextricably linked to the pedagogical aims and learner needs which inform those aims. Within the teaching context, face-to-face classroom time is quite limited and the time required for effective collaborative work on the project exceeds available classroom instructional hours. A blended design allows for a face-to-face induction period and ongoing instructor support, while providing flexible opportunities for learner reflection and online collaboration.

References

Gardner, SA, Behnham, HH and Newel, BM (1999) Oh what a tangled web we've woven! Helping students evaluate sources. *The English Journal 89/1*. Available online at www.jstor.org/stable/821354

Garrison, R and Vaughan, ND (2008) *Blended Learning in Higher Education*. San Francisco CA: Jossey-Bass.

Hedge, T (2000) *Teaching and Learning in the Language Classroom*. Oxford: Oxford University Press.

Jarvis, H (2009) Computers in EAP: change, issues, and challenges. *Modern English Teacher 18/2*. Available online at http://usir.salford.ac.uk/11266/1/METHJ2009.pdf

Jones, D (1996) *Critical Thinking in an On-line World*. Conference Proceedings, Untangling the Web, University of California. Available online at http://misc.library.ucsb.edu/untangle/jones.html

Kasper, L (2000) *Content-Based College ESL Instruction*. Mahwah NJ: Lawrence Earlbaum Associates.

Levine, A, Ferenz, O and Reves T (2000) EFL academic reading and modern technology: how can we turn our students into independent critical readers? *TESL-EJ 4/4*. Available online at www.tesl-ej.org/wordpress/issues/volume4/ej16/ej16a1/

Luzón-Marco, MJ (2010) Webtasks for learning professional and academic English: adapting the WebQuest Model. *CORELL: Computer Resources for Language Learning 3*. Available online at www.ucam.edu/corell/issues/MJLuzon2.pdf

Miller, L, Hanfer, C and Ng Kwai Fun, C (2012) Project-based learning in a technologically enhanced learning environment for second language learners: students' perceptions. *E-Learning and Digital Media 9/2*. Available online at www.wwwords.co.uk/rss/abstract.asp?j=elea&aid=4992

Ramachandran, S (2004) Integrating new technologies into language teaching: two activities for an EAP classroom. *TESL Canada Journal 22/1*. Available online at www.teslcanadajournal.ca/index.php/tesl/article/view/167/167

Slaouti, D (2002) The World Wide Web for academic purposes: old study skills for new? *English for Specific Purposes 21*. Available online at www.elsevier.com/locate/esp

Stapleton, P (2005) Evaluating web-sources: internet literacy and L2 academic writing. *ELT Journal 59/2*. Available online at http://eltj.oxfordjournals.org/content/59/2/135.abstract

2

Blended learning in English for Academic Purposes courses: A Nigerian case study

Peter A Aborisade

Introduction

When the blended learning project commenced in the Federal University of Technology Akure (FUTA), it was the blind leading the blind, a foray in the dark. Other than reading of computer assisted language learning (CALL) in the literature, none of us had first-hand experience of supporting learning with technology. Decisions were made ad hoc, and experiments carried out more in hope than in expectation. The curriculum was tinkered with from time to time. Progress was slow and challenging. The main challenges included the technical logistics of implementation and integration, as well as the academic issues of pedagogy. We did not have the advantage of learning from the experience of any institution in Nigeria; neither did we have support from any authority. Five years down the line, from a borrowed Web 1.0 of an external non-governmental organisation (the *ProjektHope*) we now have some Web 2.0 tools on our virtual learning environment (VLE). We started with one English for Academic Purposes (EAP) course and we now have six courses, EAP (2), Biology (1), Entrepreneurship (1), Computer Science (1) and Electrical Engineering (1). Uptake is expected to increase exponentially in a couple of years as we have formed a Blended Learning Research Group (BLRG) to provide training for the growing numbers of academic staff.

Context

FUTA is one of the few specialised universities in Nigeria, established in 1981. Like most universities in Nigeria, FUTA has a General Studies Unit, to cater for the arts and social science subjects with the aim of giving students of science and technology a balanced perspective of life. The 'Use of English' courses aim to remedy students' language shortfalls and assist their development of academic skills. All students take the in-sessional courses in the foundation year. Nigerian universities are low-resourced with the triple constraints of few teachers, large classes and grossly inadequate facilities. Enrolment continues to increase with freshmen now accounting for around 3,000 plus each year, but staff numbers have remained low, with facilities remaining inadequate.

The courses

The two EAP courses take place in the two semesters of the freshman year. Both courses are credit bearing and students need a pass grade in each one to graduate. Students come from various disciplines, including biological and physical sciences, and engineering. Class sizes range between 200 and 400 for each teacher, with each student receiving two contact hours a week. A course runs for about 13 weeks of a semester. In the first semester, course GNS 101 has the objective of equipping students with information literacy and study skills. Topics taught include: time management; study skills; scientific word formation; parts of speech; listening and lecture comprehension and note-taking/note-making. GNS 102 follows as an 'integrated reading and writing' course designed 'to equip students with skills in reading and writing in academic contexts and research skills.' The course covers topics such as introduction to reading for academic purposes, investigation and negotiation of meaning, critical thinking and teamwork skills development. The course culminates in writing a term paper after investigating a topical issue. At the end of the course students are expected to be able to read critically in academic contexts, raise questions, reflect on their learning processes and use basic research and internet skills.

The challenge

For the enrolled population, language teaching in the large classes remained a Herculean task. LoCastro (2001), among others, suggests that when a language class exceeds 15 in number problems arise, such as those of pedagogy, management and of the affective type, especially in a low resourced environment. In the last decade, the majority of students who enrol for university courses come with low English language proficiency on account of declining standards in pre-university education and the rising profile of Nigerian pidgin among young people. Observations and analysis of students' oral and written interactions show widespread use of pidgin and its interference in formal writing. An increasing number of youths, especially from the Niger Delta, have pidgin as their first language (Ihemere, 2006; Marchese and Shnukal, 1983).

For a language course, interaction is crucial. Therefore, the main driver of change to incorporating technology in our practice is pedagogic – the large class situation that made interaction in English, the target language (student–student, student–teacher), difficult, if not impossible. In class most students with difficulty in using English hardly spoke out but would communicate with peers in pidgin or their first language. With online discussions they would take time to compose whatever had to be said and struggle to construct their ideas in English, even if in poor English with traces of pidgin or mother tongue. Teachers were dissatisfied and frustrated with their practice in the face-to-face teaching-learning mode and felt a need for change, especially as students and core discipline colleagues ridiculed the programme for having little impact on students' English language proficiency.

All in the blend

Reports on the application of computer assisted language learning had opened the door to consideration of advances in e-learning applications. At FUTA, the first attempt was the borrowed Web 1.0 site whereby students were given access to online materials on HIV/AIDS for their term paper writing. The real attempt at applying learning technologies did not come until 2008 after a member of the teaching team had the opportunity, through the Commonwealth Academic Staff Fellowship, to attend the UK Subject Centre for Languages, Linguistics and Area Studies' e-Learning symposium at Southampton University. There, a presentation on using the wiki opened up a new vista. Relying on elaborations of the subject by Beatty (2003) and Dudeney and Hockly (2007), teachers took themselves through several sessions of professional development to decide what they needed to know and do, and how to get students using the wiki (Aborisade 2009). However, by 2009 the decision to adopt the Moodle VLE was taken as this was seen to offer a wider range of opportunities (https://futa.edu.ng/futaelearningdirect).

Why blend?

In low-resourced contexts the triple problems of inadequate classroom spaces, lack of teaching-learning facilities and few teachers create a complex mix of constraints, including timetabling. An extension of the classroom was needed. Learning technologies are reported to help extend teaching-learning flexibility. The fact that technology supported courses 'provide better support for the less able, engage students who do not respond well to 'traditional' classroom learning, provide opportunity for accelerated learning for gifted and talented students, and develop independent learning skills through a personalised learning experience is well attested to' (Boulton, 2008). Other reports (Murray, 2000) contend that computer-based technologies can be powerful pedagogical tools as extensions of human capabilities and contexts for social interactions supporting learning. Blended or hybrid learning (Rodriguez and Anicete, 2010) was therefore an appealing choice for two main reasons. First, as 'digital immigrant' teachers and students we get to keep within our comfort zone of the face-to-face mode while we learn to use the new tools of Web 2.0. Secondly, accounts in e-learning literature suggest that blended or hybrid learning has great advantages; Graham (2006) listed six: pedagogical richness, access to knowledge, social interaction, personal agency, cost effectiveness, and ease of revision. It has been found that many students preferred this mode because of the advantage of combining the affordances of face-to-face and online modes and building on their diverse learning styles (Reynard, 2007; Rodriguez and Anicete, 2010). The blended mode enables an enhanced learning experience by enabling diverse learning environments, thus fostering reinforcement, increasing accessibility of learning materials; and helping to build a sense of community and collaboration through the collaborative and communication platforms of the wiki and forums for sharing experiences of learning.

What we blend

By 1993 we were already fairly grounded in the communicative language teaching (CLT) pedagogy (Dudley-Evans, 1984; Bloor and St John, 1988; Hyland and Hyland, 1992). The requirements of this approach drew us to look for alternative methods of course delivery beyond the constraints of the face-to-face teacher-fronted, rote learning mode. The courses were already task- and skills-based, adopting the process-product and problem-based approaches. We had students working in collaborative groups to carry out investigations (for example on HIV/AIDS or climate change) and to write term papers. What remained was to enable learners to do more on their own, to help teachers be able to give more support by giving more frequent feedback and providing links to diverse materials and sources and, especially, to create avenues for greater interaction amongst learners in the target language. GNS 102, for example, followed a seven-stage process up until the writing of the term paper, and each stage had a number of steps with varied tasks: 1) raising awareness of language use, 2) choosing a topic, 3) sourcing for materials, 4) structuring the essay, 5) drafting the essay, 6) writing references, 7) using checklists. All of the stages, except 5, start off in an face-to-face meeting, presenting and explaining the ideas and principles. Tasks and samples of good practice are set, but are only available online. However, most tasks are carried out at group meetings, while answers are uploaded onto the learning site. Stage 5 takes place basically online on the groups' wiki pages but a sample writing of the introductory paragraph using 'moves' begins in the classroom. Students have the opportunity at face-to-face meetings to debate, brainstorm and raise queries on aspects of each stage while collaborating and communicating on their group tasks out of class. Online work extends students' working hours; enables flexibility of work mode and variety of work styles. Equally important is the opportunity this affords to explore materials the teacher is unable to provide as they investigate their project topics.

We use the face-to-face meetings to build the group teams after explaining and debating the course rationale, goals and learning outcomes. Also important is giving an explanation on how the online component integrates and works. Each stage of the course and the expectations are clarified. Feedback is given on issues around the tasks that students carry out. On the Moodle VLE the learning materials are available for download; links to other sites with useful materials are provided (a regular one is www.uefap.com); a news forum is provided enabling teachers to post information regularly, and a course discussion forum enables learners to share ideas, ask questions and discuss their progress on the course. Students collaborate on the group wiki pages to share information on meeting times and draft/edit their term paper; students are also encouraged to use micro-blogs on their profile pages to reflect on their learning and record ideas they have gained which they might like to develop later. The totality of the blend is a learning experience that has kept students engaged, interacting in English and interested in learning like they never have been before.

Figure 1 presents the evaluation of a first semester 2010–11 session for GNS 101 using the Constructivist On-Line Learning Environment Survey (COLLES). The format of the survey questionnaire requires the respondent to indicate a level of agreement or disagreement using a 5-point Likert scale (1 – almost never, 2 – seldom, 3 – sometimes, 4 – often and 5 – almost always). The questions ask about: (1) the course's relevance to student's interests and professional goals, (2) the level of critical or reflective thinking that the student applies to the material in the course, (3) the level of interactivity the student engages in during the course, (4) the level of tutor support, (5) peer support the student is receiving in the course, and (6) the success of both student and tutor in making good sense of each other's communication. Three hundred and twenty six (326) returns from the writer's group of 11 departments totalling about 800 students registered online were received. We interpret the outcome as suggesting that our experiment is succeeding, though a lot more needs be done in the areas of peer support and interactivity, but this represents considerable movement from near zero level.

Figure 1: COLLES survey result

Preferred options	Relevance	Reflective Thinking	Interactivity	Tutor Support	Peer Support	Interpretation
Almost Always	629	577	324	540	285	483
Often	365	410	329	418	362	393
Sometimes	246	252	497	271	476	338
Seldom	49	48	106	58	126	70
Almost Never	15	18	49	17	54	20

Lessons learned and the way forward

We have learned that the bottom-up evolutionary process works for educational development in our context. Of the seven higher education institutions in Nigeria listed in the Moodle user directory, four use the VLE for distance learning as a repository for content; one uses it for assessment only. Only in FUTA where teaching staff own and drive the process is take-up growing in a gradual but fairly steady rate. The tools in the VLE are a major boost for collaboration and communication, two key things we had longed for but lacked in our practice. With their tongues let loose, students were a source of inspiration; they knew more than we always credited them with and had skills we knew nothing about. Teachers can be learners too and students can help drive the process. A group of students that went through our courses have emerged as ICT champions, giving support to other students. We have learned that the unexpected could happen when using technology, but we were undaunted because we had our face-to-face comfort zone as a backup when the site crashed. Teacher workload increased rather than decreased as time was required for professional development in IT and pedagogy, for course design, VLE management and course facilitation. Now work has more meaning and purpose and students' motivation gives us satisfaction.

As often happens, shut-downs of universities by government, staff or students disrupt academic programmes. The VLE enables students to access materials and keep discussions going during such disruptions. Teachers are also able to continue the facilitation of learning, cover the curriculum in depth, check students' understanding of ideas and concepts, and provide feedback. We have learned that teacher roles are changing, as learners' engagement is enhanced by the creation of new learning environments and as they take more decisions in the process.

On the downside, however, poor technology infrastructure and inadequate facilities exert great pressure on the most willing students and staff, in terms of effort, time and finance. Teachers are unable to respond to all questions and posts because of large numbers. Also worth noting are the technology downtimes and inadequate bandwidth problems, coupled with not having backup servers, which make us lose data constantly. Training requirements for academic and technical staff are issues anyone in our context must pay attention to when going in for blended learning.

Conclusion

The much talked about digital divide is a reality. In a developing country such as Nigeria, the obstacles to educational change are myriad. They include the generic issues of strategy, perceptions and e-readiness; human and contextual issues, and resources of time, cost and technology. The gap can be bridged by teachers who are daring and resourceful and students can be sources of expertise. But as has been shown above, change is possible: we can increase students' work hours and help students speak English more and better, interact more and learn more independently.

References

Aborisade, PA (2009) Investigating a Nigerian XXL-cohort wiki-learning experience: observation, feedback and reflection. *Electronic Journal of e-Learning* 7/3: 191–202. Available online at www.ejel.org

Beatty, K (2003) *Teaching and Researching Computer-Assisted Language Learning*. Essex: Pearson Education Ltd.

Bloor, M and St John, MJ (1988) 'Project writing: The marriage of process and product' in *ELT Documents*: 129. Modern English Publications in association with the British Council.

Boulton, H (2008) Managing e-Learning: what are the Real Implications for Schools? *The Electronic Journal of e-Learning* 6/1: 11–18. Available online at www.ejel.org

Dudeney, G and Hockly, N (2007) *How to Teach English with Technology*. Essex: Pearson Education Ltd.

Dudley-Evans, T (1984) 'The team-teaching of writing skills' in Williams, R, Swales, J and Kirkman, J (eds) *Common Ground: Shared Interests in ESP and Communication Studies*. ELT Documents: 117, Pergamon Press.

Graham, C (2006) 'Blended learning systems: definition, current trends and future directions', in Bonk, C and Graham, C (eds) *Handbook of Blended Learning: Global Perspectives, Local Designs*. San Francisco, CA: Pfeiffer.

Hyland, K and Hyland, F (1992) Go for gold: integrating process and product in ESP. *English for Specific Purposes* 11: 225–242.

Ihemere, KU (2006) A basic description and analytic treatment of noun clauses in Nigerian pidgin. *Nordic Journal of African Studies* 15/3: 296–313.

LoCastro, V (2001) Teaching English to large classes. *TESOL Quarterly* 35/3: 493–496.

Marchese, L and Shnukal, A (1983) Creolization of Nigerian Pidgin English: a progress report. *English World-Wide* 4: 17–26.

Murray, DE (2000) Changing technologies, changing literacy communities? *Language Learning and Technology* 4/2: 43–58.

Reynard, R (2007) Hybrid learning: challenges for teachers. *THE Journal*. Available online at http://thejournal.com/Articles/2007/05/17/Hybrid-Learning-Challenges-for-Teachers.aspx

Rodriguez, MA and Anicete, RCA (2010) Students' views of a mixed hybrid ecology course. *Journal of Online Learning and Teaching* 6/4: 791–798.

3

A blended English as a Foreign Language academic writing course

Natalya Eydelman

Introduction

I would like to describe an academic writing course I am teaching for the second-year students majoring in Teaching, Translation and Interpretation or Intercultural Communication at the Department of Foreign Languages at Novosibirsk State University in Russia, discuss how it is blended and address some of the issues that have emerged in the process of designing and teaching it.

Learner characteristics

My learners are undergraduate students at the Department of Foreign Languages, majoring in Teaching English as a Foreign Language, Translation and Interpretation and Intercultural Communication.

Assumed knowledge and skills

The level of my students' English language proficiency ranges from B1/B2 (intermediate/upper-intermediate) to C1 (advanced) according to the Common European Framework of Reference for Languages (2002).

The course of academic writing the students take is a four-semester course which aims to develop the students' writing skills to help them improve their language proficiency and prepare them for writing academic papers in a number of subjects they are taught at the university, and for writing their term and graduation papers.

During the first two semesters students learn how to write one-paragraph essays of several types, such as descriptive, narrative and argumentative, with the focus on such elements of their organisation as the topic sentence, supporting examples and conclusions. It is taught in face-to-face mode only. One of the reasons for this is the level of ICT competence of the first-year course instructor and, to a certain extent, that of some of the students. During the second year of instruction the students learn how to write five-paragraph discursive essays that should be fluent and clear and meet the standard requirements for essay content, organisation, language use, the mechanics and style. The course puts an emphasis on letting the students understand different stages of the writing process, recognise their own strengths and weaknesses and use this information to their advantage when composing their essays.

Why blend?

The decision to offer this course as a blended one was made for the following reasons:

1. To motivate the students to write, which is cited in literature as one of the benefits of using Web 2.0 tools such as blogs and wikis in courses of writing (for example, Turgut, 2009; Krebs et al., 2010). It should be mentioned that though using these tools for peer-revision does not necessarily automatically motivate students to write, they can, however, contribute to the students' motivation to write for a wider audience (Lee, 2010; Richardson, 2010), to encourage them to come up with ideas for their writing that can appeal to their peers and enhance their confidence in it (Turgut, 2009; Pinkman, 2005; Zhang, 2009).

2. To create a space for them to share their experiences (Davoli et al., 2009; Richardson, 2010; Solomon and Schrum, 2010).

3. To give the students opportunities to provide each other with feedback on their writing (Davoli et al., 2009; Richardson, 2010; Solomon and Schrum, 2010).

4. To encourage informal communication (Richardson, 2010; Solomon and Schrum, 2010).

5. To support course management (Bonk and Graham, 2006; Davoli et al., 2009; Solomon and Schrum, 2010). Through the course's wiki the students can access the course materials uploaded to it and complete the course assignments they receive. The wiki is also equipped with the tools for synchronous and asynchronous communication providing additional channels for it. Besides being used for the course activities throughout the course, the wiki is also used for formative and summative assessment, with the students completing quizzes as well as creating and submitting their e-folios at the end of the semester and the academic year to the wiki.

6. To provide additional channels for interaction and opportunities for collaboration (Richardson, 2010; Solomon and Schrum, 2010).

The choice of workspace

The foreign languages department is equipped with a multimedia lab which is used to deliver the course. However, the department does not use the university's virtual learning environment for teaching, nor does it provide the finance to purchase software and tools necessary to run courses like mine. Thus in choosing the software and tools to teach my course I am limited to those available for free.

The course is taught using PBWorks, a free hosted workspace which allows collaborative editing of pages and files (http://pbworks.com). It was chosen as one of the learning environments for the course because it met this requirement. In addition, it is distinguished by a relative ease of use and accessibility, which is very important in my learning context, since in the first place my course is aimed at the development of the students' writing skills. What is also important, is that PBWorks is free from advertising, which I see as its significant advantage over some other online services.

A summary of my guiding principles

When designing the course I took into consideration my learners' needs, the skills they have and/or need to acquire and the technology available to meet these needs. When choosing the technology to support my course I was guided by the considerations of matching my learners' present and future needs with the affordances and limitations of the learning environment that was created, including its accessibility, ease of use, and the cost of maintaining it. It is important too that such course delivery can help to promote a shift towards more learner-centred teaching.

How is the course blended?

During the weekly face-to-face sessions, for the duration of two academic hours students read and discuss a variety of materials, the selection of which is made based on their interests and taking into account their learning needs. Then the students are offered a series of activities and exercises to help them to improve different aspects of writing and the language. Their choice is conditioned by the course syllabus and at the beginning of the course many decisions are based on error analysis of the students' work made by the teacher.

During the face-to-face sessions students do brainstorming and prepare their essay's outline. In addition, depending on time availability, the students are asked to work on their own to freewrite on the topic of their essay and then discuss what they have written with their peers. This work then continues to the course's wiki, hosted by PBWorks, which students can access from home during the week.

In the wiki the students post their works in progress or completed ones. Each of them has her own folder in the wiki, which makes it easier to navigate. The students are asked to post their works in the wiki at least one day before a face-to-face session to leave their peers some time for commenting on their work. In general, they are asked to comment on at least one other person's work so as to not overwhelm them with the amount of work and to encourage them to do it. After that the students should revise their essay drafts based on the comments of their peers and the teacher. This way the students go through all the stages of the writing process and can continuously work on improving their essay drafts.

It is very convenient to draft, revise and edit essay drafts in the wiki, which allows for an easy exchange of comments and for multiple ways of commenting both by editing the work and/or adding comments in the thread.

In total the students received 236 hours of instruction over the period of two years, including 34 and 68 private study hours during the two academic years of instruction, respectively.

Teacher and learner roles/interaction patterns

Traditionally the Russian system of education is more teacher than student-centered, so this course offers a way to gradually move away from a teacher-centred classroom. The teacher controls the choice of texts for discussion, and discussion questions for the reading selection. She also suggests the tasks the students have to complete during the before, while and after reading stages. The reading and discussion of texts serve as a starting point for the students' writing which can be done in response to the reading selection or in connection to it. After the discussion in the classroom, the students make suggestions about their possible essay questions and the points to consider in them. This is done in the course's wiki; thus the students can receive comments from both their peers and the teacher. It is followed by the students publishing their essay drafts in the wiki, with the students commenting on the first drafts of their peers' essays and the teacher on the second one. Generally, the students submit two essay drafts, with the second one being graded. However, the students have a further opportunity to improve their essays, if they want them to be included in the portfolio drafts at the end of the semester. So, generally, the design of this course allows for a variety of interaction patterns from those initiated by the teacher to those initiated by the student(s), as well as multiple opportunities for assessment and evaluation of the students' works both formally and informally.

Teaching methodology

Approach to teaching writing

To teach this course a combination of process and product approaches with some elements of genre approach to writing are used (Badger and White, 2000; Flower and Hayes, 1981; Kroll, 1990; Steele, 1992). In essence, the product approach as defined by Pincas is primarily concerned with the proper use of the language, with the students producing a piece of writing after analysing a model text first and imitating it next (1982, cited in Badger and White, 2000). The process approach as defined by Tribble (1996) emphasises 'Writing activities which move learners from the generation of ideas and the collection of data through to the "publication" of a finished text' (1996 p. 37), while the genre approach stresses the social nature of writing and thus focuses on producing pieces of writing ranging from letters to research articles and reports (Flowerdew, 1993 p. 307). Such a combination takes into account the students' prior experience in writing and their current and future needs, and helps to provide them with the necessary amount of guidance, while at the same time encouraging them to gradually become more independent and confident in their writing.

Peer-editing

Different aspects of peer-editing pedagogy have been widely discussed in research literature. Some of the advantages of incorporating peer revision in writing instruction include students working in a friendly environment (Hyland, 2003: 199; Villamil and de Guerro, 1996: 67), gaining a better sense of the audience (Hyland, 2003: 199; Nation, 2009: 143), assuming a more active role in the learning process (Mendonca and Johnson, 1994; Hyland, 2003: 199), and developing skills of critical reading (Hyland, 2003: 199).

All the students are new to peer-editing and revision activities, so a special training session is held at the beginning of the year to introduce them to such activities. In addition, later in the semester when the students get used to working this way, a special feedback session is run to discuss their experience in peer-editing. They are taught what they can comment on in their peers' works and what to pay attention to.

Later in the course of the academic year, students are asked to pay attention to more advanced points of essay content/organisation/style. To help them make their comments more substantial we read and discuss the comments they give to each other, so that gradually they become clearer and more specific.

Every effort is made to ensure that each student in the group receives some feedback on their work. It is stressed that working in the wiki students receive a greater level of responsibility: the students are not only responsible for themselves but also for their peers. Sometimes this is a difficult aspect of the course instruction which some students struggle with for quite some time during the course.

In accordance with the course requirements, in addition to publishing their own works each student is required to comment on a work published by at least one of their peers.

Some common activities and exercises

One of the first activities the students are offered is to share their experience in writing an essay or some other kind of work when discussing the question of the stages of the writing process in the beginning of the academic year. They are asked to describe their approach to writing an essay and share some insights into it, as well as some difficulties they can encounter with their peers. They also need to read at least one reflection written by another student and comment on it. This way the students are first introduced to one of the common activities in which they will participate regularly throughout the course.

Among the exercises the students are offered to complete are student-generated exercises. To start using them on a regular basis, the teacher first creates a worksheet with common errors students made in a particular piece of work and publishes it in the learning environment, for the students to discuss and correct the errors. Later on in the course, the students are asked to create their own worksheets for their peers based on the analysis of their own common errors. This way they are able to recycle the material with which they have problems several times, and to help each other along the way. Judging by the results of the end-of-the course survey, the majority of students found peer-generated exercises quite interesting to complete and rather useful as regards the improved level of grammar and vocabulary knowledge they were able to achieve by the end of the academic year (Nstudents = 27; approval rate 3.8). It can be considered quite a positive result considering the fact that the students' prior experience is to a very large extent teacher-centred.

Contextual challenges

When taking the course offered in the described mode the students face several kinds of challenges, some of which are associated with learning to write itself and others with the mode in which the course is delivered.

Challenges of learning to write are probably common to the majority of learners working on the development of their writing skills, such as formulating the topic for their essay, developing it with adequate support, and organising their ideas logically and consistently. Another challenge on the writing side is connected with the students' ability to write their works at an adequate level of grammar, vocabulary and style.

In addition, there are a number of challenges connected with using the wiki as one of the modes of instruction. These include:

a. Learning to work in collaboration: working in the wiki students become more dependent on their peers' feedback, so if it is not published in time the students cannot use it while revising and/or editing their essay drafts.

b. Learning to use the learning environment: for most of the students working in an online environment is a new experience, so they need some guidance and practice in using it. This is sometimes complicated by the students' prior learning experience which to a large extent is based on a teacher-centred approach to learning and teaching.

c. Learning to use the learning environment to its full potential, for which the students need to become more familiar with its affordances and limitations.

d. Learning to manage their time more efficiently: this is of general concern, and becomes even more acute than usual in the given context, for obvious reasons.

Lessons learned and advice

While designing the blend and teaching using it, it has become clear that it takes time for students to get used to both participating in peer-editing and doing it in the wiki. So, it is important to train students to comment on their peers' work and help them to learn to use the learning environment by offering activities that will allow them to learn to use it more fully. Also, it is necessary to make the students aware of the time management issues that can interfere with the learning process. In addition, students should be encouraged to take more control over some aspects of the learning environment, such as adding relevant content to it, maintaining its appearance and using its editing and commenting features to their greater potential.

Pains and gains from blending

Keeping the students motivated throughout the whole duration of the course was one of its worrying aspects. The other one was enabling the students to stick to the deadlines for wiki submissions. In the context as described this was crucial because of the students' dependence on their peers' feedback on their writing for further revision.

Among the benefits of course blending the students enumerated the following: ease of access to the course materials and work written by the students' peers, an opportunity to receive feedback on their writing from their peers in addition to that given by the teacher, and to gain more confidence in their writing thanks to the opportunity to compare their ability to write to that of their peers. Also, thanks to blending, students gain greater awareness of audience issues because peers provide a broader and more natural audience for their writing, which agrees with research on the benefits of peer-editing reviewed in this article.

Overall the attitude of the students to the described course blend was rather positive and encouraged me to work on improving it. Some possible directions for the improvement of the blend include improving the criteria for assessing the students' contributions to the wiki, improving the students' wiki submission procedures and providing them with more opportunities for collaboration.

References

Badger, R and White, G (2000) A process genre approach to teaching writing. *ELTJ* 54/2: 153–160.

Bonk, C and Graham, C (eds) (2006) *The Handbook of Blended Learning: Global Perspectives, Local Designs.* San Francisco, CA: Pfeiffer Publishing.

Common European Framework of Reference for Languages (2002) Available online at www.coe.int/t/dg4/education/elp/elp-reg/cefr_scale_EN.asp

Davoli, P, Monari, M and Eklundh, KS (2009) Peer activities on Web-learning platforms – Impact on Collaborative Writing and Usability Issues. *Education and Information Technologies* 14: 229–254.

Flower, L and Hayes, J (1981) A cognitive process theory of writing. *College Composition and Communication* 32/4: 365–387.

Flowerdew J (1993) An educational or process approach to the teaching of professional genres. *ELT Journal* 47/4: 305–316.

Hyland, K (2003) *Second Language Writing.* Cambridge: Cambridge University Press.

Krebs, M et al. (2010) Are wikis and weblogs an appropriate approach to foster collaboration, reflection and students' motivation? *IFIP Advances in Information and Communication Technology* 324: 200–209.

Kroll, B (ed) (1990) *Second Language Writing: Research Insights for the Classroom.* Cambridge: Cambridge University Press.

Lee, L (2010) Fostering reflective writing and interactive exchange through blogging in an advanced language course. *ReCALL* 22/2: 212–227.

Mendonca, C and Johnson, K (1994) Peer review negotiations: revision activities in ESL writing instruction. *TESOL Quarterly* 28: 745–769.

Nation, IS (2009) *Teaching ESL and EFL Reading and Writing.* New York/London: Routledge.

Pinkman, K (2005) Using blogs in the foreign language classroom: encouraging learner independence. *The JALT CALL Journal* 1/1.

Richardson, W (2010) *Blogs, Wikis, Podcasts and Other Powerful Web Tools for the Classroom.* Thousand Oaks, Calif: Corwin Press.

Solomon, G and Schrum, L (2010) *How 2, Web 2: How to for Educators.* Eugene, OR: International Society for Technology in Education.

Steele, V (1992) *Product and Process Writing: a Comparison.* Rowley: Newbury House.

Tribble, C (1996) *Writing.* Oxford: Oxford University Press.

Turgut, Y (2009) *'EFL learners' experience of online writing by PBWiki'*, in Proceedings of World Conference on Educational Multimedia, Hypermedia and Telecommunications 2009. AACE, Chesapeake, VA. Available online at http://0-www.editlib.org.aupac.lib.athabascau.ca/p/32033

Villamil, O and de Guerro, M (1996) Peer revision in the L2 classroom: social-cognitive activities, mediating strategies, and aspects of social behavior. *Journal of Second Language Writing* 5/1: 51–75.

Zhang, W (2009) Blogging for doing English digital: student evaluations. *Journal of Computers and Composition* 27: 266–283.

4

Incorporating blended learning in an undergraduate English course in Colombia

Juanita Pardo-Gonzalez

Context of the university

Universidad de los Andes is a Colombian higher education institution characterised by the use of technology, and English language needs. In terms of technology, los Andes has a very strong internet culture and it uses a learning management system (LMS), which is an aid for many administrative and pedagogical matters. This University also has a culture that uses English as part of the students' administrative and academic life. Students who enrol at los Andes are mainly Colombians whose native language is Spanish, and the University requires them to have a good command of a foreign language in their academic life. This is enforced by two requirements. One is to have a minimum level of reading in English by their third semester of studies, and the other is to demonstrate a high proficiency level in English or another foreign language in order to graduate. English courses are seen as an aid to fulfil academic English requirements, but are not mandatory, do not have any credits, are not graded numerically, and do not affect a student's grade point average (GPA).

Type of English courses – The English Academic Support Programme

The English programme is an English as a Foreign Language (EFL) programme that is part of Departamento de Lenguajes y Estudios Socioculturales, which has situated the practices of language learning within the study of cultural and social issues, intertwined with language. With this as a background, the English programme is a six level in-service (starting at a false beginner level) skill-based programme based on a threefold theoretical background that consists of:

- Content-based instruction (CBI), the teaching of a language and subject content. The content used involves a light approach, with more emphasis on language. It responds to the Department's perspective on cultural and social aspects of language.

- Learner training (LT), the training of students in learning strategies to empower them to learn in a more autonomous way, in line with the University's mission statement of fostering autonomy among students.

- English for Academic Purposes (EAP), the training of students for the use of English in a higher education setting. This is because most input students receive in their subject field of study is provided in English and the University wishes to prepare students to take postgraduate courses in English speaking environments. Each course focuses on one skill. Levels 1–3 have reading as the main skill, in order to have students reading in their field of study as soon as possible. Levels 4 and 6 have a strong emphasis on speaking to prepare students to participate in class, and level 5 deals with writing to enable students to write essays and papers in English when they graduate. Their exit level should be a TOEFL of 80 or IELTS 6.5.

Course for the blend

The course in which this project is based is at the fourth level of English, and is called 'Autonomy and Orality'. The aims of the course respond to the theoretical background of the programme. It is a 13-week long high-intermediate course that meets three times a week for 1.5 hours and is divided into three units. The first unit is five weeks long while the second and third units are four weeks long. In addition, each week in one of the sessions students have access to a language laboratory. When the blend began, this was the only level in the programme that had instructors who were willing to experiment with technology and there were four groups taught by two instructors. The number of groups in this level had the potential to increase, unlike in other levels. In a nutshell, it was selected as a pilot for blended learning courses because its instructors were willing to take the risk in terms of technology and the pilot would affect a limited number of participants.

Students and instructors in the blend

The population involved in this project includes students and instructors whose backgrounds are varied. On the one hand there are los Andes undergraduate students, who, as mentioned before, are technologically literate, and come from different fields of study including, but not exclusively, mathematics, engineering, medicine, law, and literature. These students need to learn English due to the foreign language requirements established by the University or because the academic environment imposes the need. On the other hand, there are instructors who are qualified in EFL and have teaching experience at undergraduate level, but are not as familiar with the use of computers as students are. All of the instructors hired in the University have a native-like command of English and have an EFL, Teaching English to Speakers of Other Languages (TESOL) or similar degree. In addition, they have taught undergraduates before and have experience of teaching in the programme. Despite the fact that some of them have been working in the University for some time, their command of information communication and technology (ICT) skills were not as good as their students. Some instructors had used computers in the classroom while others had hardly ever used them for personal reasons or outside of the classroom. The instructor turnover in the course is high: four in a year.

Rationale of our blended approach

This blended approach was incorporated considering five key issues: administration, instruction methods, flexibility, needs and wants, and infrastructure.

1. It was a top-down decision from the administration, but was favourably received by EFL instructors. This could have been due to the fact that there was a small, but new generation of EFL instructors who championed and led change and other forms of teaching that were more up to date, and former teachers were ready for a change. The administration's demand triggered the integration of ICT in the teaching of our classes. According to Graham (2006) this integration is known as blended learning. He explains it as a teaching system that combines face-to-face instruction and computer mediated instruction.

2. Graham's (2006) definition of blend supports the University's main instruction method – face-to-face – while offering students more access to their learning, which is something that we welcome in an EFL environment.

3. Blended learning offered flexibility in the learning environment, which was crucial to our context since students learning English in the University come from different majors and have different studying habits and schedules. This is in tune with Brutt-Griffler's (2007) view of e-learning that establishes technology as a means to instruction and not an end.

4. Despite the fact that we used technology (tape recorders, televisions, and a language laboratory with 45 individual workstations), instructors wanted to include more authentic material and to communicate with their students in 'their' technological language in order to motivate them and to use different methodologies that would be student centred. This is where the Department started considering online, hybrid or blended courses and realised that blended learning was most suitable. Graham (2006) argues that blended learning fosters pedagogical methodologies that use interactive strategies, which, in our context, instructors had pinpointed as necessary. These needs are what Waterhouse (2005) highlights as some of the strengths of blended learning: fosters student centred learning, fosters asynchronous and distant learning, fosters student-content interaction, fosters communication and collaboration, makes course administration simpler, and helps track student learning, among others.

5. Blended learning was desirable due to the limitations of the campus, because since it is located in downtown Bogota, it cannot grow more and classrooms and study spaces are limited. Blended learning seemed to be a solution when incorporating an online laboratory, which would reach a larger number of students. This rationale is aligned to Waterhouse's (2005) and Brutt-Griffler's (2007) claims above.

How the blend has been built

The idea of this project was to take a course that had proved to be successful and to alter the teaching conditions for the instructors as little as possible at the beginning, but to benefit the students. The outcome of the blended course would be the result of gradual incorporation of ICT through an ongoing process, which has six major stages, as shown below.

Figure 1: Stages of the incorporation process of the blend

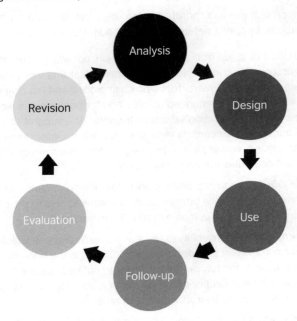

Every year the course passed through this complete cycle and triggered the work of the following year in terms of number of users, elements incorporated in the blend and benefits to the students. In terms of numbers, the blend has increased significantly in terms of number of students, instructors, and groups using the blend from the first year to 2010, when growth seemed to be stabilising. The use of the blend in hours per week reached its peak in the year 2007 both for instructor use in the classroom and student use outside the classroom. See Table 1 'Incorporations in the blend in terms of numbers per year'. The list of incorporations in the blend and student benefits are summarised in Table 2 'Incorporations in the blend and student benefit by year'.

Table 1: Incorporations in the blend in terms of numbers per year

Use of the project	2003	2004	2005	2006	2007	2008	2009	2010	2011
Number of students using the outcome	0	30	60	240	450	1,064	1,128	1,389	1,412
Number of teachers using the outcome	0	1	1	3	9	15	21	24	24
Number of groups using the outcome	0	1	2	8	13	18	42	50	55
Student usage in hours per week out of class	0	1	1	2	3	3	3	3	3
Teacher/student usage in hours per week in class	0	0	0	1	1.5	1.5	1.5	1.5	1.5

Table 2: Incorporations to the blend and student benefit by year

Year	Incorporation to the blend	Benefit to the students
2003	Use face-to-face instruction and enlarge the laboratory through a course Webpage.	Practise the language outside for longer periods of time and outside class.
2004	Manage an online voice laboratory.	Practise privately to later show themselves and classmates in the classroom they can speak in English.
2005	Create online drills as homework and quizzes.	Practise and thus gain self-confidence and boost their language ego.
2006	Reproduction of video and audio files.	Control of some resources to the students giving them independence to practise in the language.
2007	Create oral discussion boards incorporation of synchronic communication.	Respond in real time in non-face-threatening scenarios.
2008	Use the blend for evaluation.	Manage easily the recordings and keep record of their performance in English allowing them to track their progress.
2009	Use the internet and instructor production of material.	Control the use and creation of resources, fostering self-motivation.
2010	Word processing, email communication.	Use technology they are familiar with as part of the course.
2011	Written discussion boards.	Create other environments in the course to share with classmates and instructor.

The blend

Our blend can best be explained as the use and implementation of an ICT environment or tool that expands the classroom walls to the virtual ICT synchronous and asynchronous reality, thereby aiding and reinforcing classroom instruction and enhancing learning potential. Beatty (2003: 8) asserts, 'It is likely that in the future, computer-based language learning tools will become pervasive and invisible'. This is what I tried to do in the blended course. The blend is composed of several aspects that are a fact of the course; they are inseparable now from the course. It is in a sense what Chappelle (2001: 1) claims by stating that everyday language is tied to technology (emailing for example); and as a result, language learning with technology is a fact of life. Below, you will find a sample schedule that illustrates this 'invisibility' for the first unit of the course.

Table 3: Schedule for Unit 1

Week	Unit	Face-to-face activity	Online task
1–5	1	Course introduction.	Video of online laboratory.
		Laboratory orientation session.	Pronunciation profile recording on a private oral discussion board.
		Dictionary use.	Instructor feedback.
		Learning key words for self-monitoring pronunciation.	Dictionary drills – automatic feedback.
		Links to consonants and vowels and instructor guidance.	Private oral discussion boards instructor feedback.
		Using a pronunciation self-evaluation guide.	Consonant and vowel drills – automatic feedback.
		Learning styles video discussion.	Listen to a recording to self-evaluate it.
		Presentation strategies and guide for self-evaluation.	Learning styles questionnaire – link.
		Submit self-evaluation of oral presentation.	Learning styles oral presentation planning.
		Reflecting on characteristics of a good language learner.	Self-revision of the presentation.
		Discuss the advice, strategies and implications.	Public oral discussion boards instructor feedback.
			Voicemail advice to a classmate on the strategies to be a good language learner, using a determined learning style for pronunciation purposes.
			Exam 1

The blend comes to life

The technological component of the course was made possible by using a virtual facade of the course: a webpage which was WebCT based and has private access for all enrolled students.

The blend only comes to life when both instructors and students use it to carry out the course tasks, allowing for learning to take place at each individual's speed. Face-to-face instruction demands students refer to course materials or tasks that are online, thus becoming a unit. There are three types of use during the semester: the orientation session, during the semester, and evaluation.

Tools in the blend

The Department preferred to buy already made software that suited our needs and allowed us to further develop the English programme without becoming programmers or engineers. Thus, this blend uses a specialised learning management system for languages (language LMS) known as Wimba (now Collaborate), in-house designed audio/visual material, and internet projects. Each of these resources aims at different objectives and thus entails different methodologies and roles for the participants.

Online lab

The online lab is a language LMS which provides oral communication within a course or an institution. It is an empty structure that may be developed according to the type of course. In other words, this tool is a group of skeletons which we, both instructor and students, help bring to life by creating their complexion, selecting their attire, and inviting them out. We create their complexion by feeding them different types of exercises because the software does not have pre-determined exercises. Also, we dress these skeletons according to the occasion, which means that we select the course content that we want to teach. Also, we give life to these skeletons, depending on the way we use them and the role we want them to play in our course. In this LMS, there are different skeletons, each one identified with a name: oral discussion boards, drills, voicemail, and oral presentations.

Video and listening

Face-to-face instructions used video and listening input. It is not a new perspective that video can be used in ELT (Allan, 1985). What is new is the control and creation of the input since now the instructor does not control the pauses and students have unlimited access to it. The incorporation of these in the web page changed the instructors' role and shifted to a learner-controlled environment. At the moment we have more than three in-house created videos and are also using selected videos from web pages or YouTube that address course needs and goals. There is a shift towards student-created material (see the unedited student production: http://youtu.be/em30lGMn4t8, and http://youtu.be/58Pj4L0T12k).

Internet – links and WebQuests:

Some elements did not exist in the face-to-face course as it was originally designed. Students are faced with a window of opportunities on the internet and they are encouraged to look at it to enlarge their content or communication skills knowledge. This blend has incorporated and carefully selected links and inquiry oriented tasks. One example of this is the Brain Quest, which is based on the idea of WebQuests coined in ELT as TalenQuest. (Koenraad and Westhoff, 2003). These are student inquiry guided tasks in groups (usually four). Each member of the group is responsible for one of the topics in the site and learning happens collaboratively.

Future innovations – growth

Possible expansions of the blend for this course suggest tandem learning as exchange projects with other institutions. This experience is in a pilot project phase at the moment (see a compilation of pilot project unedited student material at http://youtu.be/Qg0d67IE1Do) and I have seen up to now that it could provide a new kind of socialisation in the blend, and would incorporate elements of intercultural learning in a more vivid way. Also, since students demand the use of the blend in their next levels, this process has expanded to other levels of the English programme, with successful results. In addition, the blend has become appealing to other languages in the Department and I have started a training course on how to implement blended learning in foreign language classes such as French, Italian, Japanese and Chinese.

Lessons learned, key elements, and advice

While this project was in process, during and after its implementation important issues came to light. To carry out this blend the following elements needed to be considered: analysis, process, integration, innovation, improvement, material design, and research. These elements can be summarised in the following tenets:

- Use an existing face-to-face course as the basis for the blend.
- Use the context (campus limitations, infrastructure) to promote the use of blended learning.
- Sell administrative requests as needs and desires of instructors.
- Begin with instructors that are willing, even if they are not technology oriented.
- Instructors will learn to love technology, but this is a process.
- Relax! Instructors will improve their ICT literacy on the way.
- Instructor training in the blend is also an ongoing process and depends directly on instructor turnover in the institution.
- Trained instructors will help you promote the blended learning idea to other courses.
- Students and instructors will change the roles they have in a face-to-face classroom.
- A large-scale project is achieved step-by-step; therefore clear goals per year are necessary.
- Blended learning needs to be seen as an ongoing and gradual process in which the course evolves. It is not a final product.

- Add technological changes gradually. You cannot juggle with too many variables at the same time.
- If you begin the adoption of innovation, be prepared for more work to come your way.
- Integrate technology rather than simply use it.
- Find the appropriate tools for your course. Not all tools are for all courses. If I found one way to foster oral communication skills, you will find your own way to foster the skills you wish to work with.
- More up-to-date methodologies and tendencies will fall in place in your class before you know it.
- Instructors soon discover that there is room for material design adaptation and adoption.
- This is an opportunity for research and as such it needs to be well thought out, referenced, documented, and implemented.

Blended learning over online learning and face-to-face instruction

There are three main benefits for students that combined explain why the use of blended learning was appropriate for this course, over online learning or face-to-face instruction.

Blended learning offered them:

1. Flexibility in their learning environment, which addresses different students' studying habits, schedules, and rhythms of studying. Some students do not realise that they need more time than their classmate until they get the chance to practise at home. One student said: 'It allows me to practise comfortably from home and at the speed of each learner'.

2. Personalised instructor feedback in and outside class. Some students are too shy to ask questions or to engage in a feedback session with the instructor. Blended learning provided non-face-threatening scenarios for all types of students. One student said: 'I valued the feedback given by the teachers.' Another said: 'The tool was useful since I could not recognise my mistakes on my own or did not ask. The teacher always gave feedback on my expression and on content in English.'

3. Recognition of the value of face-to-face instruction. Given the practice that students had online they gained confidence in their language ability and proved this ability in class, boosting their 'language ego'. One student said: 'It was not nice to talk to a machine and it was nice to talk to a human being from time to time, be it classmates or the teacher, to obtain immediate feedback and know that I could say it!'

References

Allan, M (1985) *Teaching English with Video*. Harlow: Longman.

Beatty, K (2003) *Teaching and Researching Computer-Assisted Language Learning*. London: Longman.

Brutt-Griffler, J (2007) 'Bilingualism and e-learning' in Andrews, R and Haythornwaite, C (eds) (2010) *The Sage Handbook of E-Learning Research*. Thousand Oaks, CA: SAGE Publications.

Chappelle, CA (2001) *Computer Applications in Second Language Acquisition*. Cambridge: Cambridge University Press.

Graham, C (2006) 'Blended learning systems. Definition, current trends, and future directions', in Bonk, C and Graham, C (eds) *Handbook of Blended Learning: Global Perspectives, Local Designs*. San Francisco CA: Pfeiffer Publishing, 3–21.

Koenraad, ALM and Westhoff, GJ (2003) *Can You Tell a LanguageQuest When You See One?* Paper presented at the European Association of Computer Assisted Language Learning. University of Limerick Ireland. Available online at www.koenraad.info/publications/my-publications-english

Waterhouse, S (2005) *The Power of e-Learning: The Essential Guide for Teaching in the Digital Age*. Boston: Pearson.

Comments on Part 1

Brian Tomlinson

The four chapters in Part 1 all describe blended learning EAP courses for university students. Their countries and contexts are very different but the chapters share many features in common. They are all reports of pioneering courses and report their procedures, problems, solutions and ongoing development in ways which should be of great help to any EAP university teachers intending to develop blended learning courses for their institutions.

All four courses reported seemed to have been developed as pragmatic solutions to problems rather than as principled attempts at pedagogic innovation. In all four institutions the main problems facing the teachers were the large size of the classes, the inadequacy of the class time allocated to the courses and the differing needs and language levels of the students. As in most EAP courses throughout the world the main challenge was for a small number of teachers to help a large number of students to become effective users of academic English in a very short time. The face-to-face elements of the courses reported in Part 1 enabled the students to get to know each other, to become familiar with the objectives and procedures of the courses, to develop a shared community, and to be provided with the reassurance and reinforcement best achievable in one-to-one and in group face-to-face interaction. The online elements of the courses added massively to the on-task time the students were able to devote to the courses, provided opportunities for far more exposure to, and use of, English than purely face-to-face courses could, allowed for individualised tasks and feedback and allowed the students to both work in their own time at their own pace and to collaborate with other students on shared projects in ways which they could not have done in the classroom.

The decision to introduce the four courses and the way they were initially developed might have been determined largely by pragmatic considerations but many pedagogic benefits of blended learning courses and many principles and guidelines for their development emerged as the courses progressed. All the courses reported positive motivation, provided the courses got the balance right between face-to-face and online delivery, they all reported the benefits of students being able to receive ongoing feedback from both their peers and their teachers and they all reported an increase in the perceived relevance of the courses. Of course, not everything which was introduced was appreciated and benefited from by all the students. Some did not like talking to machines, some did not appreciate having to post their contributions for peer feedback and collaboration to meet demanding deadlines, and some did not always appreciate the extra workload which blended learning courses can impose.

My advice to intending EAP course developers would be to take advantage of the experiences reported in the chapters in Part 1 and to design blended learning courses so as to achieve both principled learning objectives and practical solutions to problems. I would suggest that all blended learning courses should aim to:

- Maximise the students exposure to English.

- Provide experience for all students of a variety of academic genres as well as opportunities for individual students to gain further experience in those genres relevant to their academic specialisms.

- Increase the likelihood of student affective and cognitive involvement by providing choices of texts and tasks (Tomlinson, 2013).

- Cater for differing levels and aspirations by providing choices of texts and tasks.

- Provide opportunities for students to make discoveries for themselves about how features of English are used to achieve intended outcomes (Tomlinson, 2013).

- Maximise the opportunities for students to communicate in English.

- Provide opportunities for students to use English to achieve intended communicative outcomes in relation to the genres which feature in their academic specialisms.

- Provide opportunities for students to seek ongoing feedback from peers and teachers on their communicative performance.

- Provide opportunities for teachers to monitor the progress of their students in ways which enable them to provide constructive criticism and responsive teaching when it is most needed.

What is perhaps most important though is that every course has to be different because every course is composed of different students with different wants and needs. Those wants and needs are not just linguistic; they are attitudinal too and I would advise blended learning course designers to not only provide choices within a mode but wherever possible to offer choices to students of which mode(s) to work with. For example, some students could be posting a presentation for others to listen to in their own time, some could be giving a presentation through video conferencing and others could be presenting face-to-face to a group of fellow students. Versatility and flexibility are to me the key benefits of blended learning courses and they should be exploited as much as possible.

Reference

Tomlinson, B (2013) 'Second language acquisition' in Tomlinson, B (ed) *Applied Linguistics and Materials Development*. London: Bloomsbury, 11–30.

Part 2 – Teacher development

5

A blended learning teacher development course for the development of blended learning in English Language Teaching

Nik Peachey

Course overview and context

The Blended Learning in ELT course was designed for practising classroom teachers, with the aim of developing their understanding of the potential of blended learning for the development of English language skills.

The course is delivered in three parts:

- The first part is an eight-week 80-hour tutor moderated course delivered online using the Moodle learning management system (LMS) platform.

- The second part is a two-week 60-hour face-to-face workshop delivered at the Bell Teacher Campus at Homerton College in Cambridge.

- The third and final, optional, part of the course is a three-month 160-hour self study element based around the completion of two to three written assignments which will be assessed for credit towards an MA in Teaching English to Speakers of Other Languages (TESOL) at the University of Nottingham.

The course is aimed at English language teachers who already have some grounding in technology and materials design. It is for participants who want to take their understanding of technology beyond the classroom activity level and investigate the potential of blended learning for the development of complete courses. The online element of the course does not strictly have a limit on the number of participants that can be enrolled, but the limit for the face-to-face element of the course is around 20.

The course aims to develop participants' understanding of the application of blended learning within English Language Teaching (ELT), so the choice of a blended learning course format to do this lends an element of experiential learning to the course. Participants will have the opportunity to experience the kinds of methods, approaches and problems that their students will encounter and this should help to give them deeper insights into the process and systems that should help to support the students they construct their own courses for.

Designing the blend

As described earlier, the course is split into three blocks of eight weeks online (group with moderator) – two weeks face-to-face (group with workshop tutor) – three months online (individual participants with tutor).

The online section

The materials for the initial online units of the course are built within a Moodle LMS platform. This material is delivered in (at present) ten units each of four to five tasks. Many of the tasks incorporate Web 2.0 type tools which are embedded into the task templates to add an element of social interactivity. They also give participants experience of using the same tools as learners that they will then use as teachers to construct learning.

Some examples of the kinds of tools used are:

Tricider https://tricider.com/ This web-based tool enables a form of information crowdsourcing. Users can create questionnaires which recipients not only answer but also contribute to and comment on. The tool is used within the course itself to brainstorm teaching ideas for the various tools presented.

MailVu http://mailvu.com/ This is a web-based tool that enables asynchronous video communication. The user can record up to ten minutes of spoken monologue and then very easily send it via email. It does not require any form of software as it works within the user's web browser and does not require any form of registration, so is quick and simple for teachers and students to use. The tutor and participants on the course use this tool for communication and information sharing and then devise tasks to use with their students.

VYou http://vyou.com/ This allows registered users to create their own communication video booth. They simply record an introduction video clip which loops continuously, giving the impression that the person is available online for questions. Visitors to the booth can then write questions and send them to the owner of the booth, who replies with a video message. This tool is used within the course to add a human presence to the online environment and to answer any questions that course participants have. The participants then create their own booth and use it with their own students.

The participants on the course have the opportunity to evaluate activities and exercises already created with these tools and decide which can best be used within their teaching context.

The course also has built-in study resources which include links to related online journals and blogs, embedded video clips of lectures, talks and presentations from various web-based sources, and custom-made video tutorials to help develop digital skills, which help to provide background reading and a theoretical perspective to the course.

The face-to-face element

Because of the enforced limitations of the limited block of face-to-face time (the two-week attendance at Bell Teacher Campus) the initial online part of the course has been designed to prepare participants. Technology has been used to create a 'flipped' approach to instruction within a connected online platform with the tasks helping to develop and support participants' autonomous learning through video-based instruction in the use of technology. This use of the online block as a preparation for the face-to-face block should ensure that participants come to the face-to-face course with a reasonably consistent level of ability. They can then focus on the more pedagogical and creative aspects of course creation during the face-to-face workshops. The final part of the course, which goes back to the online mode should give them the chance to reflect on their learning and build up their background reading, but they will be able to view what they read in the light of the practical experience and understanding that they have built up during the course.

Teacher and learner roles and interaction

The first element of the course – online – has been developed around learning tasks which encourage participants to actively investigate aspects of technology use within the context they work. These tasks vary from exploring recommended background reading and viewing, researching different types of web-based tools and creating learning activities and materials for their students.

Having completed the tasks they should then reflect on them and share their reflections with their peers in online discussion forums. The main focus of the interaction within these forums is peer-to-peer, though these are tutor-moderated and it is the role of the tutor to stimulate discussion and interaction, draw participants' attention to salient points and additional reading and resources, and summarise and tie up discussions.

The second element of the course – face-to-face – is much more workshop based. Participants meet together for tutor-facilitated hands-on sessions which focus on developing the use of technology to create and share engaging content and explore how this can be used in varying contexts. Here the tutor acts as facilitator and technical support, helping participants to develop their own materials as they develop their technical skills and pedagogical understanding.

The third element of the course – online – is the more academic part of the course. Participants complete academic assignments which encourage them to reflect on their experiences of applying blended learning materials with their students and their reading and research into the pedagogical foundations as well as to formulate their ideas in such a way that they contribute to the professional field of English Language Teaching. Their assignments for this final part of the course include action research projects and more literature-based research which they can use to frame their more practical experiences from the course. Here the tutor's role reverts back to a more traditional one, offering support by reading through elements of the participants' academic work and offering feedback and support online.

So in this way participants move from more practical applications of blended learning towards the more theoretical exploration of the background. This gives participants the opportunity to approach and reflect on theory with a firm background in classroom practice.

Teaching methodology

There is a mixture of methods, approaches and beliefs that underpin the development of the course. In some ways the course takes a 'flipped' approach to teacher development with the initial online course pushing teachers to complete tasks and interact in a very independent way and prepare themselves and lay the groundwork for the more practical aspects of the face-to-face element of the course.

The core content of the online course is based around units containing active learning tasks. Unlike many teacher development tasks, these are not simply reading or viewing tasks but they call upon the participants to engage with the materials, try to apply what they are learning within the context they work and to reflect and share their reflections with their peer group.

Instead of recommended core texts, the core content of the course includes a wide range of online reference materials, but this material is approached in a non-prescriptive way. The range of references and recommended reading draws on ELT websites, blogs and online resource sites as well as online journals.

Participants are encouraged through directed reading to critically evaluate what they read and assess its relevance to their own context and again share their reflections with their peers within discussion forums. The aim of this approach is to develop a more inclusive but critical approach to online published literature. This is especially important in such a fast-moving field where traditional paper-based reading sources are often out of date by the time they are published and practitioners need to rely more heavily on less established and authoritative sources of information.

Within the core online course tasks participants are encouraged to develop the kinds of digital literacy skills and digital study skills that their own students would need to be successful online learners. Many of the tasks focus on helping participants to develop sound information management and knowledge sharing strategies facilitated by online tools such as RSS readers, social bookmarking and micro-blogging platforms.

RSS (really simple syndication) is a common but underused technology which allows visitors to subscribe to web-based content using a 'reader'. The reader is a personalised web page which pulls in content from the sites the user subscribes to. In this way the user can have content from tens or even hundreds of different websites delivered to their own personal web page. This helps to keep them informed of any new content or research within their field without them having to constantly waste time searching the internet and checking sites individually, although the efficiency of this process depends very much on their ability to identify useful credible sources.

Social bookmarking allows users to store and retrieve any links to useful online articles or resources they find. This process is slightly different from normal bookmarking because social bookmarking sites allow users to share their bookmarks with other groups or site users. Using this technology within the course allows participants to work in research groups to collaborate in discovering useful resources and information. This forms a strong model for the kinds of study skills and practices they need to encourage within their own classes.

Micro-blogging platforms such as Twitter enable users to build global information sharing networks. Training participants to use these kinds of platforms during the course enables them to reach out beyond their course cohort and expand the scope of their research, collaboration and learning into the global ELT community, not only for the duration of the course, but to help them to sustain learning after the course is completed.

The socially interactive nature of the tasks is designed to promote the connectivist aspects of peer-to-peer learning within the online community. Some of the main principles of connectivism outlined by Siemens (2004) in his essay 'A Learning Theory for the Digital Age' are that: 'Learning and knowledge rests in diversity of opinions. Learning is a process of connecting specialized nodes or information sources. Nurturing and maintaining connections is needed to facilitate continual learning.' So the focus is very much pushed towards building an online community of practice that works with minimal tutor support using the tools previously mentioned.

Creating the initial element of the course online enabled the integration of a number of web-based Web 2.0 type social tools as well as much greater integration of social networking, collaborative creative tasks and multimedia elements within the course.

Overall the course is a form of 'loop input', a 'style of experiential teacher training process that involves an alignment of the process and content of learning' (Woodward, 2003), in that a blended learning course is being used to develop understanding of blended learning approaches and methods based around content focused on blended learning methodology. This gives participants experiences similar to those their students will have as learners.

Using an online medium in this way as part of the blended learning course gave participants some genuine experience of online learning on which they could then reflect. This genuine experience of learning through an online medium and all the issues that emerge through it helps teachers to understand the strengths and limitations of the medium in a way that could not be achieved in the face-to-face classroom alone.

Blended benefits

The overall advantages of taking a blended learning approach to the course as opposed to doing the course completely face-to-face are many. The greatest advantage is that having considerable parts of the course online enables us to extend the period of learning over a far greater timescale than would be possible with face-to-face teaching. This means that teachers have more time to develop and absorb the materials they are studying. It also enables the teachers to learn in their own teaching context, try things out with their own students and gain genuine first-hand experience on which they can reflect when they come to approaching and understanding theory.

We are also able to make much better use of the face-to-face time that is available for the course because participants arrive with a good level of technical knowledge and sound experiences and have already had some time to absorb many of the technical and theoretical aspects during the first online block of the course.

Lastly, through exploiting the social networking and community building opportunities offered during the initial online phase of the course, the participants arrive at the face-to-face part of the course already familiar with each other and this really accelerates the bonding process that groups generally go through during the initial stages of a face-to-face course.

Design challenges

Both face-to-face and online courses can be problematic for the development of teachers' techno-pedagogical skills. Face-to-face courses generally tend to be too short and intensive for teachers to get past the 'shock and awe' impact that new technology can have, and whereas they can help to build or destroy enthusiasm for technology, it can be hard within short face-to-face courses to develop the degree of balanced critical understanding that is necessary for the effective use of technology. Online courses, on the other hand, tend to be far too theoretical with teachers lacking the practical 'hands on' guidance and experience that they can get within the physical classroom. The blended learning structure of the course was employed to address both these areas. Teachers had the opportunity to be exposed through the online course to some of the potential uses of technology to support development within an online environment, and then had the opportunity to employ their insights within a more practical face-to-face workshop environment.

Most people still have a limited concentration span for online work. This, mixed with the busy nature of teachers' lives, influenced the design of the online tasks. Most of the active tasks were developed to be short and doable in chunks of 30 minutes or less. They are also very practical so that participants can immediately implement what they are learning within their own classroom.

Future adaptations

The course has been designed to evolve as more participants do the course and as the technology changes. Because the online element of the course is Moodle-based it can easily be edited and kept up to date. It is also anticipated that digital artefacts and teaching resources produced by each cohort within the course can be archived and shared and be the basis for the development of new materials for later cohorts.

Lessons learned and advice

Time management
Blended learning is often seen as a time-saving measure both in terms of course design and tutor time for delivery, this is a huge misconception. The development

and instructional design of the online part of the blended learning course can be extremely time consuming and complex if you want to take the course beyond the delivery of simple downloadable documents. Delivering any kind of online support for blended learning can also be very time consuming for tutors as many participants feel that an online tutor is available 24/7 and they do not have the limitations of 'class time' to restrict access to their tutor. Calculating how much time to allow tutors per student and dealing with student expectations becomes significantly challenging.

Moodle limitations

Many developers use Moodle as the platform of choice for course development because it is free and has a powerful LMS which can track students' online attendance and levels of participation. Developing materials using Moodle though can be very limiting as the platform tends to lack structural depth (though much has been done to address this with the more recent versions of Moodle).

Most resources and activity types that Moodle enables have to be built from the initial course landing page, which generally means that page can become very long, difficult to navigate and slow to load. During the development of the Blended Learning for ELT course, this problem was avoided through the development of independent content templates which were built separately and then uploaded as files. This enabled an additional structural level for the course, so that Moodle's internally constructed pages could be used as unit indexes and the initial course landing page could then be a basic contents page. The use of HTML for the independently developed template pages for the tasks also enabled a much greater level of integration with Web 2.0 tools and multimedia online elements, as they could easily be embedded into the HTML templates.

Structuring course delivery

When course tasks and units depend quite heavily on peer-to-peer interaction it is difficult to decide whether to make units time-bound and only available for a designated amount of time, or whether to make all units constantly available. Making units constantly available enables participants to more easily and flexibly manage their time in a way which suits them, but can lead to some participants, who work ahead, having no one to interact with. It really becomes dependent on the tutor then to monitor this situation and provide interaction for fast-moving students as well as remembering to refer them back to earlier discussions as slower-moving participants start to catch up. It is essential that participants understand that the value of what they learn comes from the learning journey and the interaction with peers, rather than from a race to the end of the materials.

Guiding principles and practical considerations

Importance of tasks – It is impossible to overstate the importance of active tasks in the online elements of the learning. Passive reading or viewing materials that require no action, interaction or reflection soon tire online learners and do not lead to deeper engagement or learning. Tasks also need to be relevant and applicable to the working context of the course participants and once completed, some form of feedback from peers or the tutor is essential.

Generating peer-to-peer interaction – Making sure that the tasks and the moderator encourage peer-to-peer interaction increases the likelihood of successful connectivist learning.

Using freely available technology – Using free and open access apps and web-based tools ensures that participants will have access to the same tools to create their own courses and that the skills they are learning will be immediately relevant and applicable to their teaching context.

Open content – Using open web-based content such as online journals and blogs ensures that all participants have equal access to resources and even participants coming from less well-resourced areas are not disadvantaged by limited access to academic materials.

Flipping the paradigm – Using a flipped approach to core content ensures that participants come to the much shorter face-to-face element of the course readily prepared with a strong understanding of background issues and basic technical skills and experience. This helps to maximise the effectiveness of the face-to-face workshop element of the course.

Recommendations for blended learning course designers

Build online tasks around social interactivity – People do not really want to interact with a computer, they want to interact with other people, so design tasks in which the computer is the conduit and enabler of communication, not the focus of it.

Think about tutor time – Think carefully about the amount of online tutor support necessary and how to avoid tutor overload. The tutor is very important to the success of the course, use their time wisely and value it. If the tutor is unhappy or feels overwhelmed or exploited then the course is unlikely to be successful, however well you may have designed your materials.

Do not reinvent the wheel – Check to see if you can exploit freely available resources before you start to build your own. It can save you a huge amount of time and enhance the materials by including a wider perspective.

Be time realistic – Think carefully about how long it takes to build effective online resources. It takes much more time to create online learning materials than it does to create classroom materials. A good rule is to try to estimate how long it will take, double it and then add 50 per cent, then you might be close to the reality.

Integrating online and face-to-face – Make sure you think about how the online and face-to-face elements will support each other and how best they can do this. Your course still needs to have some unity and continuity even if it is delivered in very different modes and in different places.

Exploit what works best – Build online tasks that can go beyond what can be done in a book or in a classroom. The internet and the world of online communication can be used to achieve some marvellous and creative things, so do not try to imitate books and classrooms, understand what is best about online and exploit it to the full.

Encourage learner autonomy and reflection – Getting students working alone and on their own computers is a great opportunity to give them some freedom, so exploit every opportunity you can to encourage autonomous learning and reflection.

Develop online learning skills – Think about the skills participants will need to handle the course and how to build on these. Teachers and students who are new to online learning will need help to cope with the medium as well as the actual learning you want to deliver, so be prepared with videos, tutorials and FAQs to help.

Be prepared to change – Constantly evaluate, reflect and learn from your course so that you can make the next course better. Digital materials and online courses are easy to change, and update, so be prepared to change what you may have originally thought was a great design.

References

Flipped Classroom Defined. Available online at http://digitalsandbox.weebly.com/flipped-classroom.html

L is for 'Loop input'. Available online at http://elteachertrainer.com/2010/05/28/do-we-still-use-%E2%80%98loop-input%E2%80%99-these-days/

Siemens, G (2004) Connectivism: *A learning theory for the digital age*. Available online at www.elearnspace.org/Articles/connectivism.htm

The Flipped Class: Myths vs. Reality. Available online at www.thedailyriff.com/articles/the-flipped-class-conversation-689.php

Woodward, T (2003) Loop input. *ELT Journal* 57/3. Available online at http://eltj.oxfordjournals.org/content/57/3/301.full.pdf

6

Reversing the blend:
From online to blended

Gavin Dudeney and Nicky Hockly

Introduction

At The Consultants-E, we offer fully online *in-service* training courses for practising language teachers. All of our training courses focus on helping teachers to learn how to effectively integrate information and communication technologies (ICT) in a principled manner, in their face-to-face and/or online teaching.

The course

This case study looks at one of our longer courses, the Cert ICT: Certificate in Teaching Languages with Technology, which is fully validated by Trinity College London. The course itself grew from a shorter, four-week course that was the recipient of a British Council ELTon in 2007. In its current form the course was first developed and run as a *completely online* 120-hour course. We launched an additional blended version of the qualification in 2009. In the blended Cert ICT, 50 hours of the total 120 hours are offered face-to-face. This is followed by the remaining 70 hours being taken online.

Our decision to review a blended approach responded to the inherent advantages of both face-to-face and online instruction:

> *Those who use blended approaches base their pedagogy on the assumption that there are inherent benefits in face-to-face interaction (both among learners and between learner and instructor) as well as the understanding that there are some inherent advantages to using online methods in their teaching.*
> *Thus the aim of those using blended learning approaches is to find a harmonious balance between online access to knowledge and face-to-face human interaction.*

(Osguthorpe and Graham, 2003)

Added to these general notions of playing to the strengths of each method, we also identified a number of pedagogical and practical reasons for deciding to offer a blended version of the course:

■ The course content (the development of ICT skills) lends itself well to face-to-face delivery, as tutors can physically help participants while they work with a range of ICT tools, in situ. Although this is also achievable online, the process of identifying issues and providing hands-on help can be more challenging online for tutors, and require Skype calls, or developing screencasts to help with specific issues. In this respect we refer to issues with learning and manipulating software packages, setting up online accounts with Web 2.0 services and other activities that are necessary at the start of the course prior to engaging with the actual learning content within the course itself.

- A part-time blended model allows participants from similar teaching backgrounds to work together on the course, as they are usually living locally, whereas the fully online version of the course always has international cohorts. Both local and international cohorts have their advantages (one is not intrinsically 'better' than the other), but offering an additional blended version of the course allows participants to choose which group environment they would prefer to work in – by choosing a part-time blended option, they will work with local teachers.

- A blended model increases the market reach of the course, by appealing to teachers who may be concerned about embarking on a fully online training course. As one blended course participant put it in feedback:

For me as a learner, the face-to-face part was great and was a stimulus to do the course. I've never done an online only course before, so this 'blended' approach appealed to me more. I think having the 'blended' approach has alleviated this fear. I feel better prepared and more open now to the online part.

The participants

Participants on the Cert ICT are qualified in-service language teachers. The Cert ICT focuses not just on ICT tools and techniques, but also on general concepts and areas such as online assessment, integration of ICT into the curriculum, mobile learning, e-learning and blended learning. As such, the scope of the course is not restricted merely to English language teachers and we have also occasionally had teachers of other languages on the course in the past (French, Spanish, Chinese and German).

However, the Cert ICT is validated by Trinity College London, so there are clear entry requirements: teachers must hold an initial teaching qualification, and non-native speaker teachers need a minimum level of English (IELTS 5.5 or equivalent).

The needs of the participants on the Cert ICT are usually fairly defined: they want to, or need to, learn more about how to use ICT in their classrooms. Specifically, they would like to learn to use technology tools with their learners in their face-to-face teaching, and want ideas about how to do so effectively. The participants are usually fairly experienced teachers, with a minimum of two years' experience, up to 20 years or more. (See teachers talking about their course expectations on the Blended Cert ICT: http://youtu.be/M0WrjdjXTTg)

Generally, our course participants have received little or no technology training in the past. But we do get a range of teachers on the course, from those with almost no experience, to a few who are already fairly proficient users of technology. The course is, in fact, designed to take this into account, so that tasks are open ended, allowing participants to complete them to the level of their own ability. As practising (and often experienced) teachers, participants frequently realise this early on, as this comment from one more tech-savvy course participant shows:

It was good because it was viable for all levels so to speak – you could work at your own pace and also help others and get help.

Generally speaking though, very tech-savvy participants will complete tasks and find the course easier than those with no ICT experience whatsoever. What this means in practice is that unskilled participants take longer to complete tasks, and need more hands-on support from the tutor and the rest of the group. Less technically proficient participants are often aware of the skills gap if they take a course with more proficient colleagues. However, the face-to-face component enables supportive group work from the beginning of the course, and can help these participants feel more secure. Here is one (less skilled) participant's take on this in her course feedback:

> I was often amazed at how those who knew more never seemed to mind helping out people like me and often wondered if they felt that they regretted signing up for this course. One day, I asked two of them and they immediately said, 'No way!' and went on to say that they felt that they had learned/were learning A LOT!

The tutors

All of our courses, whether offered fully online, or in blended versions, have a minimum of six participants and a maximum of 15 participants. This is partly because of the nature of our courses that are all hands-on, and task-based. In other words, participants work individually, in pairs and in small groups and prepare a significant number of outputs during a course. The hands-on nature of our courses means that the tutor workload is high. Typically, for one hour of online work, we calculate 1.5 hours of tutor support for a group. For one hour of face-to-face work, the ratio may be two hours of tutor work (at least) if we include preparation time.

In addition, we assign one tutor for a single group of six to ten participants. If the group has 11 to 15 participants, there are two tutors, with one taking the lead role (about 60–70 per cent of the workload), and the other playing a support role (30–40 per cent of the workload). Again, this is due to the increased workload for tutors with larger groups, due to the additional one-to-one support that online courses need to provide to participants, especially in the area of technology, where teachers may have little or no experience.

Course design and delivery

With the blended Cert ICT, the tutor can deal with larger groups in the face-to-face component, with up to 20 participants in one face-to-face group. However, for the online component a large group of 20 is split into two separate online groups of ten, each with its own tutor. The fundamental design issue here is that online tutoring (at least for hands-on, task-based courses that require a great deal of interaction/communication) can significantly increase a tutor's workload. The online version of a face-to-face course may mean more work for a teacher – if the job is going to be done well. This is a fundamental issue when considering blended learning, and one that we find many institutions do not seem to be aware of. Clearly it has important implications for staff hours and costing.

Because all our courses are offered online, typically we have teachers from all over the world, working closely together online in groups, for the duration of their course. The blended version of the Cert ICT, however, tends to attract participants who live locally to where the face-to-face component of the course is being run.

Clearly there are advantages to having only local participants on the blended version of the course, as content can be tailored more specifically to the local context. On the other hand, the insights and fresh perspectives provided by having a range of participants from all over the world in the fully online iteration of the course are lacking in the blended iteration.

The blend

Our case study may be slightly unusual in this volume, in that our blended course was in a sense 'reverse' engineered: we looked at providing a face-to-face component of what was *already* a fully online course.

In our work giving face-to-face training workshops and short courses around the world, we have the opportunity to talk to many teachers about technology, training, and their perceptions of working face-to-face and/or online. These contacts, and emails that we received from teachers all over the world, asking whether the Cert ICT existed in face-to-face mode, informed our decision to offer the course in blended mode. We also felt that some parts of the course content (learning how to use specific technologies) lent themselves especially well to being taught face-to-face: for example, learning how to set up a blog, or how to create a podcast, or how to contribute to a wiki, can easily and effectively be modelled and practised face-to-face.

In short, offering the Cert ICT as a blended option, with the initial 50 course hours taking place face-to-face, was seen as an easier and less threatening 'way in' to learning about technology for many teachers. The blended course starts with a one-week online orientation period in the course Moodle platform, in which participants complete three very short introductory tasks: they complete their profile page with personal information; share their attitudes to technology; and outline their expectations for the course. These tasks aim to familiarise the participants with the Moodle platform they will be using during the course, and they also help them get to know a bit about their course colleagues before meeting face-to-face. The course then officially starts with the face-to-face component. There are a number of reasons for starting with the face-to-face component, rather than the online component:

- The content of the course, especially in the initial stages where participants are building up their ICT skills, lends itself well to a face-to-face delivery mode, as noted previously. The online component of the course then deals with more theoretical issues (such as online assessment, integration into the curriculum, e-learning and m-learning). It also makes sense to start the course with the more practical training, so that by the time the more theoretical issues are considered in the online component, participants have some experience in using ICT on which to reflect.

- The group dynamic and relationships built up face-to-face help sustain participants through the online part of the course. Feedback from participants after the face-to-face component of a blended iteration reflects this perception:

  I think that due to the face-to-face component, our future interaction via emails will be much more relaxed and fruitful now that we've all had the chance to get to know each other a bit. We are people with faces and life stories now, not just online cyberspace companions.

It makes it much easier to interact with people you have met face-to-face, even though it's sometimes easier to be more anonymous, more distant. I have used (I think!) a Moodle before ... or something very similar, with the Open University so this wasn't, or should I say isn't, my first time.

The face-to-face part of the course was particularly helpful in creating a good relationship between the course participants.

■ As previously noted, participants with no online learning experience can find the idea of online training intimidating. Starting with the face-to-face component can help allay these fears, and provide a more gentle introduction to online training for more reluctant participants. In addition, participants may feel that a face-to-face approach simply suits them better:

I feel I have learned and progressed satisfactorily in the course, but that given my learning style I preferred the face-to-face component more than the online one.

Design decisions

The blended version of the Cert ICT offers the first 50 of the 120 hours as a face-to-face option – either intensively over two weeks, or part-time over ten weeks (depending on the local market and the time of year of delivery). Once those 50 hours have been completed face-to-face, the remaining 70 hours of the course are taken online in a virtual learning environment (VLE) called Moodle (www.moodle.org).

The face-to-face component uses a communicative training approach. Participants each bring a laptop to the face-to-face sessions, and they work on these throughout the course, learning how to use certain ICT tools and producing regular outputs. The face-to-face component is also paperless – all handouts/worksheets/resources are found on the course Moodle. Participants download these as needed during the face-to-face sessions, and save them on their own computers. Thus, the course Moodle functions as a course repository in the face-to-face component of the course, which is slowly built up over the 50 hours face-to-face. At the beginning of each face-to-face session, handouts are made available in the Moodle, which are then used as necessary. In the next session, more materials are made available. It is important not to overload participants by providing all the course resources at once in Moodle – by slowly revealing them session-by-session, participants are far more able to digest and use the resources provided. This is something that participants often appreciate:

Very clear layout, loved having only one week's tasks and content at a time, not too much stuff at once.

One of the design decisions we made is to introduce Moodle before the face-to-face component starts (with a few very simple tasks for participants to complete – see above), and then to use it as a repository of materials, and also to share work produced in each face-to-face session. This means that by the time participants get to the online component of the course, they are already familiar with the basic functions of Moodle, and use it on a regular basis.

Lessons learned

When deciding what part of a *teacher training* course to offer online, and what parts face-to-face, we find it makes sense to offer the most practical/hands-on elements of course content face-to-face. More theoretical discussions can easily take place online, for example via asynchronous forum discussions. In fact, it has been argued that online asynchronous forum discussions lead to more thoughtful contributions:

> *...asynchronous discussions allow for a higher level of cognitive questions that encourage critical thinking. Learners have more time to process questions and develop responses, and the learner's cognitive level of response often matches the cognitive level of the questions asked. Higher level cognitive and affective questions encourage learners to interpret, analyse, evaluate, infer, explain and self regulate.*

(Walker, 2005)

We also learned that it makes sense to introduce the VLE either before or early in the face-to-face component, rather than springing it on participants just before they are going to start the online component. In other words, the introduction of the online platform is scaffolded.

We learned that the use of a VLE in the face-to-face part works best as a repository, or for sharing outputs that are created. It doesn't make much sense to have participants completing extra tasks at home in the VLE during our face-to-face component, when we have a clearly separate 70-hour online component to follow.

One key question we have considered is whether the blended learning approach for the Cert ICT is more beneficial to the learners than the fully online approach. We have come to the conclusion that it is extremely difficult to make comparisons between these two modes, because they are so different. Of major importance are participants' attitudes towards the blended versus online approach, as we have seen above. Although the blended course participants claim that they would have found the online component difficult or impossible without a previous face-to-face component, the reality is that participants on our fully online component have no such difficulty; indeed online participants have no face-to-face component experience with which to compare. Feedback on the fully online version of the same course is equally positive, and frequently includes surprise and praise for the very supportive online group dynamic that is developed:

> *Interaction with colleagues was great overall. Initial fears about online interaction were quickly dispelled.*

> *Interaction with colleagues was excellent. Maybe ours was just a good group, but it worked very well. I found everyone very helpful and supportive. Certainly some 'friendships' arose between participants, where interests, help, advice, experience and support all played their parts. A virtual classroom also has an atmosphere.*

At the same time the fully online participants were aware of some of the challenges involved in online communication, for example when this involved pair work:

It was frustrating a couple of times when I had to do pair work with someone who communicated late or not at all.

Pair work was sometimes tricky, due to geographical/time differences, e.g. my contact Switzerland-Singapore.

The lesson here is that online pair and group work needs to be carefully designed and judiciously applied, with clear guidelines for how to carry it out (for example, what participants should do if they don't hear from a task partner).

It is interesting to note that we have never received feedback from a fully online participant regretting that they did not take the blended version. Of course, frequently the blended version is simply not an option for an online participant, due to location.

In addition, when comparing the results of the blended versus online versions of the Cert ICT, they are very similar. The dropout rate on both versions is extremely low (one per cent – two per cent), and frequently due to similar causes – typically an excessive workload at school making it difficult to keep up with course work. The pass rate is also similar across the two modes, with a low rate of referrals (around two per cent), and a similar percentage of distinctions (20 per cent – 25 per cent).

Summary and recommendations

Clearly, having identified a need for a blended version of the course, it was then a question of deciding what percentage to blend, and which activities and content to timetable into each part of the blend. Ensuring that participants are comfortable with embedded technologies is a key factor in the success of a course like this, so the initial face-to-face component not only ensures that group bonding takes place, but also introduces all the technologies that will be used in the online part.

Maximising the potential of the different delivery modes is also key. Using face-to-face time for confidence building, socialising, group activities and critical input sessions makes efficient use of group communication opportunities, whilst research, discussion, reflection and project work can more productively be done online, at a distance.

In many ways it is still not clear to us why some participants choose the fully online version, and some the blended one. Clearly external factors play a large part in the decision-making process: timetables, travel restrictions, home and family life and a whole slew of parameters influence the final decision, though it is worth noting that the majority of those who choose the blended model are perhaps less familiar with technologies before they come to the course, and need more support and encouragement at the start of their training journey. After four years of running both options, the fully online course is still by far the most popular choice, and we feel that more research will be needed in order to fully identify success factors and decision criteria for both models.

References

Osguthorpe, RT and Graham, CR (2003) Blended learning environments: Definitions and directions. *The Quarterly Review of Distance Education* 4/3: 227–233.

Walker, G (2005) Critical thinking in asynchronous discussion. *International Journal of Instructional Technology and Distance Learning* 2/6. Available online at http://itdl.org/journal/jun_05/article02.htm

Further Reading

Harrell, PE and Harris M (2006) Teacher preparation without boundaries: A two-year study of an online teacher certification program. *Journal of Technology and Teacher Education* 14/4: 755–774. Available online at www.editlib.org/p/18913

King, KP (2002) Identifying success in online teacher education and professional development. *The Internet and Higher Education* 5: 231–246. Available online at www.sciencedirect.com/science/article/pii/S1096751602001045

Kupetz, R and Ziegenmeyer, B (2005) Blended learning in a teacher training course: Integrated interactive e-learning and contact learning. *ReCALL* 17/2: 179–196. Available online at http://journals.cambridge.org/action/displayAbstract?fromPage=online&aid=355478

Motteram, G (2006) Blended education and the transformation of teachers: A long-term case study in postgraduate UK higher education. *British Journal of Educational Technology* 37/1: 17–30. Available online at http://onlinelibrary.wiley.com/doi/10.1111/j.1467-8535.2005.00511.x/abstract;jsessionid=486CA11E152793B9CEA873C548175DE9.d03t01

Young, A and Lewis, CW (2008) Teacher education programmes delivered at a distance: An examination of distance student perceptions. *Teaching and Teacher Education* 24/3: 601–609. Available online at www.sciencedirect.com/science/article/pii/S0742051X07000509

7

A case study of blended learning: The 'Communicative Assessment – Development of Testing Skills' project

Keith O'Hare and Xu Bo

Background

In 2010, the British Council in China decided to use a blended learning approach for a training course to develop testing skills, targeting test-writers and key teachers in secondary schools in certain cities and provinces across the country.

Whilst it could be argued that all learning is blended, through the use of any combination of instructional modalities (Bersin et al., 2003), such as videos or books, or instructional methods (Driscoll, 2002), such as problem solving or case studies, this was the first time the British Council in China had attempted combining online and face-to-face instruction.

This article outlines why we decided to take this approach, the challenges we met and the learning points of this training project, with particular reference to blended learning. As will be seen, the socio-cultural and educational context of China plays an important role and may be of interest for other organisations working in so-called 'Confucius-heritage' contexts.

The need

In the Chinese teacher education system, teacher researchers (responsible for writing higher-stake tests) and key teachers (responsible for writing lower-stake tests, and for supporting other teachers in their schools and neighbourhoods) are given little formal training in how to write tests. Tests are often written by teacher researchers drawing on their experience as a student or novice teacher when teaching was largely based on a grammar–translation approach, and so tests tend to reflect that approach.

Thus, with the backdrop of a new national curriculum that encouraged communicative teaching and learning of English, a clear need was identified to train this group of test writers in the basic skills to develop communicative tests that had a positive backwash on teaching. They needed knowledge of the latest theories of assessment and its relation to testing and teaching, skills development (to write better tests), and a change in mind-set to believe that a different type of test would be beneficial for them, their teachers and their students.

The learner and the context

Although China has in recent years adopted online learning approaches for students and teachers, it has not been seen as particularly successful. 'Many universities and colleges in China have carried out numerous experiments with e-learning but have not achieved the expected results' (Huang and Zhou, 2007). One of the expected results was to use online learning to train teachers and students across vast distances. These expected results though, were not really met due to a variety of reasons including weak independent learning strategies of students and teachers, and teachers not being used to taking courses online. What is more, the quality of online courses is often seen as being inferior to face-to-face instruction. In addition, there is still an overwhelming preference by education authorities and teachers to have a foreign trainer (a native-speaker), in person, deliver the training. There is an assumption that the foreign trainer will have access to the most recent knowledge the participants need, and a high value is placed on the cultural and linguistic interaction the participants will have with that foreign trainer.

In addition, the UK is seen by Chinese education authorities as being a leader in education, especially in the field of assessment.

Why a blended approach?

Before designing the training programme we assessed the needs of the participants, taking into account the local context and expectations of all stakeholders, in particular the local education authorities we would be working with. This needs analysis led us to identify a series of lower level objectives, underneath the wider objective to improve the test writing skills of the participants.

When we addressed course design, it seemed clear to us that there were three objectives that would be best achieved via face-to-face interaction, and these needed to happen at the beginning of the course. They were:

1. Participants would need to make a shift in their mind-set (that they needed communicative tests and the impact of such tests would be positive).
2. Participants would need to build trust with the trainer and each other.
3. It was important to satisfy the cultural demand for the 'foreign trainer'.

We therefore designed a four-day, face-to-face course that would give participants the learning opportunities to meet those objectives.

However, there were more objectives that we felt would be best met by some form of online interaction and study. These were:

1. To provide information and the latest up-to-date knowledge on assessment from the UK.
2. To appeal to a variety of learning styles.
3. To connect the learning to the participants' workplace and local context.
4. To allow participants to develop their own tests and to learn at their own pace.

Delivery media and instructional strategies

In order to reach these objectives, a Moodle platform was set up where participants could read articles on assessment, watch videos of experts talking about different areas of assessment and testing, and link to a variety of other related websites. All of this could be done after the face-to-face training when the participants had returned to their workplaces.

The two stages have different focuses; stage one focuses on general knowledge around testing while stage two has an in-depth look at testing the four skills. So, in the stage two face-to-face training, participants learn key concepts, how to use different models, such as Weir's model of reading (Weir and Khalifa, 2008), and how to write test items. The e-moderated online courses serve as a supplementary part to the face-to-face training; helping participants to review main ideas, to put new ideas into practice via doing assignments that are marked, and to reflect on the returned assignment and identify areas in their work to be improved.

The third objective was derived from research and our own experience. There is research into teacher learning that emphasises the importance of reflective learning (Schön, 1983), so we wanted participants to reflect on their learning in the training and when back at work. This would enable them to bridge the gap between theory and practice, to evaluate their own practice, and so achieve deeper ongoing learning. In addition, we knew that all education authorities we work with want to make sure that training courses are based on the local context. It was therefore important for us that the participants took the ideas and learning from the face-to-face training, put it into practice in their work, reflected on that and discussed and shared the experience and reflection with others.

The online platform was an opportunity to support that learning process, but, initially it was just a place to share knowledge, experience and reflections. However, in hindsight, this was a mistake. We overlooked the fact that most teachers were still powerfully influenced by a transmission approach to learning, and so the desire to have a structured online course, that gave a sense of progress, was so strong that most teachers did not engage in the platform, and many cited the lack of structure as the key factor. After the first few courses, the platform was changed into a more structured, e-moderated course. This was hugely important since most Chinese teachers on the course told us they had an expectation that an authority figure would explicitly guide and lead them through their learning.

Simultaneously, in other training projects, courses had followed a skill theory view of learning. It was decided that this approach should be applied to this new online platform too. Malderez and Wedell (2007) describe a five-step process that begins with the participant describing an experience, interpreting it, being exposed to other people's ideas or interpretations, making sense of that new input, and finally taking that new understanding into their teaching or work. So, in our course, participants would review their face-to-face study and their interpretation of it, then read new articles or get new ideas from videos, make sense of that new input on the forums and wikis, and finally apply that new understanding in an assignment that would typically involve writing or applying tests in their workplace. Then the cycle would begin again, covering five or six units of online study.

When participants were enrolled on the courses, for most courses they were divided into groups, since it is widely recognised that test writing is best done in groups, rather than as an individual activity. All examination boards have a 'peer' review process for items, including Cambridge, Pearson, and Trinity. Bachman and Palmer (1996) talk about collecting feedback from a wide variety of sources both on specifications, items and on processes and procedures. The forums of the e-moderated Moodle platform gave participants and the e-moderator opportunity to do that.

Course structure

As mentioned above, the development of testing skills is a long-term process, as it requires not only necessary theoretical knowledge, but also continued practice and reflection. What is more, our goal of getting participants to change their attitude to the value of communicative testing, and to become co-constructors of knowledge through dynamic interactions, rather than passive recipients, would be a radical change in pedagogy for them. This could start in the four-day face-to-face training, but would need more time to be achieved. So, the course was designed with two stages, with each stage consisting of four days' face-to-face training, followed by around six weeks' online e-moderated training. This kind of blend that allows a radical transformation of pedagogy is what Bonk and Graham call 'transforming blends' (2006: 13).

Finally, there were practical factors to consider. Whilst it was possible to gather together in one city a group of in-service teacher researchers for four days' training, it was extremely difficult to release them from their work for a longer stretch of time, as they have many responsibilities beyond teaching. Due to the size of China, and the fact that training was offered at a provincial level, participants had to travel anything up to 12 hours by train or bus to get to the face-to-face training.

Assessing learning

In order to evaluate the new tests that participants were making, assignments for each online unit were submitted and marked by the e-moderator. This was returned to the participant and they were asked to reflect on the result and trainer comments and comment on future changes they would make or action they would take. In addition, the level of participation on the online platforms was assessed. The latter, it was hoped, would have a positive backwash on contributions to the forums. Moodle tools enable all of the above to be done, recorded and shared accurately and effectively.

Lessons learned

1. Course design

a. Originally, we started with the face-to-face training, and then on the last day of training participants were given an hour's introduction to the online platform and expected to use it appropriately. However, the course design overlooked the fact that several had never followed an online course before, let alone used a Moodle platform. It also ignored the importance of online social engagement.

The course was therefore re-designed so that two weeks before the face-to-face training, participants had a half day introduction to the platform and were shown how it works. Then, following the first two stages of Salmon's (2000) five-stage model, they then had two weeks to build a profile, socialise and do some background reading for the course.

Summary of Salmon's (2000) five-stage model

Stage	Student activities	Tutor activities
Stage 1 Access and motivation	• Setting up system and accessing.	• Welcome and encouragement. • Guidance on where to find technical support.
Stage 2 Online socialisation	• Sending and receiving messages.	• Introductions. • Ice-breakers. • Ground rules. • Netiquette.
Stage 3 Information exchange	• Carrying out activities. • Reporting and discussing findings.	• Facilitate structured activities. • Assign roles and responsibilities. • Support use of learning materials. • Encourage discussions. • Summarise findings and/or outcomes.
Stage 4 Knowledge construction	• Conferencing. • Course-related discussions. • Critical thinking applied to subject material. • Making connections between models and work-based learning experiences.	• Facilitate open activities. • Facilitate the process. • Asking questions. • Encourage reflection. • Tutor is very active at this stage.
Stage 5 Development	• Use of conferencing in a strategic way. • Integration of CMC into other forms of learning. • Reflection on learning processes. • Students become critical of the medium.	• Support. • Respond only when required. • Encourage reflection. • Tutor is less active and hands over to the students.

b. The programme was divided into two stages. As mentioned previously, one of the reasons for this was to facilitate a 'transformational blend', i.e. one that would achieve a radical change in pedagogy where participants' attitude to, and adoption of, communicative testing changes, as well as connecting the learning with the workplace. Another reason was partly cultural. Chinese teachers, as mentioned previously, are used to being led in their learning, but also they are often not allowed to regulate their own time. They often have to react to last-minute demands of their head teacher, parents, subject leader, or even colleagues, and it is expected that requests will be seen to immediately. This meant many participants would fall behind with the online study and assignments. Several partners would therefore hold informal meetings of the participants, where possible, to bring them together to tackle such issues, and also to boost motivation. Also, bringing the trainer in real contact again helped them understand the local context even more deeply, and so build more trust with the participants.

2. Delivery media and instructional modalities

a. The face-to-face trainer was also the e-moderator. It was essential that the participants had a high level of trust and faith in the online trainer, feeling that person knew their context and their learning needs. That trust could only be gained effectively during the face-to-face training.

b. The internet is very slow for some links to resources outside China, so for video tasks, if videos (with copyright) could not be stored directly on our China server, tape scripts were provided to help participants.

c. The course design had to take cultural differences into consideration. For instance, Chinese teachers are not used to group tasks and would be reluctant to adapt or change other groups' or participants' work directly. Therefore, the wiki was not successful, and discussion forums were used for post-work comments instead.

Conclusions

Feedback has been very positive, with the varied learning modes proving particularly popular among participants.

Since its first pilot in 2010, the project has been delivered with six different partners at municipal or provincial level. The blended learning style has been welcomed by both participants and partners, who are mainly local education authorities:

I find this mode helpful and effective as it allows me to learn and practice after work.

Shen Qing (participant from Shanghai)

Through the Moodle online I really have learned a lot! I have got efficient help from Jeff (the trainer and E-moderator) and I have searched the internet for PDFs and much information about testing. I will try my best to help my colleagues and students know more about tests.

One participant from Nanjing

The blended learning approach has met the needs of the project and enabled participants to learn new skills in test writing such as:

■ developing test specifications

■ using their understanding of the advantages of certain test items to enable them to use a wider range of items

■ using statistical tools like a discrimination index and item analysis

■ being confident in their ability to write reliable and valid tests that will have a positive impact on communicative classroom teaching.

It is hoped that this development of awareness, confidence and skills will have a positive impact on communicative classroom teaching in China.

References

Bachman, LF and Palmer, AS (1996) *Language Testing in Practice*. Oxford: Oxford University Press.

Bersin and Associates (2003) *Blended Learning: What Works? An Industry Study of the Strategy, Implementation, and Impact of Blended Learning.*

Bonk, C and Graham, C (eds) (2006) *Handbook of Blended Learning: Global Perspectives, Local Designs*. San Francisco: Jossey-Bass.

Driscoll, M (2002) Blended learning: Let's get beyond the hype. *E-learning* 3/3: 54.

Huang, RH and Zhou YL (2007) 'Designing blended learning focused on knowledge category and learning activities', in Bonk, C and Graham, C (eds) (2006) *Handbook of Blended Learning: Global Perspectives, Local Designs*. San Francisco: Jossey-Bass, 296–310.

Malderez, A and Wedell, M (2007) *Teaching Teachers Processes and Practices*. London: Continuum.

Salmon, G (2000) *E-moderating: The Key to Teaching and Learning*. London: Kogan Page.

Schön, D (1983) *The Reflective Practitioner: How Professionals Think in Action*. New York: Basic Books.

Tu, CH (2001) How Chinese perceive social presence: An examination of interaction in online learning environment. *Educational Media International* 38/1: 45–60.

Vygotsky, L (1978) *Mind in Society*. London: Harvard University Press.

Weir, C and Khalifa, H (2008) A model of reading *Research Notes* 31/3.

8

Blended learning:
The IDLTM experience

Ron White, Andy Hockley, Stephen Heap and George Pickering

Background

Ten years ago, the International Diploma in Language Teaching Management (IDLTM), whose origins are based on an earlier advanced diploma (ADLTM), was launched. With tripartite design and ownership, viz., Cambridge ESOL, ICTE-UQ, SIT World Learning, the certificates are triple badged. The course has been delivered by ICTE-UQ (Australia), SIT (US) and International House Barcelona, in Australia, Brazil, Oman, Spain, Turkey and Vietnam. Typically, it is individuals who enrol, but courses for closed groups are also provided.

The course attracts managers/leaders and prospective managers locally and internationally, both native and non-native English speakers (the latter with a minimum of IELTS 7 or equivalent). There is a maximum of 12 participants per course and well over 200 have successfully completed the course since 2001.

The IDLTM was designed in response to indications that there was a demand for a management course which, by being made available in blended learning mode would enable participants to combine study with work, a benefit valued by the students surveyed by Heinze and Procter (2004). In the IDLTM, such blending also facilitates professional development by being relatively long term, collaborative and school based (Hiebert, Gallimore and Stigler, 2002, cited by Owston, Sinclair and Wideman, 2008). It was also felt that a blended learning approach would allow participants more time to study management theory and to relate it to their own context. Furthermore, as Garrison and Kanuka (2004) argue 'the combination of face-to-face and online learning can result in a transformative learning experience ... because course participants can benefit from being connected to a learning community regardless of whether they are physically apart and together' (Owston, Sinclair and Wideman, 2008). Finally, with the predicted expansion of computer mediated training and learning, there was a belief that blended learning course delivery would contribute to the information literacy of participants, and that, as Dziuban, Hatman, and Moskal (2004: 3) point out, albeit in the context of undergraduate teaching, this would be of 'benefit to them throughout their entire academic and employment careers'.

After several iterations, the current model was established:

- A two-week face-to-face phase, usually of two consecutive weeks, this being the maximum time most managers can be away from work.

- Six-month online tuition and assessment for the eight course modules.

- A one-week online simulation (to form the basis of the final so-called 'capstone' or end of course assignment).

The course consists of six core modules: organisational management, human resource management, financial management, marketing, customer service management and academic management, with optional modules, such as project management and managing change. The course is intended to be closely tied to work experience and all assignments are directly based on workplace requirements, for example, the marketing module involves preparing a marketing plan for a new service to be offered by the candidate's language teaching organisation (LTO).

Pedagogical resources

In overall structure, the course involves two different modes of presentation: face-to-face and online. The course package consists of a syllabus, and a main coursebook (White et al., 2008), which itself is closely based on both the structure of the course and experience of teaching it. This book is supplemented by other publications covering the topics of the modules, as well as articles and materials downloadable from the virtual learning environment (VLE) or from recommended online sources. Prior to the publication of this particular book, the main coursebook was White et al. (1991), supplemented by other more general management coursebooks, such as Robbins and Judge (2012). However, these books played a slightly different role than the newer book, being more supplemental than central.

The VLE is a critical component, being the main channel by which online material is made available to participants, as well as being the vehicle through which communication is managed between trainers and participants, and among participants themselves. The choice of VLE is dependent on the delivery institution for most courses, though trainers are able to exercise individual preference for some courses. ICTE at the University of Queensland uses Blackboard, while other IDLTMs these days typically use Moodle. Institutional provision and back-up are significant benefits, since large organisations have the means to acquire, manage and support sophisticated IT provision. However, in such an institutional context, the IDLTM course will be just one of many and ultimately trainers and participants are dependent on the efficiency and goodwill of IT services.

Managing the mix

The face-to-face phase involves input in the form of presentations as well as activities and tasks involving collaboration among participants. The activities in this phase provide participants with the opportunity to develop as a social group as they proceed through some of the stages involved in team formation, and they establish norms of working together. Forming a social group and becoming a professional learning community is important in order to support the online phase, when participants themselves act as sources of information and ideas and sharers of experience.

Feedback such as the following from participants confirms the value of the face-to-face phase: 'From the point of view of building up a class dynamic, interaction at the "forming" stage of our group's development, getting to know each others' ways of learning and characteristics, and knowing who the people we later spent six months or so learning with purely online were really helpful aspects and "humanised" the course'. However, as participants themselves have become more experienced and sophisticated in blended learning, they are more critical, as shown in comments such as 'Blended Learning has plenty of potential but I get the feeling that most courses utilise very little of the available technology. The entire Blackboard and blended learning environment was nothing more complex than a forum or blog. Not exactly cutting edge.' Another IDLTM graduate, now following a blended learning master's course, suggested 'Changing the focus of the F2F two weeks to hands on coursework with a variety of tasks would also give notice to the instructors to differentiate their teaching and make it more engaging for the students', a view which was not, however, at all widespread and possibly reflects unfavourably on the teaching style of some trainers (see the comment below by Dziuban, Hatman and Moskal (2004: 10) on re-learning how to teach). Overall, the consensus was that 'the blended learning model worked well for me ...[and].... I think the online tasks were useful and although sometimes they didn't seem connected to the assignments they were definitely linked to growth as a manager'.

The blending of modalities is illustrated in the work on the first module, on organisational management. During the face-to-face phase, participants discuss, compare and contrast their own LTOs in terms of the key organisational concepts being covered on the module. This work is continued and extended during the online phase when they elaborate such analysis as set out in the assignment task, and during online discussion clarify their understanding of concepts and demonstrate their use in opening up their organisation to new levels of understanding. In turn, this contributes to the written assignment.

Here is an example of a task as part of the work leading up to the assignment in the Customer Service Management module:

> Participants are asked to read two documents as preparation for the activity outlined below. Having posted their descriptions, they then comment on each other's accounts and the trainer moderates the discussion and provides a summing up.

> A good metric for measuring customer satisfaction is one that:
> 1. Yields new insights.
> 2. Is based on user actions (what they have experienced) not just opinions.
> 3. Is actionable (you can do something to improve the service).

> Having read the two documents and done whatever other follow-up reading you want to do:
> 1. Describe the survey procedures used in your LTO (you can give actual examples if you like).
> 2. Comment on their effectiveness in the light of the three points listed above.
> 3. Suggest how the procedures could be improved.

> Post your comments to Blackboard.

Online phase activities

Both asynchronous and synchronous modes have been employed. Asynchronous activities involve three main elements: text, task and outcome. The simplest and most straightforward task involves a set text or texts which participants read and summarise, comment upon or apply to a specific situation or issue (the task), the outcome being an extension of knowledge and application in the management area concerned. Either the text is common to all participants, or is unique to each one. The latter is more problematic, since it can be difficult to find up to a dozen different texts which are all relevant to the specific module topic common to all participants.

An example of a task with shared texts – participants are directed to read a number of texts on the idea of the learning organisation, and then respond to the following questions in the discussion forum:

1. What do you think the ideas of Personal Mastery; Shared Vision; Team Learning; Mental Models and Systems Thinking mean to your organisation?

2. Do you think your organisation possesses any or all of these characteristics? (which? give examples?)

3. How could you go about instigating these ideas into your LTO?

A more complex task involves a pro forma or template of some sort (the text) which is then completed with data from each participant's situation (the task). These are then posted and form the basis of discussion in which participants compare and contrast their completions. The outcome is an increased understanding of the concepts and analytical or management procedures involved. All participants follow a uniform set of procedures but the outcomes vary since each participant will be drawing on data unique to their own situation.

A third type of activity involves a task in the form of critical incidents and cases in a management area, the task being either to evaluate a solution described in the text, or to propose a situation if one is not offered. The evaluation or the new solution are posted and discussed. Here is an example of such a case:

Email from agent to sales executive:

Could you please help me in dealing with this case as I received the complaint from Miss Rong yesterday? She said the meals provided in the host family are bad. She got several dinners only with some bread and a plate of vegetable, and also without dessert and fruit (although there is plenty of fruit in the fridge). She doesn't feel eating full in each day.

Her host family is also very strict with all live in their house. For instance, Miss Rong wants to buy bike because the host family is very far away from the school, however, the host family doesn't allow her to put her bike in their garden, just allow her to put outside. They are not friendly enough to Miss Rong, and she feels really upset to live there.

I wonder that how we can help Miss Rong in this case, if your colleague to discuss this case with Miss Rong's host family, Miss Rong is afraid that they will unhappy with her and her life to live there will be more difficult. Can I have your advice?

There is a fourth activity type in which participants develop their own case study through the online interactions. They post the situation (in effect generating their own text), which is then commented on by their colleagues who offer possible solutions. The case and the solution(s) are then developed by the original poster (also with reference to the literature) and submitted for assessment. An example from the Human Resource Management (HRM) module, in which the assignment asks participants to:

Produce a case study of an HRM aspect of your own LTO, in which you describe the situation, identify a problem and propose and evaluate a solution.

This is achieved in the following way, as outlined to the participants themselves:

First, you should produce a description of the situation and identify the problem and post it on the discussion board.

Then everybody in the group is invited to respond to everybody else's situation with suggestions.

You complete the assignment by writing your own solution (incorporating as many or as few as you like of your classmates' ideas).

Finally, any of the above activity types can be linked closely to the assignments which participants are required to complete for each module. The closeness of the alignment between the activity and the assignment will vary, and some trainers set up tasks which will provide content for the paper, as in the last example above. Such activities involve a blend of text, task, discussion and application in a final written text produced by the participants for assessment.

The role of the trainer in the above activities will vary, although for the most part it is to act as a facilitator by setting up the activity and then clarifying the task if this appears necessary, and prompting the participants by posing questions or drawing attention to shared or contrasting issues arising from the content posted by participants.

Synchronous activities form the second type employed on the course. These typically involve chat sessions to discuss nominated topics or to deal with assignment-related issues. The trainer mediates the discussion and, where participants are seeking specific information or guidance on the assignment, answers questions. For the most part, such sessions are an online substitute for the kind of face-to-face discussion which would occur in a classroom.

A second type of synchronous activity is exemplified in the simulation, which forms the culmination of the course. Participants are put into teams of up to six members, and they are provided with briefing material which is downloaded from the VLE. This material sets the context and provides information on the management structure, staffing, services and finances of a fictitious LTO. The task is to analyse the strengths and weaknesses of the LTO, to identify potential areas for repair or development, and to prepare a medium-term business plan. The activity takes place over several days during which tasks are assigned among team members, outcomes are posted on the VLE, and texts are prepared and posted (a Powerpoint presentation and a plan in the form of a word processed document). The trainer has an essentially passive role, monitoring progress and only intervening if it appears that a team is going off the rails.

Evaluation of activities

In a course covering a wide range of management areas, some activities are more appropriate or effective than others. For instance, a task in financial management intended to apply specific processes will have an outcome which will be either right or wrong. By contrast, a critical incident in HRM may have more than one possible solution to the problem posed. The kind of online discussion in the former will be mostly concerned with the mechanics of achieving the correct outcome, whereas in the latter, the discussion will consider alternative scenarios and consequences, while also making connections to parallel issues in the participants' own work context.

By and large, tasks which are simple in design, with a minimum amount of textual material, and which are relevant to the workplace, but allow for a range of responses from simple to complex, are the most effective at encouraging participation, collaboration and lateral learning. For instance, reading articles which have an interesting angle on a topic and which can then be mapped onto the participants' own contexts seems to generate most discussion.

In fact, the key variable appears to be the group itself. Some groups establish a very productive dynamic during the face-to-face phase which they then carry over to the online part of the course, whereas in other groups, there may be one or two 'lurkers' who make limited or no contribution, regardless of the activity. The problem then is that such people are seen to be 'passengers' by active participants, and the effect on team morale and functioning can be noticeable in the simulation. However, as one of the aspects of the simulation is to actually comment on the effectiveness of online teams and problems that arise in the operation of such teams, this 'problem' is addressed in the sense that participants are able to discuss how they reacted to such situations.

In all of these activities, the VLE plays a crucial role. This is particularly well demonstrated in the fourth activity type described in the previous section. In fact, in the type of blended learning that has evolved on the IDLTM, the VLE is an integral component and virtually none of the range of blended learning activities would be possible without the use of a VLE.

When it comes to synchronous activities, some have proven to be problematic for a number of reasons. Firstly, participants are often in widely dispersed time zones, which can make scheduling of chat sessions very problematic. Secondly, managing chat sessions with more than four or five participants is difficult, and despite establishing simple procedures to facilitate optimum participation, moderating such sessions is both challenging and taxing. Different solutions or approaches have been tried, from text-based chat to full webcam-supported audio-visual chat, but no solution has proved to be all things to all people. Some participants have even commented that after a while they found it more useful to not attend the chat sessions, and instead read the transcript afterwards, as it was more conducive to their own style of learning. At their most effective, they are practically useful for participants and they serve a valuable function in reinforcing the social ties of the group.

Thirdly, the simulation generates a lot of involvement. For one thing it is high stakes (the culminating assignment depends on content from the simulation), while for another there are social pressures among each team which encourage active participation, since letting down the team is something which most participants wish to avoid. In many ways, the simulation is the most productive of the blended learning activities used on the course. Or, as one participant put it, 'The simulation was also a fantastic way to bring everything together'.

Administration

Blended learning gives rise to a number of administration demands. In a programme such as IDLTM, the trainers are employed on a freelance basis, and only the course manager and administrator are full-time employees of the provider institution. This means that, in effect, the trainers, who will usually be widely dispersed, are service providers and they are paid fixed rates according to specified teaching hours to be devoted to both the face-to-face and online phases of the course, so guaranteeing uniformity of trainer commitment is a challenge.

Trainers are recruited on the basis of their subject expertise, but among any group there is diversity of experience of blended learning pedagogy, expectations and commitment. In turn, this gives rise to a need for trainer training and the exchange of good practice among members of the teaching team. At best, this can be arranged during the face-to-face phase, under the guidance of the lead trainer who is, however, one among equals and has limited authority to direct such training or to invoke any sanctions in the event of under-performance by other trainers.

Because of the tight scheduling and sequencing of the IDLTM programme, establishing and maintaining routines, meeting deadlines and record keeping are vital for the effective management of the course. While the importance of efficient course management is not confined to blended learning, because the blend in this case is based on online work and participation among a geographically dispersed group of candidates, the effectiveness of such a blended learning programme is highly dependent on effective co-ordination and administration.

Conclusion

The IDLTM model of blended learning is successful when judged from the high retention rate – 92 per cent on the ICTE-UQ courses – and satisfaction levels. On the basis of the IDLTM experience, some guiding principles and practical considerations emerge which may have implications for blended learning provision beyond this particular case.

Firstly, there is the role, reliability and accessibility of the platform for the blended learning components. Heinze and Procter (2004) consider student concerns over technical issues with the VLE as one the perceived weaknesses of blended learning, while the importance of both teacher and student training in the use of blended learning facilities is noted repeatedly. In addition, with the growing sophistication of participants – particularly on a course like IDLTM – there is an expectation that, to coin a phrase, course provision will have moved beyond 'BL 1.0' to 'BL 2.0'.

Secondly, the course material and examples must be directly relevant to management in an LTO. Since management textbooks rarely draw on examples in an educational service context, this has meant developing a coursebook based on the course, as well as assembling a stock of examples and cases from the world of the LTO manager, such as articles from the IATEFL Leadership and Management SIG Newsletter.

Thirdly, as Dziuban, Hatman and Moskal (2004: 10) point out, with blended learning, 'Just as students have to relearn how to learn, faculty have to relearn how to teach', while in courses such as IDLTM, bringing together trainers from a range of different areas can create a forum for mentoring and the exchange of pedagogical practices and, as they also suggest, can 'revitalize senior professors by refocusing them on the process of effective instruction'.

Fourthly, because there is a high level of integration across the eight assessed course modules, it has proved beneficial to restrict the number of trainers to a maximum of four because of the close co-operation required – at least ideally – among trainers. With a small scale course like IDLTM such co-operation is feasible, but it is clear that in large-scale course provision, facilitating communication and co-operation across a teaching team becomes a more challenging and even more important requirement.

Fifthly, the trainers themselves influence how, when and what participants contribute to online tasks and discussions. If trainers are perfunctory in the way they interact with participants, the latter are disinclined to contribute in depth. Indeed, Garrison and Vaughan (2007) advocate that teachers must provide '...ongoing facilitation, monitoring, and modelling of the course expectations for students throughout the entire semester' (p. 141). What participants value is comments from trainers which are insightful, though not necessarily lengthy, and which are worth taking time off from their own busy schedules to read and reflect upon.

Finally, although blended learning tuition involves a combination of elements, inputs and activities which are greatly facilitated by the means of a VLE, ultimately the success of blended learning depends on the imagination, understanding and commitment of the trainers, the effectiveness of well-organised and reliable administration and the wholehearted engagement of learners, prepared to participate in a course that may extend over a prolonged period.

References

Dziuban, CD, Hatman, JL and Moskal, PD (2004) Blended learning. *EDUCAUSE Center for Applied Research Bulletin* Issue 7. Available online at http://net.educause.edu/ir/library/pdf/ERB0407.pdf

Garrison, D and Kanuka, H (2004) Blended learning: Uncovering its transformative potential in higher education. *Internet and Higher Education* 7: 95–105.

Garrison, D and Vaughan, ND (2007) *Blended Learning in Higher Education: Framework, Principles, and Guidelines*. San Francisco: Jossey-Bass Publishers.

Heinze, A and Procter, C (2004) *Reflections on the Use of Blended Learning*. Paper presented at 2nd Education in a Changing Environment conference 13–14 September 2004, University of Salford, UK. Available online at http://usir.salford.ac.uk/1658/

Hiebert, J, Gallimore, R and Stigler, JW (2002) A knowledge base for the teaching profession: What would it look like and how can we get one? *Educational Researcher* 31/5: 3–15.

IATEFL Leadership & Management SIG. Available online at http://eltm.iatefl.org/

International Diploma in Language Teaching Management (IDLTM). Available online at www.icte.uq.edu.au/idltm

Owston, RD, Sinclair, M and Wideman, H (2008) Learning for professional development: an evaluation of a program for middle school mathematics and science teachers. *Teachers College Record* 10/5: 1033–1064. Available online at www.tcrecord.org/content.asp?contentid=14668

Robbins, S and Judge, T (2012) *Organizational Behaviour*. Harlow: Pearson Education Limited.

White, R, Martin, M, Stimson, M and Hodge, R (1991) *Management in English Language Teaching*. Cambridge: Cambridge University Press.

White, R, Hockley, A, van der Horst Jansen, J and Laughner, M (2008) *From Teacher to Manager: Managing Language Teaching Organizations*. Cambridge: Cambridge University Press.

9

Creating a blended DELTA Module One

Sally Hirst and Tom Godfrey

The context

This chapter explores the evolution of a blended teacher training programme at a teacher training centre in Istanbul: the International Training Institute (ITI).

ITI has been delivering the Cambridge ESOL training courses to teachers in Istanbul for more than 20 years. These courses have evolved over the past five years from a traditional face-to-face format to one which incorporates and utilises online resources to the extent that some elements and some participants rely on them exclusively. The need for the addition of online elements came initially from administrative demands for more systematic purposes such as communication between tutors and participants, and as a method of submitting and storing participants' work. As trainees are located throughout the vast metropolis of Istanbul (15 million inhabitants) face-to-face contact has become less practical, but what was initially a reactive solution to practical problems has become the realisation that through blending we can provide an educational experience that is better tailored to individual need and offers greater 'intimacy and access' (Stager 2005: 1), with regard to contact between teachers and tutors.

The course, DELTA Module One, which we describe in this chapter, has evolved into an extremely flexible programme that can best be described as a flexibly blended 'omniblended' programme as it caters for and integrates the experiences of participants following the course purely online with those attending (more or less) a traditional face-to-face format course that has online support, to the other extreme of participants following the course purely online. Participants negotiate the course depending on their location, access to resources and learning preferences. What they do is paramount, how they do things is sometimes important, but which technology they use to do them (and even at times whether they use technology at all) is often a matter of choice. There can be (and have been) anything from five to 50 people on any given course in varying proportions of blended and fully online. This combination and interaction of 'real' and 'virtual world' participants is, we believe, a unique element of the course making it blended in several senses (omniblended).

The course evolution

The DELTA modules are designed and produced by Cambridge ESOL and form part of a framework of teaching awards for teachers of English. The DELTA is divided into three modules, and is aimed at experienced, practising teachers of English in a variety of teaching contexts (e.g. adult, primary) and for an international audience of both non-first language and first language teachers of English. Module One of the DELTA is gained through an exam which aims to assess participants' knowledge base with regard to (as it says in the syllabus document) the background to teaching and learning English in terms of an understanding of language, methodology and resources. Module One is assessed by an examination in which participants are required to analyse information they are given and draw on what they know to name concepts, make informed suggestions, select priorities and identify underlying structuring and beliefs. Our Module One preparation course aims to introduce key aspects of language and English Language Teaching (ELT) they need to be familiar with, and point participants to areas suggested for their own research in order to develop the knowledge base they will need to be successful in the exam. There is also a thread on how they can most effectively approach the various task types.

There were a number of influencing factors in the establishment of the blended learning training programme. When the DELTA went modular in 2008, this transformed our potential client base in two significant ways. Firstly it opened up the possibility for a greater number of practising teachers to participate, as a shorter Module became more manageable in terms of balancing work and study. Secondly it became possible to deliver the course entirely online and meet a potential global demand as Module One (and Three) no longer necessitate face-to-face elements. There existed a practical (and financial) need to digitise our face-to-face course to make it accessible to these global participants.

However, widening accessibility means that while we interview to establish minimums and avoid too much frustration or disillusionment on anyone's part, the teaching environment, length of experience, depth of knowledge and level of awareness of current issues in ELT vary enormously between course participants, even more than had previously been the case. In addition, a large proportion of participants are not native speakers of English and language competencies can vary as can digital computer literacy. Pedagogically, the course attempts to reflect this diversity and offers support which can be tapped according to a greater range of individual learning needs. The omniblended nature of this course dictates that it is both flexible in terms of meeting participants' learning needs as well as providing appropriate individual support. This makes it extremely flexible and has proved very valuable to participants. As with every innovation (White, 1991), the blended programme involved time, cost, changes in attitude and practices as well as an increase in workloads. As Jones (1986) states: 'It's not so much the program, more what you do with it'. In 2007, the year prior to the DELTA going modular (and our first year of online presence), it became clear that making our existing paper-based resources available to participants and having upload facilities for assignments might be convenient, but left all but the most curious and self-directed still in need of face-to-face contact.

The course components

In 2008 our existing face-to-face DELTA syllabus was adapted to the modular framework and the nature of Module One changed fundamentally as part of this metamorphosis. Syllabus topics were distributed into the three Modules so each could stand alone but they made a complete whole. The course is arranged in ten blocks which represented the course duration (over the ten weeks part-time or ten days intensive). One block comprises a) input (face-to-face hours or session notes with tasks), b) quizzes c) a group project, and d) an individual exam practice task, links and suggestions for further reading and research. See Appendix 1 for the schedule for the first few blocks.

Figure 1: The first block in the ten block system

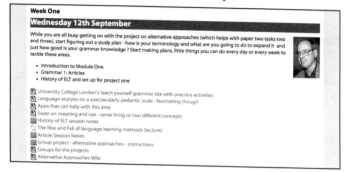

Figure 2: Exam practice in the first block

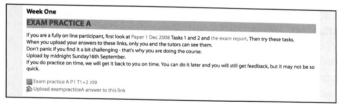

The online elements component of the course is delivered using the learning management system virtual learning environment Moodle, which brings a range of tools such as quizzes, assignment submission, blogs, wikis, forums and chat all under one roof. We chose Moodle, an open source solution, initially for economic reasons, but since then it has come to be seen as a valid and credible solution for education technology (Hill, 2011). Each course has its own Moodle room.

Figure 3: The homepage *in a Module* One Moodle room

Access to Moodle is indefinite despite the course duration. In fact many participants continue to use it as a resource during the subsequent two DELTA Modules.

a. Input

Course participants can (if they wish) attend one afternoon a week for four hours, broken into three sessions. Each of these sessions (an outline of the tutor's plan and handouts of which also can be accessed online) introduces or explores an aspect of the syllabus. Some sessions are an introduction to an area such as features of connected speech, some cover a specific aspect of something (there are grammar sessions on articles, aspects and modals). The aim is to capture interest, point participants to areas that they can and should research and suggest ways they might do this. These face-to-face sessions are delivered in a mix of group work, jigsaw activities, guided discovery and mini presentations by peers and other techniques. Online course participants have access to notes that outline the areas the same day the sessions take place, have links to reading where it is accessible online and suggestions for books where it is not. Notes include tasks features such as guided discovery activities that were used in sessions. Having access to materials online can be empowering (Sharma and Barrett, 2007: 45), as participants can work through the material at their own speed. However, as where material is being presented in face-to-face sessions, the programme allows some materials to be hidden and then time released by the tutors.

b. Mini quizzes

These are quick 'click through' activities that course participants can use to check what they have understood so far and what they need to work on. At present there are one or two for most of the weeks and they are one of the most heavily used components, but they only cover a small number of areas. These components aim to act as a self assessment learning tool. We also encourage course participants to make their own quizzes and share links using sites like Quizlet and to explore tasks in wikis that have been set up for that purpose, for example Kubbu or Zondle.

Figure 4: Quizzes can be in hot potatoes, Moodle's own quiz format or an external site such as Quizlet or Zondle.

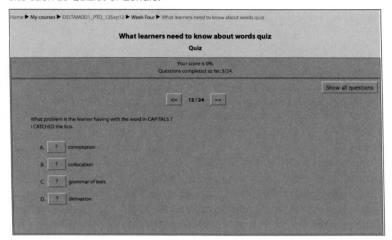

c. Projects

We designed a series of group projects. These have several purposes:

- To encourage everyone to interact, online and face-to-face, and engender a sense of community, we designed a series of group projects.

- We also need to get across the message that we are not delivering all the information that they need to know, nor could we, but that they have to become aware of what they should work on and set out to augment their knowledge accordingly.

- Lastly we wanted to foster the sense that if they work together on some tasks there could be a positive synergy, that they could help each other in useful ways and that they could go on to use what has been created by others.

To all of the above ends, each week (or block) there is a group project. Groups are set up with a mix of face-to-face and online participants and they are remixed every week. Each project is set up to get them to create something that they can publish through wikis or forums and will help other groups to revise in future. Projects are not evaluated by tutors. Moodle facilitates online collaborations (Stanford, 2008: 58), which can be teacher-to-student or student-to-student. Asynchronous forums and wikis allow participants time to compose their messages, which encourages reflection as well as 'deeper' more considered thinking than in synchronous exchanges (Sharma and Barrett, 2007: 107). Presentations can be crafted by several people together before being published. End results vary enormously but are always interesting.

Figure 5: The projects page carries links to a variety of different formats for input and presentation of finished products.

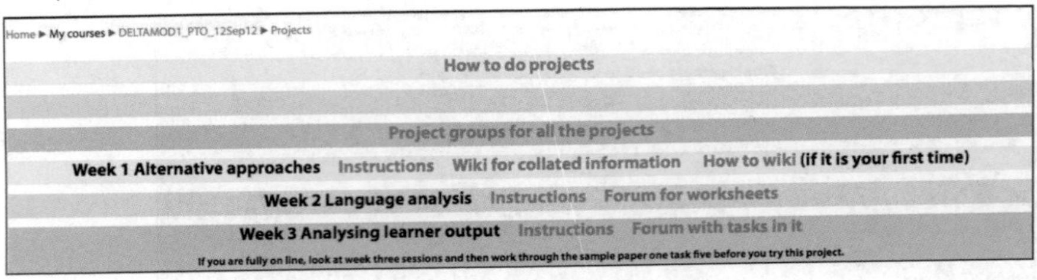

Home ► My courses ► DELTAMOD1_PTO_12Sep12 ► Projects

How to do projects

Project groups for all the projects

Week 1 Alternative approaches   Instructions   Wiki for collated information   How to wiki **(if it is your first time)**

Week 2 Language analysis   Instructions   Forum for worksheets

Week 3 Analysing learner output   Instructions   Forum with tasks in it

If you are fully on line, look at week three sessions and then work through the sample paper one task five before you try this project.

d. Exam practice

There are one or two exam task types in each block for individual exam practice. These are from past papers. Participants are free to do them under exam conditions or not as they see fit, but are strongly encouraged to upload them for feedback from a tutor. This includes individualised comments on what they have done well, where they need to change their approach and things they might do to work on an area.

Course development

The process so far has been one of organic development rather than of having an end goal 'grand design'. Prior to the Modular DELTA our online support was a matter of electronic access to documents. The change to Modular came at a time when we were beginning to realise that the ubiquity of the web and Web 2.0 were things we should explore and exploit, not just regard as potential storage. Reworking the course to break it into three meant additions and some of those additions could be in ways we had not previously been able to consider. There are still things that were part of the original ideas that have not yet been written; every new run of the course throws up questions, things that need to be tweaked, new ideas that could and should be developed. It has worked well for a lot of teachers and even now is working well, but there are always further things we would like to do to make it better and it is the online side of the course that has made this a more organic process. The technology has demonstrated many advantages: access to resources, a medium through which to interact and collaborate, provision for individual learning pathways in a secure environment. We can monitor and see how people are interacting with the online components and can react accordingly. It is easy to trace what is being accessed more, by whom and when. It is far more flexible than books; we can adjust individual components to meet need or demand within a course while it is being used.

Some matters that have been perennial issues have been exaggerated by blended courses

The training ethos at ITI is 'do as you would be done by'. The approach of the tutors is to guide trainees to rational positions/answers/conclusions rather than to tell them. The materials on the websites are designed in the same way. However, the reaction of trainees to the more digitised delivery is that more should be delivered. Exhaustive and comprehensive lists of what should be 'learned' are sometimes asked for. Such lists are neither available, nor in a sense desirable. Participants need to become familiar with a range of reading and to apply that knowledge to the texts and problems they are presented with. Being able to access more and more content, but not interacting with it/using it/applying it, is unlikely to have the desired effect. We hope to put across the idea that in the same way that teachers cannot 'deliver' English to learners, (but only show them how they might go about learning), we cannot deliver the complete knowledge participants (personally) need for the exam. More instant online access to some of the materials means they then need other things in place to allow them to take in and retain content from those materials. What once might have been achieved by taking notes on something, if the notes are provided (as is the popular demand) must now be addressed in a different way – through features like the online quiz facilities. It is still a difficult task, though, to persuade some that in fact it would be more productive for them to make the quiz themselves, so much ends up duplicated (the course provider-supplied version and the versions participants go on to make themselves, once they see the benefit).

Trainees (and tutors) have very different relationships with, and awareness of, technology. Some cope well with exploring on their own and have a natural instinct to try and forge their own path through the course. Others want considerably more support and to be told what to do and in what order. Over time we have put more and more in place to support people as they get started, to show them how they might start. Despite this there are still those who fall by the wayside and see the technology as the cause. Emails come in saying 'I've never done an online course before and I'm feeling very lost'. In fact the difficulties of getting started with the pro-active approach that would make them most successful are about time management, self awareness and research skills and have always been needed (and have always been a challenge for some). Lack of familiarity with the technology makes it an easy scapegoat, but it may also be an additional obstacle to be overcome. The more we add, the more time is required to work through things that are actually only in place to ensure people are equipped with the study skills they may need to deal with the course. 'Perhaps the greatest of all pedagogical fallacies is the notion that a person learns only the particular thing he is studying at the time.' (Dewey, 1998: 49). Some participants make the meta-leap and realise that they have also been covertly shown how they could deliver some or all of the language learning process to their students in a blended format.

Issues for the future

Our aim is to deliver a training course that promotes participant interaction and self responsibility and in which tasks are optional. The premise behind the approach is supported by sociocultural theory (Vygotsky, 1978, 1986) which sees learning (and language) as a social process. Put simply, language use is shaped by what kind of activity we are doing and who we are doing it with (Halliday, 1993), and for Vygotsky and socio-constructivists, such language use with others is the essential mediating tool in our cognitive development. However, in a blended programme, as well as in a face-to-face format, there are participants who prefer information delivered in a transmission mode rather than a more participant-centred 'learning through discussion' style. The very flexible nature of the formats and the ability to keep adding things in response to feedback *and in response* to how the course is used means we are more able to deliver more options and a greater variety of learning experiences in a way *that* was not feasible in the purely face-to-face version of the course.

However, we wonder if we are barking up the wrong tree in trying to deliver a socio-constructivist style course, when in fact much of the time participants mutter darkly about not wanting to work in groups and would prefer a more top-down transmission mode of delivery.

Conclusion

A blended training course is one where face-to-face and online components are blended to deliver uniform opportunity in a uniform training provision. Our course, which we have described as 'omniblended', offers participants a resource in which they can choose how the course is blended to meet their needs. The course attempts to cater to a range of participants' learning styles and preferences; it provides interaction between local teachers following a traditional blending of face-to-face and online interaction with teachers solely online from a range of teaching contexts and cultures, negotiating the course simultaneously.

Was using a blended learning approach more beneficial to participants than only using a face-to-face approach? The results in the Appendix 1 shows the respective pass rates.

What have we learned about blended learning? The online elements of our courses enable us to offer a far wider range of learning options, but simultaneously require a far more complex system of help, guidance and support. Storage, flexibility and access mean more can be presented and learning pathways can be better individualised, but that means more work not less for us as course providers. 'Basing education upon personal experience may mean more multiplied and more intimate contacts between the mature and the immature than ever existed in the traditional school, and consequently more, rather than less, guidance by others' (Dewey 1998: 8). Guidance may include guidance as to how the course works, supplementing study skills/time management, and help with some digital literacies. Both participants and tutors need support in using various facets of the technologies and as the Open University has shown, need is not age related (Jones et al., 2010). To be convincing, online material has to be updated regularly and links have to be checked thoroughly before each course and there needs to be a fast response to changes on the web that impact on access to resources. There is no such thing as a 'finished' course. The more we learn, the more we are aware of what more we need to do.

References

Dewey, J (1998) *Experience and Education: the 60th anniversary edition*. Kappa Delta Pi.

Halliday, M (1993) Towards a language-based theory of language. *Linguistics and Education* 5/2: 93–116.

Hill, P (2011) *Emerging Trends in LMS /Ed Tech market in e-Literate*. Available online at http://mfeldstein.com/emerging-trends-in-lms-ed-tech-market/

Jones, C (1986) It's not so much the program, more what you do with it: the importance of methodology in CALL. *System* 14/2: 171–178.

Jones, C, Ruslan, R, Cross, S and Healing, G (2010) Net generation or Digital Natives: Is there a distinct new generation entering university? *Computers and Education* 54/3: 722–732.

Sharma, P and Barrett, B (2007) *Blended Learning*. Oxford: Macmillan.

Stager, G (2005) *Towards a pedagogy of online constructionist learning*. Proceedings of the 2005 World Conference on Computers in Education. Stellenbosch, South Africa. Available online at www.stager.org/articles/onlineconstructionism.pdf

Stanford, J (2008) In the mood for Moodle. *English Teaching Professional* 24: 58–60.

Vygotsky, LS (1978) *Mind in Society: The Development of Higher Psychological Processes*. Cambridge, MA: Harvard University Press.

Vygotsky, LS (1986) *Thought and Language*. Massachusetts Institute of Technology.

White, R (1991) *Management in English Language Teaching*. Cambridge: Cambridge University Press.

Appendix 1

Extract showing first three blocks from the session schedule
DELTA MODULE ONE Wednesday 1.00–5.30
Reading suggestions, links and self practice tests available each week on the Moodle

Week one Wednesday 12 September			
1.00–2.00	Student	Introduction to Module One	
2.15–3.45	Student	Grammar 1: Articles	Syllabus unit 3 language systems (grammar)
4.00–5.30	Teacher	A history of ELT Developments from grammar translation to CLT (and set up for online homework)	Syllabus unit 1 theoretical perspectives and unit 2 approaches
Collaborative online homework Preparing for mini demonstrations of alternative approaches.			Syllabus unit 1, 2 and 5 materials and resources
Self study focus on phonemic script – choose from on site links or work your way through Pronunciation in Use or the Headway Pronunciation series.			Syllabus unit 3 language systems (phonology)

Complete online exam practice A, by last thing Sunday 16 September.
Further details on the Moodle.

Week two Wednesday 19 September			
1.00–2.30	Teacher	Demonstration lessons of alternative approaches	Syllabus unit 2 approaches
2.45–4.00	Student	Skills 1: Speaking – what the skill involves	Syllabus unit 4 language skills (speaking)
4.15–5.30	Teacher	Phonology 1: Sounds	Syllabus unit 3 language systems (phonology)
Collaborative online homework Creating online information pages for other groups on specified grammar areas.			Syllabus unit 3 language systems (grammar)
Self study, read about speaking.			Syllabus unit 4 language skills (speaking)

Complete online exam practice B, by last thing Sunday 23 September.
Further details on the Moodle.

Week three Wednesday 26 September			
1.00–2.15	Student	L1/L2 (use/contrastive analysis)	Syllabus unit 2 approaches and 3 systems
2.30–4.00	Student	Learner output/error analysis (set up online homework)	Syllabus unit 3 systems (error analysis)
4.15–5.30	Teacher	Phonology 2: Stress and rhythm	Syllabus unit 3 language systems (phonology)
Collaborative online homework Working on samples of learner output to identify and prioritise strengths and weaknesses.			Syllabus unit 3 systems (error analysis), 4 skills (writing)
Self study work on identification of stress patterns.			Syllabus unit 3 language systems (phonology)

10

The Cambridge CELTA course online

Jacqueline Douglas and Colin Paton

Introduction to the CELTA Programme

CELTA (Certificate in Teaching English to Speakers of Other Languages) is an initial qualification for people learning to teach English as an additional, second or foreign language who have previous teaching experience but no formal qualification. It is one of the most widely taken qualifications of its kind. Each year, over 10,000 people take CELTA in accredited centres around the world. This qualification is validated by Cambridge ESOL.

Typically CELTA courses are run entirely face-to-face, either as an intensive four-week course or on a part-time basis over several months (or up to an academic year). Each CELTA cohort usually contains up to 18 trainees, who may differ widely in age and background.

A CELTA course teaches trainees the principles of classroom management and of teaching communication skills. They learn how to teach English through hands-on teaching practice, input sessions with a tutor, regular written assignments, and ongoing assessment and feedback by course tutors.

The CELTA Certificate has two components of assessment: teaching practice (a total of six hours to at least two different student levels) and four written assignments. To be awarded the certificate trainees must pass both components.

Why develop a new blended model?

In 2010 Cambridge ESOL wanted to develop CELTA Online, the name emphasising the innovative mode of delivery of input. It clearly shows that trainees will have the freedom to study where and when they wish, and emphasises the need for an appropriate level of IT literacy and internet connectivity. International House London (IH London) entered into partnership with Cambridge to develop a new blended format for the part-time version of the programme. IH London, due to its extensive experience designing teacher training materials, was tasked with developing the course content and overall course design.

There were a number of factors impelling us to develop a new blended course format:

- A new blended programme would increase access for teachers and trainers to the qualification.

- Cambridge ESOL was reporting significant demand for a more flexible version of CELTA.
- Other teaching awards were already deliverable fully online or in a blended format, such as the Distance DELTA.

The new blended programme would help consolidate Cambridge ESOL's competitive advantage over other English Language Teaching (ELT) awarding bodies and reinforce CELTA's status as the qualification of choice, by bringing CELTA firmly into the technological age and by reaching candidates in geographical areas not previously provided for. The blended CELTA would introduce new ELT professionals to online learning, empowering them to take advantage of other online courses and educational technology in their continued professional development. The principles behind this project have been outlined in the literature on blended learning:

1. Most writers on the subject, Garrison and Vaughan (2011), for example, describe blended learning as combining the best of face-to-face and online approaches, achieving coherence by integrating the strengths of both. Sharma and Barrett contribute that it is 'potentially greater than the sum of its parts' (2007: 7) while Bersin comments that blended courses 'extend the classroom "people-centric" experience in space and time' (2004: 12). In the words of Thorne: 'it represents an opportunity to integrate the innovative and technological advantages offered by online learning with the interaction and participation offered in the best of traditional learning' (2003: 2).

2. Glazer notes in broad terms that blended learning supports many of us who are already embracing technology and leading 'blended lives' (2012: 1). Increasingly ELT is involved and in tune with technology and course participants will find they have the opportunity to experiment with computer-mediated communication and virtual learning environments in their own teaching post-CELTA.

3. There is emphasis on exploitation of readily-available technology, Littlejohn and Pegler, for example, writing: 'Blended e-learning offers the possibility of changing our attitudes not only as to *where* and *when* learning takes place, but in terms of *what* resources and tools can support learning and the ways in which these might be used.' (2007: 2). Hofmann adds that with blended learning, institutions and individuals can minimise costs, maximise technology and increase instructional value: 'The tools are in place to support blended learning' (2011: 2) and 'there is a push to take advantage' of resources already invested in technology' (*ibid*. p.1). Bonk and Graham (2006) also refer to the cost advantages, stating that blended learning opens up the possibility of running courses with a small number of participants.

4. Glazer focuses on another efficiency benefit: 'blended learning creates time' (2012: 4), echoing the point made by Sharma and Barrett that course participants can 'continue working and take a course' (2007: 7).

5. Sharma and Barrett also make the point that 'the use of technology outside the classroom can make learners more autonomous' (*ibid*. 11) and this is something beneficial for a CELTA trainee, both for the tutors and for trainees themselves,

during and beyond the course. Indeed, the online input material remains available to the trainee for a year following the end of the course.

The course was first piloted at IH London in April 2011 and in September 2011 the course was available to other CELTA centres.

The blended model compared with the face-to-face model

The main course elements of the face-to-face CELTA programme (120 hours) are as follows:

a. input sessions on teaching methodology

b. teaching practice (a total of six hours to at least two different levels) with feedback from tutors

c. supervised lesson planning

d. four written assignments

e. observation of experienced teachers (six hours)

f. mid-course tutorials

g. a written record of all trainees' work.

The new blended programme (also 120 hours) is distributed across web-based and face-to-face elements as follows:

Online elements	Face-to-face elements
• 30 interactive and multimedia online units on teaching methodology and language analysis. • Asynchronous collaborative online tasks (in discussion forums). • Video observations of experienced teachers (three hours). • Synchronous sessions using a live classroom. • Four written assignments. • Online portfolio of work. • Additional key resources.	• Teaching practice and tutor feedback (six hours). • Supervised lesson planning. • Observations of experienced teachers (three hours).
Either online or face-to-face	
Mid-course tutorials	

The sequence of the 30 online units was chosen with these considerations:

■ Offering 'Focus on the Learner' as the first unit emphasised for trainees the place of the learner at the centre of the learning process.

■ It follows a 'whole to part' training model, in which trainees watch complete lessons and then these are explored for the useful elements of effective teaching they demonstrate, for instance classroom management issues and dealing with meaning, form and pronunciation. An example of a 'thread' over several units is that the trainees watch a teacher use an authentic news story about a five-year old wandering into an unlocked bank. The trainees see the teacher first create interest in the story, then exploit it to develop reading skills and finally to allow learners to explore and experiment with language from the text.

- Including later units on, for example, productive skills and professional development, which mirror the broad sequence followed by many face-to-face CELTA courses.

To try to replicate the stimulus and energy that are familiar and important elements on a face-to-face course, the various forums play an essential part and these will be discussed below. The good models that trainees usually receive through demonstration lessons on face-to-face courses take the form of recorded lessons with a teacher and a group of students, which are threaded through the initial units. The online course tutor (OCT) on the pilot course overcame initial reservations about the lack of live models from trainers, realising that 'video clips show authentic teaching you don't get in the input room' (Paton and Rea, 2012).

Whilst the distribution of the course elements above remains fixed, centres running the course are able to customise the timetable to meet their local needs within certain parameters (and subject to approval from Cambridge ESOL), determining, for example, over how many weeks the course is run or when teaching practice will take place. The online course units, video observations, online collaborative tasks and assignments remain fixed. At IH London the course is run over 13 weeks and the quality assurance is equal to the face-to-face model in terms of assessment of the course. The assessment by a Cambridge external assessor is exactly the same regarding scrutiny of course documents, portfolios (in this case in online format) and observing live teaching practice with group feedback. The grading meeting that customarily takes place during the assessor's visit is done via conference call with the tutors.

There is an OCT who manages the progress of trainees through the online components of the course, and a minimum of two different teaching practice tutors (TPT), one of whom can be the OCT, who manage the face-to-face components. The OCT must be approved by Cambridge ESOL and have a qualification/experience in e-moderating. The OCT may be based at the centre where the course is run or, if not also adopting the role of TPT, may work on the course at distance from anywhere in the world.

Technology

The platform for the online component is *Fronter* from Pearson, which brings together all the online course elements into one coherent whole.

Figure 1: The course homepage in Fronter

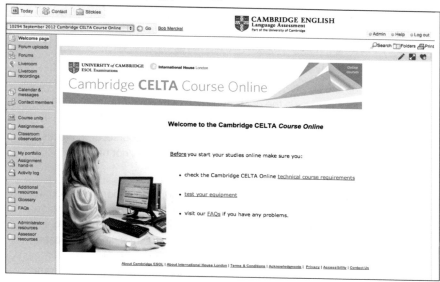

The online course environment provides key course tools such as:

a. 30 interactive online units

b. discussion forums

c. an assignment drop box

d. a live classroom using *Elluminate Live*

e. an e-portfolio for trainees (PDF and Word based)

f. an observations section with a series of videos of experienced teachers and observation tasks for trainees

g. community features such as messaging

h. full tracking of usage and performance

i. trainee tools such as a calendar and glossary.

The rationale behind the blend

The key underlying objective when designing the course was to create a programme that played to the strengths of the online medium (providing flexibility and creating opportunities for reflective and collaborative online learning) whilst maintaining the integrity and validity of a very well established qualification and the key inter-relationship between theory and practice. Possible models of the course can be found at www.esolcentrenet.org, but in summary, there is a basis of flexibility provided by the parameters of the course structure:

- it can be run over any period from ten weeks to a year
- the 30 modules can be offered by the individual CELTA centre at a rate of either two, three or four per week, the only stipulation being that the Orientation Module and Units 1–6 are released before teaching practice begins
- teaching practice can be scheduled evenly through the course, or in blocks, the latter allowing centres to 'reach out to people in areas not near you' (Swabey et al., 2012).

The course web page emphasises: 'You have the freedom to choose how you work. As long as assignments are completed on time and you contribute to discussion forums and live room discussions, the online format allows you to work at your own pace, when and where you choose.' (Cambridge ESOL Teaching Qualifications, 2012a) and this is supported by the literature. As Hofmann writes: in 'a learner-centred program ... there are opportunities for participants to learn at their own pace' (2011: 4) and Thorne comments: there is opportunity to 'undertake your own development at a time, place and pace to suit you' (2003: ix). Glazer comments that 'The asynchronous nature of the blended component of the courses has the salutary effect of expanding the time the students spend on course material' (2012: 3). Littlejohn and Pegler (2007) refer to the use of online spaces for formation of communities that can interact in exciting new ways. Glazer (2012: 3) extends this: 'Discussions conducted online encourage reflection and usually reach 100 per cent participation. As a result, the face-to-face time can be used more effectively, with students extending the material beyond what might be achieved in a conventional face-to-face course. The students in a blended course make more and richer connections between what they are learning and what they already know, creating a robust scaffold to organize the information.... Effective blended learning courses require students to interact with each other, the content, and their own thoughts.' Bonk and Graham (2006) comment that blending learning allows the learner to retain more of what is learned.

These points are borne out by the feedback from trainees on the pilot course. Emphasising the value of working independently, one says in an interview post-course: 'I work better in the evenings, shut myself away with my computer ... for assignments, I've gone back to online units, tried to include all tips...' (Cambridge ESOL: Teaching Qualifications, 2012b) and another: 'it wasn't practical to take a month off work, this was the only way my employer would have let me do it, it's fantastic it exists' (ibid.). The OCT on their course emphasises the shared nature of the discussion and assignment forums available to trainees: 'once all trainees see an answer, individual trainees don't need to ask ... there was peer teaching going on' (*ibid*.). On a face-to-face CELTA, peer support is, of course, also channelled through the closeness of a teaching practice group, and following the pilot online course, one of the TPTs noted 'the TP groups supported each other as much as any TP group would' (Cambridge ESOL Teaching Qualifications, 2012b). This point is echoed by a trainee on the course: 'the TP group bonded quickly', though she noted the frustration of limited contact time.

While there is an obvious risk that some trainees may not contribute sufficiently to the forums to develop as teachers, the OCT can readily 'track' each participant in terms of which units they have accessed and their activity on forums, and provide appropriate support encouragement via email and TPTs to any falling behind accordingly. Communication between the OCT and TPTs is vital to maintain a connection between theory and practice and one of the TPTs on the pilot course says: 'we were aware with where they were in input and referred to that, we channelled their queries through the online course tutor ... and got the online tutor's emails' (*ibid*.). Additionally, as the OCT asserts: 'the tutor can send a trainee struggling with classroom management back to that unit' (Paton and Rea, 2012) and 'they noticed things they hadn't before, so we can target their needs more than on the face to face' (Cambridge ESOL Teaching Qualifications, 2012b). Furthermore, centres have the option of conducting mid-course tutorials face-to-face as would customarily happen.

The online units and collaborative tasks

The online course units and collaborative tasks replace what in a normal face-to-face CELTA would be the input sessions. A total of 30 units were created (one of which allows trainees to choose an elective specialism) and each unit combines:

- input
- video and audio segments
- a variety of self-study activities with feedback or commentaries
- collaborative tasks (discussion forum)
- exposure to English as a foreign language (EFL) published materials
- additional useful online resources and reading.

Figure 2: An example screen from a unit

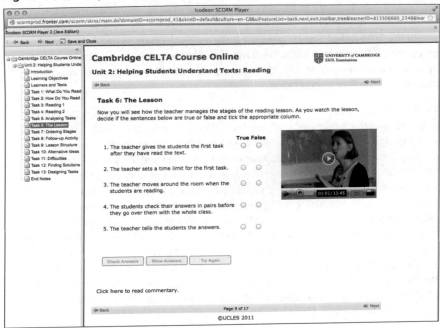

There were special challenges in moving this element of the course online. For trainees the face-to-face sessions do not just provide key input on methodology but are also a key source of loop-input experiential learning, as trainees are themselves taught whilst reflecting upon the experience and observing the techniques used by the tutor. We set out to replicate this experience online by designing online learning activities and materials that give the trainee an authentic learning experience whilst still modelling good teaching practice. It is useful to apply to trainers the point Sharma and Barrett make about the teacher: 'positive learning outcomes are most apparent when clear roles are assigned to the teacher and to the technology' (2007: 7). Garrison and Vaughan (2011) assert the need for learners to feel freedom of self expression in the virtual learning environment without negative consequences.

As Sharma (2006: 59) writes: 'The technology should not "lead"' and it is essential that human attributes such as empathy, patience and a sense of humour which are vital in ELT are evident in online components of the course. They can be found in the way the TPTs, who have a greater degree of communication with trainees on day one than is standard on many face-to-face courses, manage observation and feedback, both group and written. These attributes also emerge in the virtual learning environment, firstly, in the way that the model lessons that form part of early input sessions show the teacher dealing with real students and real classroom management issues. As the OCT from the pilot course says: 'It's really useful for trainees to see a lesson where a teacher's struggling to get the meaning across, using, for example, concept questions, students aren't immediately responding and seeing that that's ok and real teaching can be a bit messy' (Paton and Rea, 2012).

Secondly, through the work of the OCT, who will adopt an appropriate tone when communicating with trainees online and who will foster the use of the site as a 'warm' online community. The OCT on the pilot refers to the possibility of encouraging trainees by clicking on 'smileys' in the Liveroom as useful but not particularly spontaneous. A more effective approach to building rapport developed naturally: 'the main way you can do it is what you write in the discussion forums and what you write in the emails, so the written style you need to use, I think, has to be really enthusiastic, very warm and very friendly ... when you have discussion forums, when you weave together everyone's opinions at the end, you can make clear, positive references to what different people have contributed and I think that also helps to develop a sort of sense of an online community' (Cambridge ESOL Teaching Qualifications, 2012b). One of the course participants interviewed supports this point, commenting that 'the online tutor always responded to emails quickly and the technical support has been amazing' (ibid). Furthermore, Klímová, writing on the distance learning element of blended learning, asserts that it 'can offer more information to students, better and faster feedback and richer communication between a tutor and a student.' (2008: 58).

The development of the online materials presented an opportunity to re-think the nature and content of face-to-face input sessions and design materials that would not just try to replicate the face-to-face input sessions, but in key areas improve upon them by:

■ weaving throughout all the materials the voice of the language learner and trainer – through video, audio, image and text

■ allowing trainees to work through key methodological areas at their own pace

■ allowing trainees to return to work through units in a linear fashion but also jump ahead and go back to materials when needed

■ providing a permanent resource trainees could use long after the course had finished[1]

■ encouraging active and reflective learning through materials that ask trainees to process information, test their understanding through activities and receive feedback

■ making full use of multimedia (audio and video) to provide lots of exposure to the views and practices of a wide range of experienced teaching professionals, in a range of contexts

■ fostering a socio-constructivist approach to learning through integrated collaborative activities.

Teaching practice

Teaching practice is one of the cornerstones of CELTA assessment and candidates rely on the centre to provide classes to teach. Therefore candidates are obliged to come into the centre to teach, be assessed by the TP tutor(s) and receive feedback. As with face-to-face courses, before this assessment begins, they have the opportunity in unobserved lessons to familiarise themselves with the classroom

[1] Trainees are given access to the materials and all discussion forums for one year after the course has finished.

environment and to meet the students. This opportunity is also provided when trainees change to a new group of students.

Observations of experienced teachers

As part of the programme requirements CELTA trainees have to observe six hours of teaching from experienced teachers and complete, for each observation, a set observation task. Typically this is conducted by coming into the CELTA centre and watching face-to-face lessons (although up to three hours can be via video).

With a view to both reducing the need for candidates to come into centres for observations and to provide candidates with additional exposure to multi-lingual classes taught at IH London, we moved three hours of observation and observation tasks online as videos (drawing upon IH London's extensive archive of video footage from experienced teachers giving classes in a variety of EFL contexts). Trainees then complement this with three hours of local face-to-face observation of classes taught in their own centre.

Live classrooms

In addition to the asynchronous collaborative tasks we felt that there was a need for 'surgeries' that would allow:

■ tutors to deal with common problems they had observed in teaching practice (such as difficulties in giving instructions) and to respond to local needs

■ trainees to raise questions they have with course materials or other aspects of the course.

It was felt that a live classroom would be the most efficient means of dealing with these two areas, especially as the live classroom (with audio/video-conferencing and a whiteboard) would allow the tutor to demonstrate techniques. The frequency of these sessions is up to each centre, as is the content of each session, although we recommend that sessions be fortnightly on a 13-week course such as IH London's.

Assignments

It made sense to move all assignments online, especially as trainees would naturally be writing these using a word processor. Fronter provides an assignment drop box, providing alerts to trainees of impending deadlines and allowing them to easily upload assignments. Additionally tutors are provided with a full record of trainee submissions, and can easily add comments and grades and receive alerts for outstanding assignments.

Online portfolio

On a face-to-face course trainees and tutors complete a folder which contains a record of all the trainee's work as well as evaluations from the tutor and self-evaluations by trainees. For the blended programme we created an e-portfolio section where all trainees' marked assignments, lesson plans and evaluated lessons, as well as their reflections, are placed online. Trainees are given the responsibility for maintaining this section and keeping this up to date. The big advantage of such an approach is to:

a. create a permanent electronic record of trainees' work

b. allow easy access to trainees' work by all tutors and the course assessor[2]

Tutorials

There is considerable flexibility over how these can be delivered. They can be given face-to-face, over the telephone or online using the Live Classroom.

Conclusions

We ran the pilot course at IH London from April to July 2011. Formal feedback overall was extremely positive from trainees and tutors and trainee performance on the blended course was comparable to a 'traditional' face-to-face CELTA. This also appears to be true of the second course (September 2011 – December 2011). Therefore, early indications do appear to suggest that the blended design form is a successful one. With the programme being this new, little has made its way into the literature thus far, but we may extrapolate points from courses run to date:

■ Where the OCT does not also act as TPT, there is a certain objectivity that will not be true of a face-to-face course, as without meeting the trainees, he or she will build up a picture of each through the e-portfolio: 'you have complete objectivity on their performance because you basically have access to the teaching practice documents ... email contact with the teaching practice tutors ... you get a lot of information about the trainees but because you've never met them, you don't have a strong relationship with them ... so when you come to do a tutorial ... you collate all this data and see if there's enough information there to suggest they are meeting the criteria ... and I think that really does help with the tutorials' (Cambridge ESOL Teaching Qualifications, 2012b).

■ One of the TPTs commented: 'I think teaching practice in the first week, we had some classroom management issues, too much teacher talking, or too much fidgeting, just like you would have on a face-to-face course. It didn't throw up different issues, and I think if somebody landed from Mars into our TP room, they wouldn't necessarily think "ah, this is a different kind of course"' (ibid.).

■ There is more time to reflect on and return to input sessions later.

■ The results of the first two courses at IH London show that among the 26 trainees, there were two A grades, nine B grades, ten passes, three withdrawals and two fails. These grades and those on courses at other centres show that candidates are performing at least at the same level as typical face-to-face courses.

Nevertheless following feedback from trainees and tutors on the pilot we had to make significant adjustments in the following areas:

[2] Each CELTA course is externally moderated by Cambridge ESOL and having materials online, such as discussion forums, course units and the candidates' portfolios, greatly facilitates this process.

- Fine-tuning of online course materials and collaborative activities, for example, in the new version of the course (released in September 2012), interviews with respected industry practitioners on various aspects of language and methodology, fewer discussion forum tasks and less repetition.
- Refining activity design for live classroom sessions, with more streamlined functionality.
- Improving functionality in the e-portfolio, a new CELTA5 progress record document, launched in September 2012.
- Ironing out technical bugs.

Cambridge ESOL has noted an issue with the name of the course and in its recent CELTA Online Special Edition, under the heading 'Messaging to improve quality of enquiries', announced the following change to its promotion of the course to prospective trainees: 'All the new marketing material emphasises that *Cambridge CELTA Course Online* is a blended learning course, combining collaborative online study and face-to-face teaching practice. This will help reduce the number of enquiries from potential trainees who only want to study on a 100 per cent online course, as well as help further position *Cambridge CELTA Course Online* as a flexible route to gain a high-quality teaching qualification.' (Cambridge ESOL Teaching Qualifications, 2012b). However, the use of the word 'online' rather than 'blended' in the course title has been vindicated in the sense that it has been seen that trainees do need to be independent and effective time managers.

As additional courses are run at IH London and other centres the programme will continue to evolve and at regular intervals the course materials will be upgraded based on user feedback.

References

Bersin, J (2004) *The Blended Learning Book: Best Practices, Proven Methodologies, and Lessons Learned.* San Francisco: John Wiley and Sons.

Bonk, C and Graham, C (2006) *The Handbook of Blended Learning: Global Perspectives, Local Designs.* San Francisco: Pfeiffer.

Cambridge ESOL Teaching Qualifications (2012a) *A flexible new route to CELTA.* Available online at www.cambridgeenglish.org/exams-and-qualifications/celta/ways-to-take-celta/

Cambridge ESOL Teaching Qualifications (2012b) *Special Edition Teaching Qualifications Bulletin: Cambridge CELTA Course Online. Issue 11.* Cambridge: Cambridge ESOL.

Garrison, DR and Vaughan, ND (2011) *Blended Learning in Higher Education: Framework, Principles, and Guidelines.* San Francisco: John Wiley and Sons.

Glazer, F (ed) (2012) *Blended Learning: Across the Disciplines, Across the Academy.* Sterling: Stylus Publishing.

Hofmann, J (2011) *Blended learning: Infoline Tips, Tools and Intelligence for Trainers* August/1108. ASTD Press.

Klímová, BF (2008) Blended learning. *English Teaching Professional* 58: 58–60.

Littlejohn, A and Pegler, C (2007) *Preparing for Blended e-Learning.* Abingdon: Routledge.

Paton, C and Rea, D (2012) *Interview: Head of E-learning and CELTA Online Course Tutor.* Interview recorded at the IATEFL Conference, March 2012, Glasgow, UK.

Sharma, P (2006) Future in the balance. *English Teaching Professional* 42: 58–59.

Sharma, P and Barrett, P (2007) *Blended Learning: Using Technology in and Beyond the Language Classroom.* Oxford: Macmillan.

Swabey, MT, Rea, D and Paton, C (2012) *CELTA Online: one year on.* Paper presented at the IATEFL Conference, March 2012, Glasgow, UK.

Thorne, K (2003) *Blended Learning: How to Integrate Online and Traditional Learning.* London: Kogan Page.

Comments on Part 2

Brian Tomlinson

A blended learning approach seems to be ideal for developing teacher development courses. Whether the courses are initial or in-service the trainees are typically very busy, geographically spread, with different levels and types of experience, with different amounts of time available to complete their course, with convictions about their preferred styles and modes of learning and with the need for varying amounts of feedback and support. Face-to-face courses can satisfy many of these needs but they do require all the trainees to be together at the same location and at the same predetermined time, and it is not easy for the trainers to provide sufficient individual feedback and support. Online courses can solve many of the logistical problems, can help the trainees to focus on their individual needs and can provide individualised feedback and support. However, they cannot really provide the reality and stimulus that live experience of observing classes, being observed teaching classes and interacting with peers can. Blended learning can achieve all that is needed though, by dividing the course into those components which require face-to-face interaction and those which can be best delivered online. This is what all the courses described in Part 2 have done and all of them seem to have been successful. It would, of course though, be very informative if one group of trainees followed a purely face-to-face course, an equivalent group followed an online course with the same content and another equivalent group followed a blended course with the same content. If the trainees were shadowed after their courses we could find indications as to the actual benefits of blended learning teacher development courses in relation to the outcomes of the experience for the trainees.

One of the many bonuses of a blended learning approach to teacher development is the affordance of choice to the trainees. Many of the teacher development courses reported in Part 2 offer the trainees the choice of doing the course face-to-face, online or in a blended version. This is a great advantage as some trainees cannot afford the time or money to do a course away from home, some are already electronically proficient and want to make use of this proficiency and others have a strong preference for learning face-to-face or an antipathy towards electronic learning. Also a number of the blended learning courses in Part 2 encourage the trainees to decide for themselves how much and which components of a course they want to do in online modes, and which they want to do face-to-face. This choice of modes is very important as trainees who are comfortable with, and positive about, where and how they learn are more likely to benefit from a course than those who are not (Tomlinson, 2013a).

Another bonus reported in a number of chapters in Part 2 is that blended learning teacher development courses can stimulate trainees to think of making use of blended learning approaches in their own teaching. Experiencing different modes of delivery and different resources and procedures within each mode can help trainees to evaluate these possibilities not only in relation to their own development but in relation to their post-course teaching too. It is arguable therefore, that the teacher development courses should provide trainees with as much experience as possible of different modes, resources, procedures and techniques and to help the trainees through reflection and constructive criticism to consciously consider their application to the teaching of languages in the contexts within which the trainees will be operating in after the course.

Having summarised some of the undoubted benefits of blended teacher development courses reported in Part 2, I would now like to point out what I think are the dangers of delivering too much of a course electronically in order to solve practical problems of time and attendance. I have been a teacher developer for 40 years and I am convinced that there are some aspects of a development course that can only be delivered effectively face-to-face and others which are better delivered face-to-face than online.

In my view it is important that trainees observe experienced teachers live in the classroom. Videos can give the trainees useful vicarious experience of teaching techniques but videos are often edited and carefully selected versions of the classroom and (unless the centre has multiple cameras and microphones available) they cannot provide a complete picture of the effect of the 'teaching' on the learners. Trainees need to be present in the classroom to listen to and observe learners, as well as teachers (especially if the learners are working in groups and pairs), as well as to experience what being in a school is like. I know of one initial training course which is actually delivered live in a school and the trainees really appreciate observing teachers and learners both inside and outside their classrooms.

I also think that it is necessary for trainees to be monitored and assessed live in the classroom, as that way the observer can take into account the formal and informal interaction between teacher and learners, the formal and informal interaction between learners and the effect of the lesson on the learners, rather than just focusing on the teacher and his/her techniques. I also think that the feedback on a trainee's lesson needs to be delivered live. In order to give feedback in the sensitive, supportive and constructive ways that will maintain trainee esteem and encourage development the monitor/assessor needs to relate to the trainee as a fellow human being who happens to have greater experience and the advantage of observing the lesson impartially. This could possibly be achieved electronically but you would need to have the writing skills of Shakespeare to achieve it.

In my experience, developing materials in small groups can be a very effective way of helping trainees to think about and apply what they have learned on the course about language and its acquisition (Tomlinson, 2013b). This can be done usefully online but I think it is far more valuable for trainees to collaborate and spark each other off face-to-face. The excitement and raising of self-esteem which quick and effective face-to-face group development of materials can stimulate far exceeds that which collaborative online materials development typically achieves. Excellent materials can be developed collaboratively online but in my experience it can be a frustrating and time-consuming process and not as much is gained from the experience as developing the materials face-to-face.

Learning a new language and reflecting on the process of doing so can be an extremely useful component of a teacher development course. Of course, the new language could be learned online but this experience would have less value in terms of professional development. I act as moderator for an initial teacher training certificate and trainees on its courses all over the world are very appreciative of the insights learning a new language face-to-face gave them about such human attributes of the good language teacher as empathy, a sense of humour, patience and the ability to interact informally with the learners. It is appreciation of these human attributes (Tomlinson, 2008) that is a pre-requisite for the personal and professional development of the trainees and I think they can only be truly appreciated through reflection on live experience.

References

Tomlinson, B (2008) The good language teacher. *Folio* 12/2: 20–23.

Tomlinson, B (2013a) Second language acquisition, in Tomlinson, B (ed) *Applied Linguistics and Materials Development*. London: Bloomsbury, 11–30.

Tomlinson, B (2013b) 'Materials development courses', in Tomlinson, B (ed) *Developing Materials for Language Teaching*. Second edition. London: Bloomsbury.

Part 3 – English for Specific Purposes

11

Blended learning: Podcasts for taxi drivers

Nergiz Kern

Introduction

When I was working for a vocational training institution of the Metropolitan Municipality of Bursa in Turkey, which provides free courses to adults, I sometimes had to develop and teach English for Specific Purposes (ESP) courses for which there were no or few course materials readily available. In spring 2010, we were approached by the taxi association of Bursa who, as part of an initiative to improve the experience of tourists who visit Bursa, requested an English course for their taxi drivers.

The students

For the pilot course 15 taxi drivers aged between 26 and 56 who come into contact with tourists the most were chosen as participants. They were high school graduates with a traditional educational background. They had some basic English knowledge which they had been using together with gestures to communicate with tourists. Some had a strong Turkish accent. They worked at the same taxi stand and the rapport was very good, almost family like. They were highly motivated as they saw the benefits of learning English ('Tourists prefer and trust drivers who speak English.'), had an immediate use for English and saw fast improvements ('I did some small talk with a tourist and the tip was good.').

The students needed to improve their listening and speaking skills in a relatively short time to be able to communicate with tourists more effectively.

Turkish learners of English tend to have difficulties pronouncing English words, not so much because the sounds are so difficult but because they often pronounce English phonetically like Turkish. Their intonation is also often 'flat' as English is a stress-timed and Turkish a syllable-timed language. Therefore, my students needed a lot of exposure to spoken English.

The students were not able to attend face-to-face classes frequently so an intensive course would not have been possible. They often even missed the scheduled lessons.

The course

The course lasted two and a half months. Lessons took place twice a week and lasted for two hours.

Facilities and available technology

The course took place in a classroom at the taxi association. There was a whiteboard, a projector and screen, and wireless internet access. All students had mobile phones, and internet at home.

The syllabus

The syllabus was based on functional and emergent language (for example, providing information about the fare, offering assistance) with only brief grammar explanations related to the context and usually as a summary at the end of a lesson or topic.

The content

As there was very little time for me to prepare the course, I did some research online to find ready course material like coursebooks or videos with short dialogues but there was not much there, other than a few useful phrases. Therefore, I decided to structure the course around the typical stages of a taxi ride – from when the passengers get into a taxi until they are dropped off. I wrote a few sentences which I, as a potential passenger could think of, for each stage and also used some phrases I found on the internet. I planned to have the taxi drivers add more sentences and develop the dialogues fully. I was the English language expert but they knew much better what kind of conversations take place during a ride.

At certain intervals, I asked students to create new dialogues from what we had done so far in order to review the language. They recorded these on their mobile phones, sent the files to me and exchanged them among each other for feedback in class.

Blended approach

I took a blended learning approach for this course, which will be described in detail below.

Why a blended approach?

A thoughtful blend of synchronous and asynchronous communication and integration of tools can enhance learning (Garrison and Kanuka, 2004).

Situative perspective

In the above context, the situative perspective of learning (Mayes and de Freitas, 2007) fits very well. It states that the socio-cultural setting influences the learning and the learning outcome (*ibid.*). According to this socio-psychological view, 'learning must be personally meaningful' (*ibid.*: 18). The activities should be 'authentic to the social context in which the skills or knowledge are normally embedded' (*ibid.*).

This is certainly the case with my taxi driver students, with strong personal ties between co-workers. They have been a learning community (*ibid.*: 19) for many years, helping each other learn the trade and now learning and practising English together. As stated above, they derive motivation from the fact that the course content is meaningful and immediately applicable. This is also ensured by their contributions to the content (see below). Additionally, the course takes place in their social context – at the taxi association during synchronous sessions and at their workplace through the mobile component. This 'blend' of locations is made possible through the use of various online and mobile tools.

Flexibility and responsiveness

The above context made it necessary to take a flexible approach and be responsive to my students' needs throughout the course. Collis and Moonen (2002) list five dimensions of flexibility:

1. programme

2. study material

3. location

4. forms of communication

5. types of interaction.

All of these were relevant for my course and I aimed to realise this flexibility through a blended approach, which I will describe in detail in the next section.

The blend

There are two kinds of blends in my courseware: a) of interaction and b) of tools (see Figure 1).

Figure 1: A blend of interaction and tools used for the taxi English course

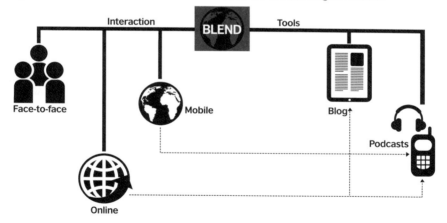

a. Interaction

The face-to-face component
As the learners had a traditional educational background, the face-to-face class met their expectations. It was also more personal and served to create good rapport with them. In addition, it was the learners' work environment, which is important in the situated learning perspective (see above). In class, the learners could work in

pairs and groups on collaborative tasks or as a whole class and I was able to provide immediate feedback and help, which is important for learners who have been out of class for a long time and with the needs mentioned above.

The online component

I only used the internet once or twice to show and explain the blog and its features. Almost all of the class time was used to elicit and introduce new language, collaboratively build dialogues and practise the language to make the most of the limited time we were together.

The online component was meant to extend classroom time and provide students with a record of coursework giving them the opportunity to review and practise the language on their own between the lessons and after the course had finished.

The mobile component

Taxi drivers have a lot of downtime. As my students could not attend face-to-face classes so often but needed a lot of practice, I wanted them to make use of this time when they were waiting for passengers. The technology – their mobile phones – was already available and they knew how to use them. So, the technology was 'normalized', as Bax (2003) calls it, and no additional cost or technology training was needed. Listening to the recordings in their work environment could also help them relate to, and retain, the material better (Mayes and De Freitas, 2007).

b. Tools

The podcasts

Originally, only the face-to-face component was planned. The idea of the podcasts occurred to me after the course had started and I saw that the four hours a week would not be sufficient to provide the learners with enough practice. Also, the break between the lessons was too long and without anybody to model the language for them outside class, they would not be able to practise on their own. Moreover, almost none of the drivers could attend every lesson due to their work. This is why I started taking snapshots of the board work in class and typing them up neatly with a word processor. I saved these as PDF files. Then, I recorded myself speaking the dialogues, words and phrases and uploaded them together with the transcripts to the blog.

In a typical lesson we would focus on one of the stages of a taxi ride or typical conversations between the passengers and the taxi driver. I would elicit information and language from the taxi drivers and help them with the language, and we would construct the dialogue together on the board. For example, one lesson was about making recommendations for hotels and places to visit. When writing the script for the recording, I would add a brief introduction in order to lead into the topic, provide a context, and to give students some new language to listen to besides the review of what we had done in class. I also sometimes added alternative phrases or sentences that could be used in the same situations. This way, there was always something new to learn from the podcasts, too. The transcript of the audio recording based on the 'Making Recommendations' lesson looked like this:

Hi! This is English for Taxi Drivers recording 18.

Making recommendations

My friend Andy is visiting Bursa. He sent me a message and asked: 'Do you know of any reasonably priced hotels in Bursa?' Many passengers ask taxi drivers for recommendations, right? So, how do you ask and make recommendations?

You can make recommendations about hotels, shops, museums, restaurants, places to see, places for entertainment, food, and many other things.

Here is how you can make recommendations:

Passenger: Do you know of any reasonably priced hotels?

Passenger: Can you recommend a good hotel?

Taxi driver: I can recommend the Boyugüzel Hotel.
It's not far from/near the city centre.

Passenger: How much does it cost?

Taxi driver: It costs between 60 and 90 Turkish liras for a single/double room.

Passenger: That's reasonable. Is it clean?

Taxi driver: Yes, it's clean and comfortable.

Passenger: How far is it from the Congress Centre?

Taxi driver: Not so far. Ten minutes by taxi.

Passenger: Thanks!

Taxi driver: You're welcome.

Passenger: Can you recommend any interesting places to see?

Taxi driver: Yes, I can recommend the historic plane tree/Yes, the historic plane tree is very interesting/Yes, you should see the historic plane tree.

Passenger: Oh, good. Thanks! Is it far from here? I have only three hours.

Taxi driver: No, it's (quite) near/No, it's not (that) far away.
It's about 20 minutes from here.

Passenger: Thanks! Let's go there, then/That sounds good. Thanks!

Taxi driver: You're welcome.

'A podcast (or non-streamed webcast) is a series of digital media files (either audio or video) that are released episodically and often downloaded through web syndication' (http://en.wikipedia.org/wiki/Podcast). Using podcasts in a blended environment helped my students with all the identified needs mentioned above.

Podcasts provide flexibility, portability and autonomy and promote active, mobile learning (Kukulska-Hulme and Shield, 2008), which is important in adult education and lifelong learning. Several studies report that students' speaking and listening skills have improved through podcasting (Sze, 2006; Abdous et al., 2009). Abdous et al. (2009) also mentions vocabulary and grammar skills improvement. Furthermore, transcripts help students with speaking and pronunciation (Rosell-Aguilar, 2007). They can also allow students to organise learning into manageable chunks (Chinnery,

2006) and are good revision tools (Evans, 2008), as they can be listened to outside class and repeatedly so, which is important to develop automaticity (Alonso et al. 2005: 221). Other advantages of podcasts are that they allow for flexibility, they are portable and they allow students to learn autonomously (Edirisingha, Salmon and Fothergill, 2007). Finally, podcasting is sustainable as it is a low cost, low barrier technology (Rosell-Aguilar, 2007).

The blog

The blog, for which I chose the easy-to-use Posterous platform which can be updated via email, served mainly as a delivery platform, which allowed students to access the podcasts and transcripts in a fast and simple way to either read and listen online or download them to their computers or mobile phones for offline listening and reading. I also occasionally provided additional exercises and links to useful websites.

Figure 2: Blog for the taxi English course on the Posterous platform

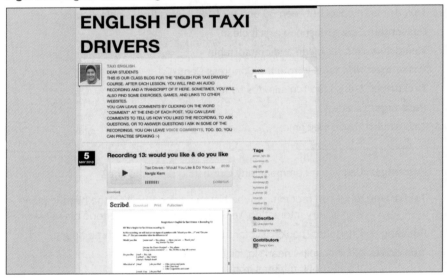

As can be seen in Figure 2, the blog had a search function (top right) so that students could find the topics they were interested in reviewing easily. I also tagged each blog post/podcast episode with relevant keywords, which were automatically listed on the right sidebar of the blog under the heading 'Tags'. Clicking on any of the tags or keywords brings up a list of all the blog posts/podcasts with related content.

The blog also allowed students to subscribe to it via RSS, which informs blog readers about new blog posts or podcast episodes and allows them to see the content with so-called 'aggregators' or 'RSS readers' on the web, a computer, or on a mobile device without having to visit the website itself. I did not specifically explain this feature because my students knew when I would upload a new podcast. This feature is more interesting for those who follow or subscribe to several blogs and podcasts.

Sustainability

Blended learning often means more investment in resources (e.g. financial, human, technical) (Garrison and Kanuka, 2004; Littlejohn, 2004), which neither my students nor I had as it was a low-budget course and my learners were busy. Therefore, I created sustainable courseware with the following features:

- short recordings, chunked material
- reusable learning objects
- easy to update, reorganise, reassemble or copy
- limited number of easy-to-use tools
- easy familiarisation with tools, tasks, and layout
- RSS, tagging, search tool (see above for an explanation)
- easy and flexible access to material.

Further planned adaptations

I considered adding students as contributors to the blog so that they could continue recording themselves, upload the files to the blog and ask for peer feedback even after the course, but due to the short duration of the course this was not possible.

Another idea was to develop a second module of the course for those taxi drivers who wanted to take it a bit further with their English language skills because they are also sometimes booked for private tours and then often serve as guides as well, or at least have to do more small talk. Connected to this was my idea to conduct short interviews with tourists in Bursa about Bursa, and make audio or video recordings which would then be posted on the blog. Ideally, they would be made by students (for example, when waiting for passengers or on a tour during breaks) and I could create tasks around them.

Lessons learned and advice

I believe the blended approach helped make this course a success. The short duration of the course and the few hours I had with these particular students with their needs as described above would not have been enough to give them sufficient help and practice in order to enable them to actually use the language at work.

I believe the blended approach helped my students to develop their language skills in a shorter time and become more confident in using them in real-life situations as we can see from the comments they made about improving and using some of what they had learned with passengers, even while the course was still going on (see Introduction).

Although all students had mobile phones, most of them were not smartphones. This meant the learners had to go to the blog, download the podcast episode, transfer it to their mobile phones and print out the transcript. There was no way of doing this automatically unless they only wanted to listen to the podcasts on their computer. The other alternative was to transfer the recordings to the students' mobile phones via Bluetooth from my laptop and provide the transcripts as hardcopy. The set-up and materials allow for this flexibility so that they can be used in low-tech and high-tech situations.

When recording the introduction of each episode, the small talk and the actual dialogues, it is good to pause between the sections so that later on, when reusing them for future courses, the sections can easily be cut and reassembled as needed.

Keeping the podcast episodes short makes it easier for the learners to listen to them even when they only have short breaks. It is also less intimidating for beginner learners and can give them a sense of achievement when they finish an episode and understand it. The risk of 'getting lost' in the recording is lower too.

Finally, one mistake that many podcast creators make is that the language used to explain the episode, language or grammar is often more complicated than the actual language or grammar point explained, which makes it difficult for the learners to understand. In this course, I wanted to avoid this trap but I also wanted to include an additional challenge. Therefore, I chose a middle way and did include some more complicated or unknown language in the introduction or 'small talk' part. Weaker students were helped by the transcript, they could ask me or at least learn to cope with situations in which they did not understand everything that was said in English (a common situation at work), and stronger students had some additional language to take away from the episodes.

References

Abdous, M, Camarena, MM and Facer, BR (2009) MALL Technology: Use of Academic Podcasting in the Foreign Language Classroom. *ReCALL* 21: 76–95.

Alonso, F, López, G, Manrique, D and Viñes, JM (2005) An instructional model for web-based e-learning education with a blended learning process approach. *British Journal of Educational Technology* 36/2: 217–235.

Bax, S (2003) CALL– past, present and future. *System* 31: 13–28.

Chinnery, GM (2006) Emerging technologies – Going to the MALL: Mobile Assisted Language Learning. *Language Learning & Technology* 10/1: 9–16.

Collis, B and Moonen, J (2002) Flexible learning in a digital world. *Open Learning: The Journal of Open and Distance Learning* 17/3: 217–230.

Edirisingha, P, Salmon, G and Fothergill, J (2007) 'Profcasting – a pilot study and guidance for integrating podcasts in a blended learning environment', in Bernath, U and Sangrà, A (eds) *Research on Competence Development in Online Distance Education and E-learning*. Oldenburg: BIS-Verlag, 127–137.

Evans, C (2008) The effectiveness of m-learning in the form of podcast revision lectures in higher education. *Computers & Education* 50: 491–498.

Garrison, D and Kanuka, H (2004) Blended Learning: Uncovering its transformative potential in higher education. *The Internet and Higher Education* 7: 95–105.

Kukulska-Hulme, A and Shield, A (2008) An overview of mobile assisted language learning: From content delivery to supported collaboration and interaction. *ReCALL* 20/3: 271–289.

Littlejohn, A (2004) *Reusing Online Resources: A Sustainable Approach to E-learning.* London: Routledge.

Mayes, T and de Freitas, S (2007) 'Learning and e-learning: the role of theory', in Beetham, H and Sharpe, R (eds) *Rethinking Pedagogy for a Digital Age: Designing and Delivering E-Learning.* Routledge, 13–25.

Rosell-Aguilar, F (2007) Top of the Pods – In search of a podcasting 'Podagogy' for language learning. *Computer Assisted Language Learning* 20/5: 471–492.

Sze, PM (2006) 'Developing students listening and speaking skills through ELT podcasts'. *Educational Journal* 34/2, 115–134.

12

A blended learning course for the aviation industry: A case study

Lynda Beagle and Graeme Davies

Course overview

RMIT English Worldwide (REW) is an English language centre owned by RMIT University in Melbourne, Australia. REW has been developing and publishing courseware and assessment for use at the Melbourne campus and for offshore partners for the last 12 years.

REW has developed two English for Specific Purposes (ESP) courses, one for pilots and the other for air traffic controllers, which employ a blended learning approach and focus on extending English language speaking and listening skills in aviation contexts. The courses, named *Beyond Level 4* (BL4), are targeted at practising aviation professionals who work in international airspace, and are designed to assist them to move from Operational Level 4 to Extended Level 5 or Expert Level 6 according to the International Civil Aviation Organisation (ICAO) Language Proficiency Rating Scale. It should be emphasised that the BL4 courses are focused on developing industry-specific language for learners who already have good functional and operational competency in aviation English.

Each course is accompanied by a supplementary grammar book, a guide to monitoring and assessing performance for the language instructor, and a separate script and answer guide to assist in administering the parallel face-to-face component of the course.

Course description

A review of the literature shows there is no single accepted definition of blended learning, but it can be understood to combine computer-mediated delivery and face-to-face interaction. Garrison and Vaughan suggest that in blended learning 'face-to-face oral communication and online written communication are optimally integrated such that the strengths of each are blended into a unique learning experience congruent with the context and intended educational purpose' (2008: 5).

The use of e-learning resources in the BL4 courses is ideal for the aviation industry, as it enables pilots and air traffic controllers to study without interrupting their work schedules. The online platform not only facilitates convenient and efficient delivery of content, but also has the clear benefit of replicating the context in which aviation personnel primarily use the language; that is, via radio telephony. Online delivery reproduces the challenges of this medium, namely oral interaction without the benefit of visual cues.

The face-to-face aspect of the courses is created through the interaction between the learner and the instructor, a trained English language teacher, who monitors the learner's progress, evaluates their speaking output and gives feedback via tutorials held at the organisation's training centre. The tutorials, which are conducted in English, provide the opportunity for support, targeted advice, feedback on performance and suggested strategies to help reach the desired outcomes. Wagner refers to interaction as 'the so-called glue that holds together all of those variables being blended' (2006: 44), and it would seem that as a large part of the BL4 course is undertaken independently by the learner, the interactive component is essential in facilitating learner engagement, motivation and satisfaction. However, at this point, the course has not been in use for sufficient time to evaluate the benefits of tutor-mediated support, and we await feedback on this element from course users.

The design of the courses is essentially the same for the pilot and the air traffic controller streams, and both are structured to provide 80–100 hours of online material delivered in eight units, each containing three sessions. Each session provides listening skills development, grammar and vocabulary input, and speaking skills in the following format:

Figure 1

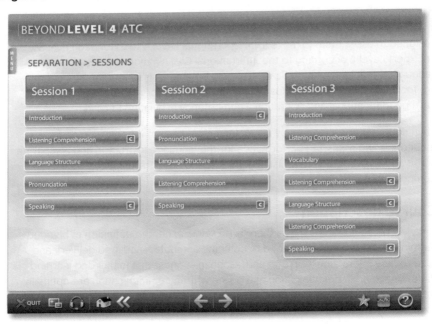

 = Check Activities

The course is designed for the learner to work through the material at his or her own pace, typically over three or four months. Check activities have been included to monitor and assess the learner's listening and speaking performance, as well as their performance with grammatical structures and vocabulary (overall, 56 of the 280 total activities are check activities).

Listening, grammar and vocabulary check activities are scored directly into the software database, and both the course user and the instructor can access progress reports, graded as Competent, Satisfactory or Not Satisfactory. For the speaking check activities, the learner can listen to recordings of their own performance and can repeat activities before submitting them if they are not satisfied with their first attempt. Once the audio files have been submitted, they are stored in the software database ready for assessment.

The check activities form the basis of the interaction with the instructor, whose role includes monitoring the learner's general progress in the course, evaluating the learner's speaking performance and delivering the structured face-to-face (tutorial) course components. It is recommended that tutorials take place at the end of each unit, or at least twice during the course, in order to provide formative feedback that enables the learner to target areas of need. The frequency of the tutorials is determined by the resources available in the training organisation. As Oliver et al. (2006: 506) note, 'in most settings, there can be unlimited scope for technology-mediated communication but far more restrictive amounts of face-to-face communication'. The decision to restrict the face-to-face component of the course to one-on-one tutorials was based on the difficulty of timetabling classes that all learners could attend, given the scheduling constraints of the aviation industry.

The course is written in Flash, which is considered the most readily accessible online tool for multimedia development, and is also ideal for the presentation of realistic animations and plausible aviation training material, in particular flight and radar or control tower simulations. Flash provides effective compression of large files and enables the audio file management process through a remote database, both of which are critical for efficient online delivery. It is also recognised as the software language that can deliver the widest cross-platform compatibility, whereas rival languages may not perform equally well in different operating systems or browsers. Although some more recently developed online hardware products (e.g. iPads) do not support Flash, software applications are now available to overcome this limitation.

Teaching methodology

The course was designed for independent, self-paced study partly because of the time and scheduling constraints experienced by those working in the aviation industry. However, an additional strength of the online delivery is that it simulates the context in which pilots and air traffic controllers use English in the workplace, namely communicating via radio telephony. The course utilises situations in which learners must build on the standardised phraseology required for routine flight operations and extend their use of general English to deal with non-routine and emergency events. This replicates the real world environment, where pilots and controllers are separated from their interlocutors and must rely on verbal communication aided by the visual information typical of their workstation; for example, charts, radar or cockpit displays and views from the cockpit or control tower.

The course covers listening, speaking and language discretely, but each session of the course is presented as a coherent progression from receptive input to productive output. Typically, each session is based around a core non-routine listening scenario. It begins with a context-setting activity that prepares the learner for the situation, pre-teaching of key vocabulary, pronunciation exercises and grammar activities, all of which focus on the target language featured in the listening text.

The speaking activities are the culmination of each session's language focus and are a form of role play designed to extend the contexts covered in the earlier listening activities. The learner is assigned a role, e.g. first officer, and interacts with the computer, which fills the other role. The learner listens to the transmissions and must make appropriate replies based on prompt cards provided onscreen. The responses are recorded and the learner can listen to each recorded response before moving on. There are typically four or five stimulus-response exchanges in each conversation. In this way, the target language is embedded in all the activities, but is presented in different ways and recycled in the final speaking activity. The learner is guided from an initial receptive focus through to quite demanding language production in a realistic context, with the aim of ultimately spontaneously and accurately producing language forms appropriate to the situation.

Considerations that influenced the design process

The motivation of learners doing this course is high, as it serves as preparation to take an ICAO-endorsed language proficiency test, success in which leads to expanded work opportunities, for example, flying on international rather than domestic routes. Without the structure imposed by scheduled classes, motivation is an essential element of successful online study. The learner needs to study independently so, as noted by Macdonald, success in the blended learning environment requires the learner to be self-directed and reflective (2008: 121). However, the nature of the learners' work in the aviation industry means that consistency in study patterns is difficult to maintain. For this reason, it is important that the course comprises digestible modules of reasonable duration, is portable and also clearly engages learners in highly plausible simulated work contexts. The aviation industry is very much dependent on melding visual cues with other communications; therefore, the design of the course emphasises its visual impact to inspire and maintain engagement.

Another consideration was that, in general, the learners would be working in isolation, rather than as part of a dedicated cohort. This makes the contact with the language instructor extremely important in order to ensure that each learner progresses appropriately, to provide tailored feedback and also to give direction to the learner's broader language acquisition or maintenance needs. Macdonald argues convincingly that face-to-face support is important in a blended learning context to reduce feelings of isolation and to maintain motivation when a course is fully online (2008: 50).

However, the course developers can only recommend the amount and level of contact between the learner and the instructor, and this ultimately depends on how much importance the client organisation places on training, and on the resources available to them. Thus, an inherent limitation of the course is that it requires instructors with both the language skills and requisite time to maximise the benefits of the course's inbuilt tracking and assessment system.

As has been discussed, online delivery provides many advantages, but obviously also poses some inherent limitations in language learning. One possible weakness is that an online interface cannot reproduce the interactions entailed in true two-way communications. This once again underlines the importance of the face-to-face component of the design, where a skilled instructor can judge a learner's capacity to clarify, confirm, and respond to a live interlocutor.

A final limitation of the course is the lack of community, which precludes any kind of collaborative learning or collaborative problem-solving. In many computer-mediated courses an online community is developed, with the learners interacting via discussion boards and/or email. Equally, in a traditional English language classroom, there is strong focus on interaction and use of the target language. However, the blend of online activity and one-on-one interaction in the BL4 courses is in keeping with the work context in which the learners use English, and therefore enhances the intended learning outcome. The focus of the BL4 courses is relatively narrow, i.e. to achieve Level 5 or Level 6 on the ICAO rating scale, and learners have not expressed any desire to have increased interaction within their cohort.

Lessons learned and advice

In terms of lessons learned, it became apparent during the development process that good online design includes interactive elements on every screen the learner sees. Whereas traditional book-based programmes can provide explanations and examples followed up by related exercises, online design precludes extended expository material and has very definite real estate limits. Although a supplementary grammar book was not part of the original design concept, it was decided during the building of the courses to develop this print-based material. The extra resource provides learners with extended explanations of particular grammar points and a range of exercises to practise and reinforce these.

The supplementary grammar materials can be used as an intervention (prompted by the learner and/or the instructor) when a learner is struggling with a particular aspect of language, as identified by course performance. It also means that the instructor can recommend directly relevant material to supplement the online course, keeping in mind the need for language educator resources and skills to be available within client organisations. As noted previously, the course design should not place unrealistic demands on the capabilities and resources of the client organisation providing the training.

Another lesson pertinent to internet-based courses is that the field of online design is dynamic and both the hardware and software are ever-changing. Therefore, it is important to ensure that design decisions, such as using Flash as the programming language for the course, are made with full readiness to move with the evolution of the technology. This means being responsive to issues such as the Flash/iPad compatibility problem, proactively seeking workarounds and ensuring that only the latest, most secure and flexible programming language is used. The unpredictability of internet developments is an occupational hazard, and the only remedy is to maintain constant responsiveness.

Conclusion

In conclusion, this example of a blended learning course may serve as a suitable model for other industry-based ESP courses where learners need to develop specific language competencies. The use of online delivery incorporates self-paced learning that enables flexibility and does not disrupt the learners' work routines, which is a key concern for the aviation industry. The course provides targeted English language input and practice, as well as check activities that are recorded and subsequently assessed. Regular tutorials with the course instructor provide formative feedback and direction for subsequent engagement with the course materials. Although second-language learning is traditionally undertaken in a wholly face-to-face environment, the BL4 courses aim to achieve specified language development using the possibilities offered by new technologies.

References

Garrison, D and Vaughan, N (2008) *Blended Learning in Higher Education*. San Francisco: Jossey-Bass.

Macdonald, J (2008) *Blended Learning and Online Tutoring*. Aldershot, Hampshire: Gower.

Oliver, R, Herrington, J and Reeves, TC (2006) 'Creating authentic learning environments through blended learning approaches' in Bonk, C and Graham, C (eds) *The Handbook of Blended Learning*. San Francisco: Pfeiffer.

Wagner, E (2006) 'On designing interaction experiences for the next generation of blended learning' in Bonk, C and Graham, C (eds) *The Handbook of Blended Learning*. San Francisco: Pfeiffer.

13

Blended learning for English for Occupational Purposes: No frills, soft skills, gaps filled

Andy Keedwell

Background

While definitions differ, it is generally agreed that blended learning involves an effective combination of different modes of delivery, models of teaching and styles of learning (Procter, 2003: 3). Staker and Horn (2012: 3) make a helpful distinction between online delivery of content and instruction (with a degree of student control) and delivery at a 'bricks and mortar location away from home'. However, a common misconception of blended learning is that it implies large-scale, international programmes, designed by a centralised expert unit, with cohort upon cohort of students studying general English. I will describe here an alternative in which blended learning was used as a small-scale, delicate tool to reach a specialist market through highly-targeted materials developed locally and delivered in a comparatively low-tech way.

To some extent, this account is of historical interest as the programme was designed in 2003 and delivered 2004–05, in Armenia, where the concept of learning in any way other than face-to-face was very new. Armenia has changed rapidly since then and so is receptive to an online element of learning, as shown by the range of non-face-to-face courses on offer there today. Nevertheless, I hope that some of the lessons learned from programme design and delivery might be of use to others.

Blended learning described here was implemented by the British Council, which did not begin to engage fully with Armenia until 2002–03, unlike elsewhere in Eastern Europe. As a new, ambitious British Council centre, we were approached by the Armenian Ministry of Foreign Affairs (AMFA) to support language upgrading for diplomatic staff. AMFA did not have any resources of its own to support this but, in terms of relationship building, it made a great deal of sense for the British Council in Armenia to meet the request. As ELT Support Manager (the sole member of a small staff to deal with English) I opened discussions with the very co-operative AMFA Liaison Officer.

Assessing needs

Some aspects of course design were straightforward. A target audience of 40 junior diplomats who served regularly on overseas missions, with a serviceable B1+/B2 level of English, was quickly identified. Needs analysis showed that the need was not so much for language improvement but training in the soft skills of a) delivering presentations/briefings and b) producing reports.

I faced, however, a number of challenges. As professionals, trainees spent considerable time out of the country in locations ranging from Minsk to Riga to Bangkok. This precluded regular standard course delivery. Secondly, as a project manager with a wide, varied portfolio (and a relatively small budget), I could not commit to regular classroom teaching. Neither was there a pool of local teachers on whom to draw: one of my roles was to enhance teacher skills to a point at which there would be. Blended learning, therefore, was not just a good idea but a necessity.

Rationale for course design

The AMFA requested soft skills training, in particular report-writing and presentation-delivery. An often subtle mix of language and skills, this type of training delivery is located on that intriguing, vast and sometimes forgotten branch of Hutchinson and Water's ESP tree as English for Occupational Purposes (Hutchinson and Waters, 1987: 13) or perhaps more helpfully, English for the world of work. Content of such a course needs to directly target workplace needs and both AMFA administration and the trainer agreed that the focus of training should not be on the language itself but what could be done with the language.

Looking at genre

Like many course-designers, I find it useful to think in terms of genre, generic features and generic moves: identification of, and hands-on practice by, generic features by learners seems to me to provide a common-sense rather than a theoretical route to enable novice writers/speakers to handle the discourse they aspire to use effectively. In our context, 'presentations' and 'reports' are often very loosely-used terms which cover a wide variety of genres and one challenge to the course designer is to determine which specific generic features are of relevance. However, I would argue that both genres have a great deal in common, a fact which nicely lends itself to course design. Discussion and needs analysis showed the target group would be expected to:

- give briefings/produce reports to highlight information which had been gathered in some way
- describe how that information had been identified
- outline what should be done based on that information.

Topped and tailed with introduction and conclusion, this gave a familiar generic structure for both oral and written forms of:

I	Introduction
M	Methodology
F	Findings
R	Recommendations
C	Conclusion

The presentations and reports participants were expected to give in the workplace had a clearly defined purpose (to inform and often to persuade). In addition, effective delivery in both cases depends on accurate analysis of the audience's needs. All these aspects helped to build links between the two strands of the training.

Looking at skills

Success in giving an effective briefing or writing a report depends on:

- Being organised – organising information and ideas through language to meet the needs of the audience/reader.

- Being clear – highlighting information, clarifying argument, avoiding ambiguity.

- Being precise and exact – distinguishing fact from opinion, avoiding undue generalisation and perhaps an element of hedging.

- Being economical – using language and presenting information with the audience's needs in mind: neither too much or too little.

Identification of these characteristics produced a happy (if rather corny) acronym of COPE – clarity, organisation, precision and economy – and the suggestion that the course would help trainees COPE with real-life tasks. The underlying principle of COPE also helped unify the two strands of training.

Choice of face-to-face and blended learning

Quite logically, the real-life differences between oral briefings and written reports suggested a face-to-face briefings course and an online writing course. I would argue that presentation skills can only be learned through doing, through trainees interacting with peers, providing evaluations of each others' performance and practising and refining these skills through face-to-face interaction. Trainee development can only come from within but the presence of the trainer as coach can provide immediate input and act as catalyst. Progress can be rapid and can have a significant impact within a short period.

In real life, report writing is much more of a reflective, solitary activity in which the report-writer, sometimes with others but often alone, collects, marshals and organises data, makes choices in grammar and lexis to present it and manipulates a range of rhetorical functions to meet the needs of an unseen, if often clearly defined, reader. As such, it clearly lends itself to a situation unfolding over time where trainer and trainee do not work face-to-face. In practical terms, it also clearly met participants' needs as the entire course could be completed during overseas service.

Course design

Effective course design depended on a harmonious combination of the two strands so that one course component complemented rather than supplemented the other in the sense of a 'good Scotch whisky' (Isackson, 2002). The IMFRC structure and COPE principles unified the course (at the risk of overloading participants with acronyms) but equally so did the fact that both courses took as their starting point the imperative to meet the needs of the audience (the writer/speaker as writer, the reader/listener as customer) and the 'politeness' of being concise/avoiding redundancy. Both courses emphasised the importance of language as an organising and highlighting tool, and developed language awareness of ways to describe how findings were obtained, classifying and integrating visuals into text or presentation.

Technicalities and timetabling

Both courses began with an introduction to the blended learning approach and it was possible to run the face-to-face course over the two months that the participants were in country. Timelines were more fluid for the online element of the course. With a flexible approach to timetabling, the majority of trainees were able to attend seven three-hour face-to-face sessions on presentation skills. Sessions were occasionally repeated to accommodate everybody. As trainees were engaged in giving real-life briefings outside the classroom, it was possible to maintain pace despite the sessions being widely spaced.

Had I been developing the online report writing course today, I would have made more use of virtual learning environment technology, Moodle in particular. At the time, not all of today's technology was accessible and my own technical knowledge was quite limited. The solution was therefore simple. Thirty hours of materials (partly adapted from previous face-to-face courses, much of it innovated) were developed and issued to trainees in hard/soft copy form, with keys for self-access tasks and commentaries on possible answers to more open-ended tasks (see Tomlinson, 1998: 322). Trainees undertook self-access tasks throughout each unit and completed an assignment at the end of each module (generally a report sub-section of 150–200 words) which they emailed to me. I guaranteed to provide feedback by email within three days. Trainees were also asked to complete a final assignment of around 400 words, working to guidelines but on a topic of their own choice, which I also received by email and which contributed to final assessment.

By today's standards, the system was rudimentary and there are of course a multitude of ways in which the course could be developed further. If we accept though that technical platforms are only a means to an end, I would argue that the relative simplicity of this no-frills approach is effective in situations where (for whatever reason: time, cost, or lack of technical skills) a full range of IT resources cannot be exploited.

Lessons learned

'Did it work?' is the fundamental question. Certainly, within limited parameters, it seemed to be effective in meeting trainees' needs:

a. All 40 trainees completed final assignments for the course which were assessed according to a simple but usable set of criteria as ranging from excellent to satisfactory.

b. Trainee post-course evaluations were very positive (90 per cent rating the course as high quality) and contrasted with an element of initial scepticism. Trainees consistently stated in end-of-course questionnaires that they had enjoyed the flexibility and asynchronicity of the course and could fit it around their busy lives and foreign service.

c. Feedback from AMFA administration in post-course informal discussion was very positive and identified tangible improvement in staff skills in terms of clarity and comprehensiveness of presentations and reports.

d. I was delighted to be invited to several (unclassified) presentations by trainees after course completion, which substantiated AMFA comments – presenters were clearly taking a much more structured and economical approach.

e. The agreement with AMFA went a considerable way to cementing relationships with the British Council in Armenia. Later AMFA proposed similar training for officials from Nagorno-Karabakh (an independent republic recognised by no country except Armenia) – although (for various complex political reasons) this did not happen, it would have been a useful way to engage with the country while respecting diplomatic protocol.

Challenges

■ Local development of a local course by a materials designer working alone has advantages – but course design would no doubt have benefited from one or more second opinion. It is probably impossible to predict every need of every trainee: the email format allowed for some flexible troubleshooting, however, and I also acted as consultant to trainees on job-related report writing during and after the course. This provided insights which were fed back later into course design, including requests for support from participants for developing skills at elementary hedging. Their questions included advice, for example, on how to qualify predictions for the future in situations which were uncertain or how to present findings when the results of fact-finding had been rather disappointing.

■ Designing and delivering blended learning locally also has the potential to swamp an individual online provider. The specific context meant that I engaged with two batches of 20 trainees – quite manageable, but a different matter had an entire government department asked for training.

■ One design flaw in the online course was that I had initially visualised the course as a two-way dialogue between trainer and trainee and neglected the critical element of peer interaction. In the early stages of the course, participants missed out on the vital aspects of information exchange and knowledge construction (Salmon, 2000: 5). During the course, I and the trainees found ways to remedy this but online mechanisms (however simple) for peer support, evaluation and discussion needed to have been built into the course from the start.

■ The greatest challenge lay in replicating the success of the course with other organisations. Unlike AMFA, these proved to be resistant to the idea of blended learning (and in some cases resistant to the idea of providing any training for their staff). The situation has doubtless changed in Armenia since then.

Some principles for course design

1. The choice of how to 'fill the gap' often lies on a continuum between large, standardised 'global products' and something locally/individually produced for a small, highly specific, mobile audience. Both forms have their advantages and disadvantages.

2. 'Technology is only important to the degree that it helps us get where we want to go' (Mehlinger, 1996). Blended learning does not necessarily imply high-tech resources or skills. Simple, comparatively low-tech solutions can serve a purpose while not exploiting the full range of what is available.

3. This chapter has discussed soft skills development in which the oral skill lends itself logically to face-to-face training and the written skill to online learning, with structural features of IMFRC and the underlying principles of COPE (unifying the two strands, so consolidating learning). There are many other ways in which this could be done: a blended learning course to link negotiation skills and proposal writing, for example, or the oral and written aspects of participative project management.

4. Blended learning for the world of work functions effectively when there is an immediate pay-off for the trainee. AMFA participants were conscious throughout the programme of the progress they were making and the impact of the course on their success in everyday work-related tasks.

5. Blended learning is still an unfamiliar concept to many: the course described here included an introductory face-to-face session to blended learning in which principles were explained and discussed and this, I think, is essential.

6. Learners do not only learn from the trainer. One oversight in course design (rectified to some extent during course delivery) was to neglect to provide trainees with ways to discuss issues and support each other and it is this level of interaction that means that what is provided is more than a mere online correspondence course (Muilenburg and Berge, 2000: 1). Blended learning is a three-way and not a two-way process.

I hope that this chapter has shown sufficiently that 'do-it-yourself' is certainly one valid approach to blended learning. While it has its disadvantages (and may even appear a little rudimentary at times), it also has the potential to meet very specific needs quickly, fairly comprehensively and with substantial smaller-scale impact.

References

Hutchinson, T and Waters, A (1987) *English for Specific Purposes*. Cambridge, Cambridge University Press.

Isackson, P, August 2002 Blog. Available online at www.internettime.com/itimegroup/astd/lc_blog.htm

Mehlinger, HD (1996) School reform in the information age. *Phi Delta Kappan 77*, Bloomington, USA. Available online at www.questia.com/library/1G1-18084235/school-reform-in-the-information-age

Muilenburg, L and Berge, ZL (2000) A framework for designing questions for online learning. *DEOSNEWS* 10/2, ISSN 1062-9416, Pennsylvania, USA. Available online at http://smcm.academia.edu/LinMuilenburg/Papers/440394/A_Framework_for_Designing_Questions_for_Online_Learning

Procter, C (2003) *Blended Learning in Practice.* Paper presented at the Education in a Changing Environment Conference, 2003, Salford, UK. Available online at www.ece.salford.ac.uk/proceedings/papers/cp_03.rtf

Salmon, G (2000) *E-Moderating: The Key to Teaching and Learning Online.* Kogan Page Limited: London.

Staker, H and Horn, B (2012) *Classifying K-12 Blended Learning.* Innosight Institute White Paper, May 2012, New York, USA. Available online at www.innosightinstitute.org/innosight/wp-content/uploads/2012/05/Classifying-K-12-blended-learning2.pdf

Tomlinson, B (1998) *Materials Development in Language Teaching.* Cambridge, Cambridge University Press.

14

A longitudinal case study of the 'blends' used on courses between the British Council in Bulgaria and Siemens Enterprise Communications Bulgaria

Edward Russell

Context

The British Council in Bulgaria developed a new kind of course in response to changes in the local market's demands over a six-year period. Our corporate clients, mostly from the information technology and telecommunications sectors, demanded a unique mix of English language support and business skills, such as those relating to customer services, to improve their engagement with new customers. This mix of input, is in a way a blend as described by Oliver and Trigwell (2005: 17): 'the combination of a number of pedagogic approaches, irrespective of the learning technology used'. The blend we used over a series of courses was a mix of pedagogy (drawing on content and language integrated learning and task based language learning), and a mixture of technologies. Our teaching centre sought to meet these mixed needs and we began experimenting with the delivery of a Customised Business English Course (CBEC) developed initially by Jamie Mann of the British Council in Bulgaria. Later we sought to overcome timing issues by using face-to-face and online tools, the classic 'blend' that Oliver and Trigwell (*ibid.*) describe as 'the integrated combination of traditional learning with web based online approaches'.

A CBEC delivers a blend of language, soft skills and content instruction, the idea being that in order to improve the clients return on investment we could take the opportunity to combine business skills with language instruction and write each course based on the client's unique specification. It allowed us to borrow key components from free-standing workshops and embed relevant elements within these.

In this case, the needs were initially seen as being support with speaking (to clients on the telephone), writing (emails, reports), customer service skills, and general English language training. This was to be delivered for 150 of Siemens' telecommunication engineers who supported clients in the US market. Courses were developed through needs analysis of participants and input from the clients. The results showed that participants would benefit not only from language input and practice, but also from greater awareness of the modes and text types that are used to communicate externally and internally. The fact that the partnership with Siemens was longitudinal in nature meant that each time we were able to respond to feedback from all stakeholders both during and after each course, in an attempt to further improve and refine the package.

The need for a CBEC arose from discussion with the client stakeholders about the need for improved English combined with a focus on US-style customer services delivery to their expectant clients. This would enable the company to retain clients, exceed expectations and meet their corporate objectives. The course participants were usually male, under 30, graduates of technical universities, and mainly Bulgarian first language speakers, but there were also a number of Turkish and Armenian speakers. Despite generally having CEFR B1 and above levels of English, many service engineers had limited overseas experiences in English-speaking contexts.

Our small Bulgarian teaching centre had an excellent mix of experienced, well-qualified trainers, managers and a teaching centre manager who was supportive of product innovations, provided decisions were pedagogically grounded. We worked hard to develop relationships with clients and met prior to and after every course to discuss feedback and improvements. We also conducted a mid-course satisfaction survey to enable us to monitor, and respond to, participant concerns. This structured approach to client/service provider relationships meant we were afforded certain liberties and could innovate with the course, using experimental practices that were considered valid.

An evolving partnership

Initial (non-CBEC) courses began at Siemens in 2004, and were standard, general, or business English courses that followed a coursebook and provided training to language-level groups of up to 16 participants. These courses were 48 hours in length with 24 two-hour classes taking place face-to-face at Siemens' offices, two or three times a week, in the evening before their participants' shifts began.

From this initial stage the CBEC (v2 below) was developed in response to the participants' and client's concerns that the course was not linked to their specific needs. We added elements that were based on the functional English and soft-skill requirements of participants' working lives (for example dealing with an upset customer on the telephone, or replying to an email enquiry) as well as including a more telecoms/IT-specific language focus.

The client demanded faster and greater improvement in their engineers' performance, particularly in the quality of emails they were writing. This required us to employ our resources more flexibly to meet their demands. The participants themselves were finding the longer courses hard going, as they were either before or after their night shifts. We were seeking ways to add value to this CBEC, without increasing our peak hour workload, whilst also cutting down on the cross town travelling we were doing. The idea of using technology to add flexibility to our offer seemed to make sense, both pragmatically and potentially pedagogically. One of the ways to assist participants with their writing was to give feedback on participants' real-work writing, perhaps at an early draft stage.

In the next version (v3) of the course we experimented with screencasting (SC), which is a short video of your computer's screen with a recorded commentary as you move around and (in this case) make changes to a text. It was initially developed as a way to make short explanatory videos for users of software, and was seen as an alternative to reading an instruction booklet. We saw an opportunity to use this tool as a way of giving feedback on writing. We felt that we could give more interesting feedback on participants' writing in this way by manipulating their text while we talked about it, as opposed to pen on paper, or inserted comments in Word documents, as we had done previously.

The participants were sent a weekly email outlining activities for the week (based on a needs analysis). The tasks were opportunities to self-study on selected websites, which were thematically linked to texts from their self-study books. In addition, they were asked to send a piece of writing from their daily work tasks. The rubric stated simply: send a work-related piece of writing that you'd like feedback on (no more than 500 words). In return, a few days later, participants were sent an email with a link to their screencast, and were provided with links to websites where learners could read about, or practise, a certain linguistic area that had emerged as a potential focus. Individual follow-up work like this was suggested after each piece of submitted writing. We developed a checklist that tutors could use to track progress, and reflected the taught content in v2. This checklist offered learners another modality; if the audio and video feedback were not clear it also aided record keeping and standardisation between tutors. This initial experiment was successful and screencasting was then incorporated more fully into the blend in the next version.

Table 1: Satisfaction with progress after six weeks of v3

	Very satisfied	Quite satisfied	Neither	Quite dissatisfied	Very dissatisfied	Don't know
Writing	6	8	3	2	0	0
Grammar	4	5	2	4	0	4
Listening	3	3	8	1	1	2
Reading	2	5	4	2	0	6

The next CBEC (v4) had less face-to-face time, perhaps due to the greater efficiency of the course, and was just 36 hours long, spread over 12 weeks and included six screencasts (one every fortnight) which were incorporated as a way of giving feedback on assessed tasks. In this course one major drawback of using screencasts in this way was that it did not naturally set up a conversation about the text in question. It often led to moves resembling the following: trainer sets task, participant responds, trainer gives feedback. Although these moves are beneficial, they also replicate more traditional (input–output) procedures of the teaching/learning process.

The important methodological change in v5 was that screencasts would deliver *formative* feedback that could be implemented as learners worked towards producing a final piece, in a portfolio of their writing. This move towards portfolio assessment matches much best practice in assessment where the focus is on assessment for learning, rather than assessment of learning (Li, 2010). The global economic downturn led to many clients expecting more from less, and Siemens was no exception. With training budgets constricting we continued our push to find solutions for our partner. Towards the end of 2010 (v5) the face-to-face hours were down to 16 hours with 20 hours of material being delivered online, that included a number of writing tasks. The face-to-face sessions occurred fortnightly for two hours, and were an opportunity to react to, or set up, tasks online. We introduced a forum that served as a virtual learning environment (VLE) and screencasts were still used but links were posted as threads in the forum. This was cost effective for the client, and far more flexible for the participants. Participants were able to participate whether in the country, or overseas, whether working days or nights. The reduction in face-to-face hours meant that there were considerable cost savings involved which was one of the original motivations behind blended learning (Driscoll, 2002). For us too, it was a good way to engage participants that did not overstretch our small team's limited resources too much.

Table 2: Summary of CBECs

Version	Type	Technology used	Face-to-face hours	Notes
v1 (2004)	General and Business English	n/a	48	
v2	CBEC	n/a	36	Addition of soft, work skills component, additional preparation time for teacher.
v3	Feedback only	Emails, screencasts of work tasks. Follow up links to material.	0	Skeleton self-study programme. Screencasts as stand-alone bolt on to v2. Links and 'further reading'/ tasks assigned as part of screencasts.
v4	CBEC	Screencasts of set tasks.	36	Screencasts (+ checklists with written comments) integrated into the syllabus as feedback on assessment.
v5 (2010)	CBEC	Forum as VLE, screencasts of set tasks, portfolio assessment.	12-16	Participants produced written and spoken tasks (presentations) for portfolios. SC used formatively.
Future v6	CBEC?	Dependent on organisation, and learner needs and context.	20?	Participants taught to use SC, or other tools. Emphasis on continuing the dialogue after feedback.

Teaching methods and task types

Teachers mainly used a task-based approach on the CBEC, using real-life work tasks as the basis for many activities. However, learners tired of doing work-related tasks in addition to their actual work, and more variety was added to the later, online, versions of the course where choice was offered. This in itself is another element of a blend in Collis and Moonen's (2002) understanding of blended learning as being about 'flexibility and learner choice'. In v5 the learners nominated elective text-types to produce (including oral presentations which were recorded online). In this version, the authentic task-based approach was replaced with a process/genre analysis approach. However, the range of texts chosen by learners to cover in v5 was too varied and more focus would have produced better quality writing, particularly as some text-types (for example short stories) were less familiar to some learners, and thus more challenging to produce.

Screencasting

Screen casts, video and audio recordings of activity on a computer screen, have been used in a number of contexts both to provide feedback on writing, see for example Stannard (2008) and Brick and Holmes (2008), and also as a mode for educational instruction, for example Wigginbottom (2007).

Giving feedback in this way gave flexibility to our participants. Because it is an asynchronous tool, they could access their feedback as often, and whenever, they wished to. Likewise, we could produce these screencasts at times relatively convenient to our schedules, at off-peak hours. The participants were familiar with screencapture, and the videos were popular with participants, who found the personalised feedback useful and motivating because they were able to implement the feedback immediately in their work places. Perhaps more motivating was the support the combined 'benefits of oral and online delivery' offered with 'additional visual elements to enhance communication' (Brick and Holmes, 2008). It is the mix of modes, both giving feedback in writing, accompanying this with a spoken audio commentary and most of all being able to move the text around that increases the impact. When reorganising, for example, a sentence, a paragraph or a short text, the ability to record this process and talk through the stages and considerations is plainly more motivating and clearer than traditional forms of recast, or paper and pen feedback.

Feedback on writing (different approaches)

According to Li, now that the effect of corrective feedback on writing 'has been established, researchers should embark on the mission of investigating the factors constraining its effectiveness' (2010: 349). Indeed, feedback is widely recognised as an important part of the language learning process and can improve the quality of writing 'when it is done during the writing process, i.e. between drafts' (Krashen, 1984: 11). The impact of our efforts to focus on feedback as part of the process on this course led to significant improvements in writing style and language awareness in participants' final portfolios.

Choice of tool for screencasting

For the British Council in Sofia, the choice of screencasting provider came about after trialling a number of free providers. The available (free) choices for screencasting services varied between java enabled, web browser offers, and software installed programmes. Initially we went with an online recorder (screencast-o-matic.com), but in the later versions of the course we settled on Jing. This was not compatible with internal IT systems, but relevant tutors were willing and able to download it onto their personal laptops. It proved a more stable and versatile tool than screen-cast-o-matic. There was more functionality, and you did not have to be online to be recording screencasts.

Practicalities of making individual recordings

Screencasting was popular with both clients and participants, who gave positive feedback. It was effective (there was clear progress between pre- and post-draft writing), and it was cost effective. Screencasts took around 10–15 minutes to produce and send, thus four to six screencasts an hour was possible from a trainer. The teaching centre arranged training for involved teachers, and used administration hours for the production of these short (maximum five minutes) video clips. However, there was a question as to whether this was a sustainable enterprise, and whether the time teachers invested in this might not be spent more efficiently on other tasks that promoted learning.

The issue of teacher and learner interaction patterns

In v5, when we chose a forum this decision was strongly influenced by a sense that it would create some opportunities for a more social interactive learning environment. We knew that participants were familiar with this medium, and we felt that there would be more opportunities for conversation and reflection around the process of writing. This is in line with sociocultural perspectives on learning that 'see knowledge and understanding not as things that can be handed down but as constructed through interactive processes' (Hyland and Hyland, 2006: 88). In v5 we hoped that the learners would instigate and lead conversations about the feedback given, and talk about issues more than they had previously in direct email contact with their tutors. The expectation was that by sharing screencasts amongst a community of learners (rather than individually), and by communicating in threads, participants would read and respond to each other's writing and experiences of learning. However, the communication between participants was not as voluminous as had been hoped, and the tendency for quite static, trainer–participant–trainer moves continued.

There were broad issues with the technology and tools, and participant motivation was an issue throughout. The scalability of the project was a concern: had we needed to upscale it, it may have proven difficult. Also, there were concerns over the sustainability of such an endeavour, for example, the time tutors and managers spent administering programmes. However, as an example of flexibility and responsiveness this series of CBEC was a success in the eyes of most stakeholders.

Lessons learned and advice

We approached these courses with common sense, and an eye for improvements. We sought feedback readily. Yet, sometimes our responses to feedback were not as effective as we might have hoped. In trying to be responsive we perhaps lost sight of learning aims. For example the six genre approach in v5 was more than challenging and the relevance of tasks, like essay writing, is highly questionable to an audience of telecoms engineers, but it was what they voted for! However, it was through constant evaluation of these moves, and discussions with all stakeholders, trainers, managers, participants, and the client that we were able to innovate in a way that was 'safe', managed and palatable.

In summary, our context was key, and the stakeholders led the thinking. The technology came only in response to client needs, exploring features in our context, while at the same time working within trainers' sense of plausibility. Prabhu (1990) says that the best method is one that meets a teacher's 'sense of plausibility'. The teachers who worked on this project were the ones who were most able to grasp this use of IT, and could see how this could support language learning. We set off with a general language-learning pedagogy in mind, and learned as we went.

Practical considerations and recommendations

- Operate within teachers' sense of plausibility.
- Seek support from colleagues, managers, and other available networks.
- Be open to questions about the proposed course's learning outcomes.
- Be open about the business model.
- Seek to learn from trying to formulate answers to challenges.
- Place learning and context first, technology second.
- Create opportunities for learning.
- Carry out an IT audit to see if your proposed tools will run on your and your client's system.
- Use tools in a way that create affordances for dialogue rather than just mono-directional instruction.
- Put tools in student hands as often as possible.
- Consider how the course will evolve and change as well as how improvements will be decided on.

We responded in a transparent way to feedback at the end of each course and to input on needs at the beginning of each course. At the same time we had to deal with disappointment when certain interventions were not to the standard we hoped for, or did not reap the desired responses from participants. Each course built on the last, each time hoping to garner more positive feedback and *better* learning. This project shows how a course can develop with a partner over a longer period.

Final word

More than any course I have worked on, or designed, these CBECs afforded high levels of challenge and variety to me as an experienced and growing, DELTA qualified teacher, and later business manager. These challenges, which came about as a result of contextual realities, led to my pursuit of deeper questions about teaching and learning online that I pursued in an educational technology-focused MA. By adopting a learning mindset, and by working closely with our partner, this experience became an exemplar of not only pedagogically-minded innovation using technology, but also of collaboration and responsiveness. We did not set out to use technology; the technology helped us to get around an issue, and the resulting practice seemed to be an enhancement of our previous, paper-based, practices.

References

Brick, B and Holmes, J (2008) *Using Screen capture software for student feedback: Towards a methodology*. Paper presented at IADIS International Conference on Cognition and Exploratory Learning in Digital Age (CELDA 2008) 13–15 October 2008, Freiburg, Germany.

Collis, B and Moonen, J (2002) Flexible Learning in a Digital World. *Open Learning: The Journal of Open and Distance Learning* 17/3: 217–230.

Driscoll, M (2002) Blended learning: Let's get beyond the hype. *E-Learning* 3/3: 54. Available online at www-07.ibm.com/services/pdf/blended_learning.pdf

Hyland, K and Hyland, F (2006) Feedback on second language students' writing. *Language Teaching* 39: 83–101.

Krashen, S (1984) *Writing: Research, Theory and Applications*. Beverly Hills: Laredo.

Lee, I (2011) Feedback revolution: what gets in the way? *ELT Journal* 65/1: 1–12.

Li, S (2010) The effectiveness of corrective feedback in SLA: A meta-Analysis. *Language Learning* 60/2: 309–365.

Oliver, M and Trigwell, K (2005) Can 'Blended Learning' be redeemed? *E-learning* 2/1: 17–26.

Prabhu, N (1990) There is no best method – why? *TESOL Quarterly* 24/2: 161–176.

Stannard, R (2008) *Screen capture software for feedback in language education*. Paper presented at Second International Wireless Ready Symposium Interactivity, Collaboration and Feedback in Language Learning Technologies, 29 March 2008, NUCB Graduate School, Japan.

Wigginbottom, S (2007) Virtual lecturing: Delivering lectures using screencasting and podcasting technology. *Planet 8*.

15

Using a wiki to enhance the learning experience on a business English course

Louise Ingham

Introduction to teaching and learning context and brief course overview

The context was a part-time adult Cambridge Preliminary Business English class at intermediate level which took place in a further education college in Warrington in England. The cohort consisted of ten female learners of mixed nationalities, aged 19–35, dominated by European cultures. All were working in the UK but some were here for a limited time. The course began in September 2010 and had established a supportive atmosphere before the blend was introduced in March 2011. Learners needed to improve their knowledge and use of business vocabulary and their accuracy and fluency with English in business contexts, to prepare for an exam.

Reason for employing a blended approach

The course was restricted in the number of contact hours and in content. Adding a wiki to create a blended course would compensate for these limitations, allowing more:

- flexibility of time, place, pace and material
- responsiveness to learner needs
- opportunities for skill development including digital literacy
- practice and feedback
- collaboration
- student-centred approaches.

These benefits are possible because wikis are interactive and offer flexible spaces which can be accessed and edited by any user at any time via the internet. A wiki is a type of website where users can add and remove content, 'Wikipedia' being a famous example where users can create or update the information included on any topic. All wiki users have writer status and can easily add text, photo, hyperlink or video that they want to share, so the teacher is no longer in control of the course content if a wiki is incorporated. The balance of power may shift because any user can view and edit the contributions of others so peers as well as the teacher can correct mistakes or give feedback.

A description of the blend/materials/software used

I blended an established face-to-face class based on the coursebook Business Benchmark (Whitby 2009) with online learning via the creation of a wiki on 'PBWorks'. This was simple to achieve by following the instructions on the PBWorks website to create and name a wiki. It did not require any programming skills or knowledge as the software includes all of the design features. I invited the students to join by adding their email addresses to the wiki which sends out email invitations, including a link to create individual passwords for the site. A learner without an email address was given a username. The site was private and learners created their own passwords so only this group could see or edit the content of this wiki. Each learner had writer status so could immediately add or modify content from any internet connection which meant that the site could grow with their interests.

The online wiki provided the freedom to enhance student opportunities for learning, both in and outside the classroom. It meant more authentic materials could be shared plus it allowed asynchronous interactions between users, which all students could learn from.

The wiki

The 'front page' included a short video of the class saying 'hello' which we made in class using a flip camera so the learners would feel welcome.

I asked the learners to post a photo of themselves along with an introduction. This initial activity was not done in class but it built student confidence with the technology. It was useful as an initial step in the eventual formation of an online community where participants asked for and gave advice or made comments on the page (see Figure 1). Participants could learn from their mistakes and share those experiences because wiki is easy to add to and edit like 'Word'. This activity created a real need to communicate in English and six learners succeeded in attaching their photographs and introductions.

Figure 1: Student comments on initial activity

The 'history feature' which can show past versions of wiki pages and 'push notifications' to students' emails allowed participants to see who had created, moved or deleted content. This encouraged responsible participation.

Timetabling

The face-to-face class ran on Wednesday evenings at 6.30 p.m. for two hours in term time from September 2010 until the paper-based international exam in June 2011. It provided 60 guided learning hours, was teacher controlled and included institutional requirements (i.e. individual learning plans, register) so time was precious. In contrast, from March 2011 the wiki could be used any time asynchronously, from any place and at the learner's own pace.

How the modes were blended

The face-to-face aspects of the course were compulsory as the students had enrolled on a traditional classroom-based course which included individual, pair and group work. I planned lesson content which included activities from the coursebook, and listening tasks from CDs, responding to learner needs including exam practice. In contrast, contributing to wiki was optional as it was experimental. It would be possible to organise a fully online course or a stronger blend with more weight given to online aspects but only if learners were aware from the start about what the expectations and requirements were. I felt that it would be unethical to change the primary mode of delivery part way through a course, which is why the wiki was optional in this instance.

The wiki complemented the face-to-face class when we examined recent wiki activity during the class. A different learner each week would log into the wiki which was displayed on the interactive whiteboard for about 15 minutes. The class discussed the week's content and sometimes edited it collaboratively so that everyone had the chance to participate.

Outside class time, learners' talents were utilised on the wiki as they had freedom to organise and produce content and develop the site. One learner created a 'news page' where ideas, gossip and opinions were shared (see Figure 2).

Figure 2: News page including student-to-student interactions

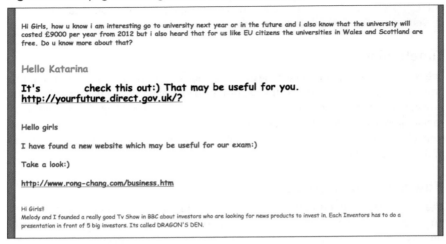

Hi Girls, how u know i am interesting go to university next year or in the future and i also know that the university will costed £9000 per year from 2012 but i also heard that for us like EU citizens the universities in Wales and Scottland are free. Do u know more about that?

Hello Katarina

It's   check this out:) That may be useful for you.
http://yourfuture.direct.gov.uk/?

Hello girls

I have found a new website which may be useful for our exam:)

Take a look:)

http://www.rong-chang.com/business.htm

Hi Girls!!
Melody and I founded a really good Tv Show in BBC about investors who are looking for news products to invest in. Each Inventors has to do a presentation in front of 5 big investors. Its called DRAGON'S DEN.

I created a 'Listening page' and added a listening track with questions about Job Centre Plus, which was relevant to a learner who had recently been made redundant (see Figure 3).

Figure 3: Listening page

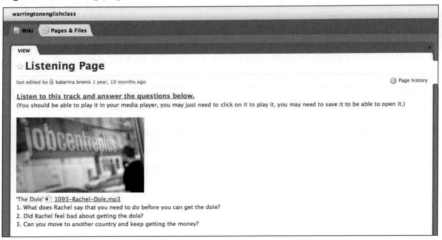

She then responded by adding a video about how to make a good impression in a job interview (see Figure 4). She created and added some questions based on that video which utilised her IT skills and her critical listening skills, and was personally motivating.

Figure 4: Student created listening task

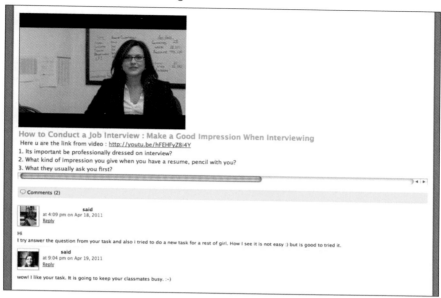

How to Conduct a Job Interview : Make a Good Impression When Interviewing
Here u are the link from video : http://youtu.be/hFEHFyZ8i4Y
1. Its important be professionally dressed on interview?
2. What kind of impression you give when you have a resume, pencil with you?
3. What they usually ask you first?

Comments (2)

said
at 4:09 pm on Apr 18, 2011
Reply

Hi
I try answer the question from your task and also i tried to do a new task for a rest of girl. How I see it is not easy :) but is good to tried it.

said
at 9:04 pm on Apr 19, 2011
Reply

wow! I like your task. It is going to keep your classmates busy. :-)

The 'exams page' held links to past papers and the exam timetable was displayed there. A 'Web resources' page included links to the television show 'The Apprentice', which was a current BBC programme about business which we discussed in class. It also included links to websites for language practice and other business resources.

I did not have data on the number of student visits per page as this was not available on my version of PBWorks, so the popularity of pages could only be judged by discussions in class and by contributions made by students.

Teacher and learner interaction patterns

In the face-to-face class there was an informal atmosphere but I set objectives, controlled tasks and set the pace. When I introduced the blend with wiki, I demonstrated it in class and closely monitored its use in order to encourage participation and troubleshoot learner difficulties. Later, tutor and individual learner involvement went through phases as learners became more competent and needs or interests developed.

As student participation increased and the wiki evolved as a result, I began to question the nature and extent of my online involvement. The challenge was to balance my presence on the site with the learner's contributions and decide how much I was going to correct or ignore mistakes and to advise on content. I wanted to minimise learner inhibition and anxiety but to encourage a collective sense of responsibility (see Figure 5). I tried not to correct mistakes but if they were significant and remained unnoticed for a few weeks I would highlight them in a different colour. I also tried to hold back in class discussions of wiki content to allow learner noticing of errors and control of the space.

Figure 5: Learner comment about correcting mistakes

said
at 11:57 am on Apr 15, 2011
Reply

Hi girls, I tried to correct all of our writings we had posted on pbwork, but despite my best try Louise still was able to find some mistakes. Any ideas how to correct remaining mistakes so we have mistake free homeworks?

Traditional exam practice activities were completed in class which required time for marking and return of papers which meant that learners would only see their own performance. As we approached the exam, I pushed the use of the wiki writing page and added new exam style writing tasks every week. This was popular and was revised (edited) a total of 51 times; 29 of these revisions were made by eight different students between 30 March and 31 May. I expect that this page was so popular as some learners felt nervous about their abilities to pass the writing paper and the wiki affords unlimited opportunities for writing, with the potential for immediate feedback from whoever logs in. I made 23 of the revisions either by adding tasks or giving feedback.

When the page began, some learners wrote individual answers to a task leading to three similar letters on the page. This may be due to a desire for recognition for individual work as in traditional assessment (Lund, 2008). To promote collaboration, in class I demonstrated editing by taking the best phrases and most suitable words from each letter to create a better answer. This seemed to convince the learners that working together with their individual strengths and weaknesses would result in better answers and they would learn more than when working alone (see Figure 6). It did require courage from learners who made the first attempt on tasks. A class needs to have trust, plus some risk takers or confident individuals.

Figure 6: Comparing student revisions of a writing task

Comparing versions of Writing task page
Showing changes between April 12, 2011 at 10:10:40 pm (crossed-out) and April 13, 2011 at 8:41:16 pm (underlined)

- asking if you can have the corporate rate
- requesting a booking form
- telling him/her which dates you prefer
Write 60–80 words
a place for my colleagues regarding^colleaguesfor Psychology of Selling course. 10 people who are interested to do interestedin this course and the for us will be ^05th on 5th of May. If the ^mentionedthementioned date won't beis not suitable for you I 12th of May. There is a thing whichisone reuest forwhich I would like to ask you for you. Can I have the please? I would also ^^requestlike to request a booking form of course if you don't mind. Kindformif it is possible.Kind regards   have tried
Hi Paulina, I am Katarina.
Ireadyour homework and i think is very good juston the end, the last sentence: ` I would also request a booking form of course ifyou don`t mind.` I think the sentence will better without this`dont mind`. They make businness and if they want have a clients then they have todo that automatically. I think they will send u the form also without any ask.
But I think is great job!!!!
Dear
course in Psychology of selling-Selling.
I saw that next month you will give aholda course in Manchester and this and book a placeroom for 10 persons.
My sales team is very busy ^busyand because of thatI would like for 5to send5 of them to attendthemon the course^courseon the first week of May and the rest for therestof them onthe third week of May. If it is not possible-Ifit isn'tpossible, could you suggest a suitable time: I woluddate.
Iwould also like to request a booking form and ^ ifyouwhetheryou are willing to offer
I looking forward to hearing from you.
^Sincerely.Your sincerely.

Video for you!

Teaching methodology

The blended design of this course was influenced by Garrison and Kanuka (2004) who suggest that by thoughtfully integrating face-to-face and online experiences learners can benefit from more active and meaningful learning experiences. Independence and increased control may also lead to development of critical thinking. The way learners and tutor shared responsibility for wiki content, error noticing, correction, editing and modifying text and the way they collaborated on activities was new to some students but encouraged deeper thinking, as well as language and skill development. The use of wiki is supported by the pedagogy of social constructivism where understanding is achieved through dialogue and collaboration with others as the social environment scaffolds learning (Beetham and Sharpe, 2007: 221).

Being able to influence the content of a course is empowering to students and values their abilities. Even learners who did not directly add content could benefit vicariously from reading the contributions of others (Sutton, 2001).

Wikis allow increased time for reflection and evaluation so writing on a wiki may cause less anxiety and pressure than is felt when producing in class. However, that anxiety may occur due to the realisation that the whole class will read any contribution. This sense of audience can be valuable as it may cause learners to pay more attention to the accuracy of their language production (Kuteeva, 2011) but there must be a supportive atmosphere or participants will not contribute.

Contextual considerations that influenced the design process

In the classroom we had a networked interactive whiteboard but not individual pcs or laptops. The area has good broadband availability and most learners were familiar with Facebook and email and had home access to personal laptops or pcs.

An initial reason for creating a wiki was because we had created interview videos in class on a flip camera and had no time to play them back. I wanted to upload them to the internet so the learners could watch them to review dialogue, notice errors and self and peer correct. I was unable to upload the videos to the college Moodle, possibly because the files were too big. The IT support team would have helped me but they are based at a different campus.

I found that it was simple to upload the videos to the free video hosting site Vimeo (Youtube would have worked too) and then create a wiki for no cost on 'PBWorks'. Then I could embed the videos on a 'video page' where comments and dialogue could be written alongside. The videos could be replayed and dialogues checked. In practice, most learners viewed their videos, two could not bear to hear themselves talk and only one listened very carefully, self-corrected and rewrote her speech so that it was greatly improved (see Figure 7).

Figure 7: Student dialogue for class produced video

---

from   on Vimeo.
Dialogue:FrontPage FrontPage
1. Dialogue;
   Who founded the company?
   The company we will talk about is insert the drinks. The company was founded by 3 boys Josh, Richard and Adam, 3 friends who decided to open the company.
   How did they get the idea?
   The idea came from considering their own hectic lifestyles. They worked hard, finishing to late, then going to the gym.
   How did they raise the money to start up?
   They raised the money to start up from business angel Mr. Maurice Pinto.
   What difficulties did they face at first?
   The first and biggest problem was distribution because the drinks were very expensive because they had not any preservatives and because of that they had a short life but oin the end they bought some vans and distributed it themselves own.
   What changes have taken place since the company started?
   They have now have turnover of £30 million and different flavours and about 10 different recipes.

---
2. Dialogue;
   How you founded the company?
   The company was founded by Harry Cragoe in 1994.
   How did they get a idea?
   Harry Cragoe spent some time working and living in USA. There he discovered the healthy smoothies and his idea come from there.

Adaptations

I am currently blending wiki and face-to-face with six different classes. I use an induction strategy and participation is strongly encouraged. It is interesting to notice the different contributions made by learners. Old pages have been archived into an accessible folder so present business English students can learn from the previous year.

Reflections on this blend

This blended approach allowed valuable flexibility and interactivity which reinforced classroom learning and empowered learners, for example with the 'News page'. Wiki allowed multiple asynchronous views of class-produced videos and allowed learners to reflect on, and offer suggestions to improve, their classmates' written work. However, the success of the online aspect depended on the personalities in the class, the friendly atmosphere, scaffolding and task design.

In order to contribute, students needed IT ability or to be well supported. For example, photos with large file sizes would not easily attach to the wiki and this could have discouraged learners if it was the first task that they attempted to achieve. Learners may come up with innovative solutions to IT problems (see Figure 8). One learner explains that they had trouble inserting text so wrote it in Word first, saved it as a picture and inserted that on the page.

Figure 8: Student reaction to problems adding text

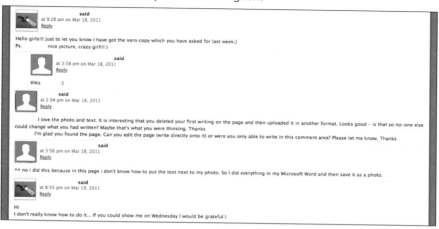

The face-to-face class had already created a supportive atmosphere which allowed the students to admit difficulties and ask for help in the comments section, and both peers and the teacher were willing to help.

Students had to be willing to share ideas and expose mistakes to the class but some were anxious and hesitated to contribute online. Students who instigated wiki content seemed to be confident autonomous learners and that type of personality will probably gain the most from this type of online learning. I would expect some passive vicarious learners in any class and they could learn from viewing the content created by others. I would try to convince all learners of the benefits of 'collaboration rather than competition' (Wheeler et al., 2008: 994).

Teachers should create relevant tasks with clear links to the face-to-face content and integrate suitable parts of those tasks in the class. Writing is particularly suited to the wiki space as the blend allowed the completion of more exam-style writing tasks than class time allowed, plus students could learn from the contributions of others and get immediate feedback from multiple users. The resulting written products can include the combined efforts of multiple students so when texts are discussed in class one individual is not responsible for the quality of a text or any mistakes.

A summary of my blended learning course design strategy

In my context it was necessary to:

- evaluate the suitability of either face-to-face or online for particular tasks
- create a supportive atmosphere
- discuss and demonstrate the benefits of collaboration and co-operation with learners in class
- recognise what was compulsory and what could be flexible
- give control to learners and become a facilitator in the online space
- be flexible and ready to respond to needs and interests
- expect a variety of learner behaviours
- ensure that internet access was reliable and provide support.

Recommendations for blended learning course designers

Notice what is lacking in the traditional classroom which may be compensated for or improved by your blend. Then, investigate the affordances of various tools and select the most suitable approach for your context. Next, decide on the strength of the different aspects of your blend and a strategy for implementing it. Discuss the reasons behind the blend with your learners so that they recognise the potential benefits to their learning.

If you select a wiki then:

- demonstrate the wiki in class and use a computer cluster to introduce the log in the process and basic functions of the wiki
- encourage students with good computer skills to mentor others
- use a mix of scaffolded, guided activities whilst still allowing freedom to create new items
- integrate the wiki into the class routine to encourage participation
- persevere, explain the purposes and show enthusiasm for the possibilities of wiki
- reward contributors with comments online and face-to-face
- react to individual needs and personalities.

References

Beetham, H and Sharpe, R (2007) *Rethinking Pedagogy for a Digital Age*. London: Routledge.

Garrison, D and Kanuka, H (2004) Blended learning: uncovering its transformative potential in higher education. *Internet and Higher Education* 7: 95–105.

Kuteeva, M (2011) Wikis and academic writing: changing the writer-reader relationship. *English for Specific Purposes* 30: 44–57.

Lund, A (2008) Wikis: a collective approach to language production. *ReCALL* 20/1: 35–54.

Sutton, L (2001) The principle of vicarious interaction in computer-mediated communications. *International Journal of Educational Telecommunications* 7/3: 223–242.

Wheeler, S, Yeomans, P and Wheeler, D (2008) The good, the bad and the wiki: evaluating student-generated content for collaborative learning. *British Journal of Educational Technology* 39/6: 987–995.

Whitby, N (2009) *Business Benchmark Student's Book Preliminary*. Cambridge: Cambridge University Press.

16

A military blend

Claire Whittaker

Introduction

This case study will describe a blend used to provide English language training to military personnel in the armed forces of Bosnia and Herzegovina (AFBiH). It will consider what the blend is comprised of, the materials and software used, how the modes complement each other, the timetable arrangement, designing for a suite of courses (elementary to upper-intermediate), and the teaching and learning methodology. It will also highlight the rationale for the decisions that were taken in relation to the design of the blend, detail the main lesson learned during the design process and offer advice to would-be blended learning course designers. Lastly, it will critically reflect on the blend and suggest areas in which it could be enhanced.

Course overview

The English courses described in this study were developed and managed by the British Council's Military English Support Project (MESP) that formed part of the wider Peacekeeping English Project. The courses provided English language training to military personnel (mainly officers) in the AFBiH primarily to enable them to partake in peace support operations. I was the Training and Systems Manager on the Project and responsible for overseeing the evolution of the blend over a three-year period.

The courses ranged in level from elementary to upper-intermediate and were taught in 13 centres across the country to accommodate the geographical spread of the AFBiH personnel. The low-level courses (elementary and pre-intermediate) were taught by unqualified officer instructors, who received extensive pre-service and in-service training from MESP, and the higher level courses (intermediate and upper-intermediate) by qualified English language teachers employed by MESP. I am unsure what the rationale for this split was as it was in place when I took up my post, but I assume it was to do with the differing levels of linguistic competence and pedagogic ability between the officer instructors and teachers. All the courses were intensive, 23 hours per week, and ran for 12 weeks, totalling 276 hours per level. The number of learners on each course ranged from 12 to 16, with an annual turnover of 600 learners per annum.

Why the blend was introduced

A version of the blend was in place when I took up post and it is my understanding that this approach was primarily adopted to support the unqualified officer instructors with their teaching. The reason for employing a blended approach as opposed to a purely computer-led course is unknown to me, although I would hazard a guess that it was over concerns that the latter would be too unfamiliar to the learners in this context for it to be effective. That is purely conjecture though. The lead mode in the blend at that time was the computer and the software used in the computer sessions led the course and determined the syllabus. The officer instructors followed up these sessions with practice and extension activities that did not demand much of them as 'teachers' but more as 'facilitators'. Adopting this approach also meant that it was cost effective (as the officer instructors were already employed by the AFBiH) and enabled the centres to start working almost immediately with very little financial outlay on pre-service teacher training. It was also cost effective because the learners – military personnel – could be trained at their place of work. However, it could be argued that the initial financial outlay to set up the centres and provide them with the computers and materials for the self-access centres was not cost-effective.

The blend

The blend was unusual in that it was comprised of three modes of delivery: face-to-face, computer and self-study. The definitions provided in the literature on blended learning in relation to language teaching and learning typically only refer to two modes: face-to-face and computer. Sharma and Barrett (2007: 7) for example, state that 'blended learning refers to a language course which combines a face-to-face (F2F) classroom component with an appropriate use of technology'. Dudeney and Hockly (2007: 137) provide a similar definition in that blended learning 'is a mixture of online and face-to face course delivery.' What becomes apparent when conducting a wider literature review is that blended learning can mean different things to different people so for the purposes of this case study I would define it as being a combination of face-to-face, computer and self-study modes.

The lead mode in our resultant blend was the face-to-face mode because in AFBiH this would be the most recognisable form of course delivery and because the coursebooks would essentially provide the syllabus in terms of content and sequencing. Therefore, it was the mode in which the core materials were initially presented and practised. Moreover, the lead mode regulated the pacing of the course by ensuring that all the learners covered the core material at the same time before the follow-up activities that they could then complete at their own pace on the computers or in self-study. Tasks conducted in the computer or self-study mode supplemented the syllabus and provided the learners with controlled practice and extension activities (Figure 1). This resulted in a cyclical approach to language teaching and learning where the learners had the opportunity to recycle and review what was presented in the face-to-face mode.

Figure 1: How the modes complement each other

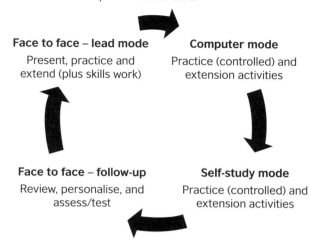

Face to face – lead mode
Present, practice and
extend (plus skills work)

Computer mode
Practice (controlled) and
extension activities

Face to face – follow-up
Review, personalise, and
assess/test

Self-study mode
Practice (controlled) and
extension activities

Materials and software

With regard to materials, a combination of general (*Headway,* Soars and Soars, 2006 and *Going for Gold,* Acklam and Crace, 2003) and military English coursebooks (*Campaign,* Mellor-Clark and Baker de Altamirano, 2005 and *Breakthrough,* Kosalkova et al., 2005) were used in the face-to-face mode. Although coursebooks have been heavily criticised in the literature for being reductionist, bland, safe, and constrictive (Tomlinson cited in Toms, 2004; Brumfit cited in Sheldon 1988; Williams, 1983), in this blend they were chosen as a step towards ensuring standardisation in terms of course content across the centres, to support the relatively inexperienced officer instructors and to help them develop pedagogically. The criteria for selection with regard to the general English coursebooks at lower levels were how 'easy' they were perceived to be to teach and the quality of the teacher's book in terms of the support it provided for relatively inexperienced instructors, plus the quality of the add-ons, for example workbook, resource packs. Availability also played an important role in the selection process. At higher levels the choice for the general English coursebook was left to the teachers and I cannot recall the criteria that they used. With regard to the military English coursebooks the choice was so limited that there was no call for extensive selection criteria.

In the computer mode the learners worked independently with one learner to one computer using REWARD (Greenall, 2002) software. It was my belief that the learners would benefit from working individually at the computer as in a previous blend where they had worked in pairs, using different software, there had been a tendency for one student to be 'active' (controlling the mouse/keyboard and completing the exercises) whilst the other remained 'passive' (watching on, rarely collaborating, and at times even leaving the room). Therefore I was trying to prevent this in the revised blend. REWARD (Greenall, 2002) was chosen primarily for two reasons. Firstly, it only required a one-off purchase, thereby ensuring to a large extent post-project sustainability in terms of cost-effectiveness. (Sustainability was of paramount importance in the design as the UK-funded MESP had a fixed end date after which the management of the centres would be handed over to the AFBiH). Secondly, it did not require an internet connection which was not available at the time the blend was developed in the centres. Moreover, REWARD (Greenall, 2002) was readily available in Bosnia and Herzegovina; it could be linked relatively easily to the coursebooks; the content was attractively presented; it appeared straightforward to use in design terms for the students; and because there was little else on the market that suited our needs if we were to address sustainability.

Self-study was comprised of eight 'strands' (my terminology) that were rotated across a two-week period with Fridays being left as 'free-choice' for the learners. The eight strands at pre-intermediate level are outlined in Table 1. The rationale for employing different strands was to provide the learners with a range of task types to appeal to a variety of learning styles and to maintain as far as possible their motivation. The materials for these strands were developed from published English Language Teaching (ELT) resources and coursebooks, or downloaded from ELT websites, and worksheets were created or the book itself used.

Table 1: Self-study strands at pre-intermediate

Pre-intermediate self-study			
Strands	**Weeks 1, 3, 5, 7, 9 and 11**	**Strands**	**Weeks 2, 4, 6, 8, 10 and 12**
Vocabulary	Monday	Video	Monday
Listening audio packs	Tuesday	Task work	Tuesday
Campaign 1 workbook	Wednesday	Vocabulary wordlists	Wednesday
Grammar	Thursday	Reading	Thursday
Free choice	Friday	Free choice	Friday

Complementarity

The content of the three modes was linked to a relatively high degree either by grammar, vocabulary or topic. For example REWARD (Greenall, 2002), which was used in the computer mode, was grammatically linked to the general English coursebooks *Headway* (Soars and Soars, 2006) and *Going for Gold* (Acklam and Crace, 2003) that were used in the face-to-face mode. Such 'complementarity' between modes has been identified as an important factor in blended learning course design and we felt it to be a guiding principle in our design too. This seems to be supported by the findings from a study into student retention conducted by Stracke (2007: 57). The results indicated that one of the three main reasons that learners left the blended learning course they were attending was 'a perceived lack of support and connection/complementarity between the face-to-face and computer-assisted components of the "blend"'.

Timetabling/sequencing the modes

During the design process a great deal of consideration was given to the arrangement of the timetable in terms of how to sequence the modes, the optimal amount of time to spend on the modes, and the optimal number of modes to sequence during a day. We believed that the learners would value the face-to-face mode more highly than the other modes (based on their feedback and our knowledge of their previous learning experiences). Therefore time spent on the face-to-face mode needed to outweigh or at least balance the amount of time spent on the other two modes. We also believed that an equal amount of time needed to be spent in the computer and self-study mode as we considered them to be as beneficial as each other, and partly because of logistics in terms of space and student rotation between the modes. Lastly, we considered the optimal length of the sessions in each mode, which we felt varied according to learners' level. Based on this rationale, combined with the fact that the face-to-face mode was the 'lead mode', we devised the timetables for the four levels as seen in Table 2.

Table 2: Timetables for the four levels

Elementary and Pre-intermediate		Intermediate and Upper-intermediate	
Duration of session	Mode	Duration of session	Mode
60 minutes	Class	90 minutes	Class
60 minutes	Computer/self-study	45 minutes	Computer
60 minutes	Class	45 minutes	Self-study
60 minutes	Self-study/computer	60 minutes	Class
60 minutes	Class	30 minutes	Computer
		30 minutes	Self-study

Designing for a suite of courses

In our context a high percentage of the learners worked their way through the levels often from elementary to graduate from upper-intermediate. With these learners in mind the content and design of the course altered in an effort to realise their increased abilities as language learners, to cater for their needs, to maintain their interest, and to fulfil our course aims, as in Figure 2.

Figure 2: Course changes in terms of design and content

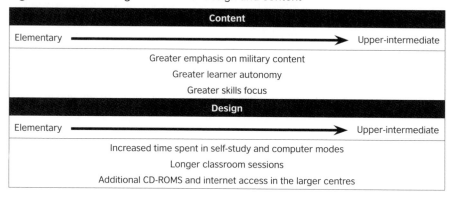

There was a steady increase in the amount of class time spent covering military English from elementary to upper-intermediate, accompanied by a decrease in the amount of time dedicated to general English (see Figure 3). Moreover, at higher levels there was less class time and more computer and self-study time as the belief was that students at these levels were capable of a higher degree of autonomy, especially if they had attended the preceding courses which should have prepared them in some way for it. Despite these changes there was still a high degree of 'horizontal integration' where there is 'some continuity in learning tools across programs and courses as [this] is clearly advantageous from the student's point of view' (Levy and Stockwell, 2006: 30).

Figure 3: Hours per week spent in the modes

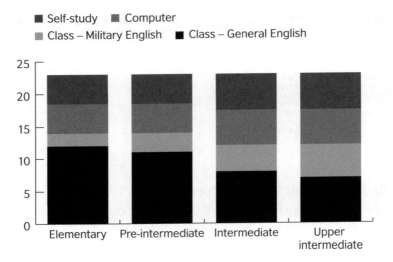

Methodology

One of blended learning's strengths is the methodological variety that the different modes can provide. In our blend the general English coursebooks supported the largely communicative approach to language teaching and learning that we advocated with elements of task-based and problem-based learning being provided by the military English coursebooks. Problem-based learning is a relatively new methodology to ELT and it allows 'students to work together in order to find solutions to real world problems' (Boyle and Mellor-Clarke, 2006: 3) which are situated in their professional field and to which there are no fixed solutions. Self-study promoted a type of autonomous learning where the primary objective was that learners were 'engaged in self-directed work' Littlewood (1996: 433). However, a criticism may be levelled at the design of this mode as the choice of materials was prescribed apart from the 'free choice' session on Fridays. This in essence restricted the learners' level of autonomy, if autonomy is defined as 'the ability to take charge of one's own learning' (Holec cited in Benson, 2006: 22). A number of relatively simple changes could be made to the design to amend this, such as increasing the number of tasks within each self-study strand and by including more 'free-choice' strands.

REWARD (Greenall, 2002) is not explicit regarding the nature of its learning theory, simply stating that it 'sets a new standard for computer-assisted language learning methods', with no indication as to what these may be. However, we can deduce from the type of offline activities that REWARD (Greenall, 2002) employs, such as drag and drop, gap fill, and matching activities, which provide immediate feedback and are linear by design, that the approach is essentially behaviourist. (Behaviourism is a theory of learning based upon the idea that all behaviours are acquired through conditioning, for example Pavlov's work with animals that resulted in what became known as 'classical conditioning' or Skinner's 'operant conditioning' which acknowledged that the learner could 'operate' on the environment, for example by pressing a lever to receive food [a reward]). This could be perceived as a weakness in the blend as according to reviews of pedagogic literature constructivism is currently the favoured model of learning. (In this theoretical approach it is believed that learners construct their own knowledge or understanding based on their prior experience rather than simply receiving it). If the centres had an internet connection this could be addressed by incorporating online activities using email, chat, wikis and podcasts for example, that encourage a more constructivist and collaborative approach to language learning. However, even by allowing the learners to work in pairs at the computer rather than individually whilst using REWARD (Greenall, 2002) a degree of co-operation may take place resulting in a more constructivist approach.

Lessons learned

The blend that I have described evolved over a three-year period so the first lesson that I learned is that effective blending can be a time-consuming process. Although I believe that this was largely contextual, given the number of centres and their widespread geographical distribution, the number of users (officer instructors/teachers) involved in the redesign process, and my inexperience as a blended learning course designer. Moreover, it was influenced by the fact that I employed an iterative approach to the redesign process in that small changes were made, implemented, and then evaluated before moving on to the next one. Most of these changes were accompanied by meetings with the users (officer instructors/teachers) as I believed it was vital to have their input in the decision making process, and/or training for them, for example coursebook familiarisation. Beetham and Sharpe (2007: 8) recognise this iterative approach and claim that 'effective designs will evolve only through cycles of practice, evaluation and reflection'.

Advice for blended learning course designers

Before embarking on a design or redesign process, identify your drivers for change, that is ask yourself why change is necessary, what the driving factors behind it are and what the limiting factors will be. In other words thoroughly acquaint yourself with your context. There were four situational drivers for change in my context:

1. Goal direction – what the learners ultimately needed their English for.
2. Sustainability in terms of content stability (i.e. how long the course content would be valid for), instructor fit (i.e. that the courses would be relatively straightforward for unqualified officer instructors to teach) and cost effectiveness (i.e. that the centres/courses would be inexpensive to run/maintain).

3. User experience – feedback on the shortcomings of the original blend.

4. My belief on how to design a blended learning course in our context to provide an optimal learning experience, which was supported by my somewhat limited knowledge and previous experience.

These drivers influenced all the decisions that we took and helped ensure that the final blend was suitable for, and therefore worked in, our context. This supports Shaw and Igneri's (2006: 3) belief that there is '...no single optimal mix. What configuration is best can only be determined relative to whatever goals and constraints are presented in a given situation'.

Conclusion

Numerous factors need to be taken into consideration when designing a blended learning course and as Hofmann (2001: 3) rightly says 'determining the right blend isn't easy or to be taken lightly'. Moreover the blend has to reflect the teaching and learning environment and recognise its contextual limitations. The key contextual factor we had to consider when designing our blend was post-project sustainability. To that end the blend I believe can be deemed a success as it is still operational, and equally if not more importantly it produced good results too, although unfortunately I no longer have these to hand. With hindsight there are a couple of areas of the blend that could be enhanced. Firstly, the learners should be allowed more options in the self-study mode to develop their autonomy. Secondly, internet access should be provided to ensure more constructivist and collaborative learning. Lastly, the learners should be allowed to work in pairs at the computer as 'when two or more learners sit at a computer and discuss process and content in the target language, they often engage in scaffold learning, helping each other improve their learning' (Beatty, 2003: 99). Apart from these areas I believe our model was highly effective, is easily replicable and inexpensive to maintain once established.

References

Acklam, R and Crace, A (2003) *Going for Gold Intermediate Coursebook*. Harlow: Pearson Longman.

Beatty, K (2003) *Teaching and Researching Computer-Assisted Language Learning*. Harlow: Pearson Education.

Beetham, H and Sharpe, R (2007) 'An introduction to rethinking pedagogy for a digital age', in Beetham, H and Sharpe, R (eds) *Rethinking Pedagogy for a Digital Age*. Abingdon, Oxon: Routledge, 1–10.

Benson, P (2006) Autonomy in language teaching and learning. *Language Teaching* 40: 21–40.

Boyle, C and Mellor-Clark, S (2006) *Campaign 3 Teacher's Book*. Oxford: Macmillan.

Dudeney, G and Hockly, N (2007) *How to... Teach English with Technology*. Harlow: Pearson Education Limited.

Greenall, S (2002) *Reward* CD-ROM. Oxford: Macmillan Education.

Hofmann, J (2001) *Blended Learning Case Study.* Available online at www.pttmedia.com/newmedia_knowhow/KnowHow_Design/Instructional%20Design/iLive/Blended%20Learning%20Case%20Study.htm

Kosalkova, Z, Ondruš, L, Koláčková, L, Šobaň, V, Pasztelyak, A, Olah-Toth, T Hafner, T and Krasovsky, V (2005) *Breakthrough.* Prague: Ministry of Defence of the Czech Republic.

Levy, M and Stockwell, G (2006) *CALL Dimensions. Options and Issues in Computer-Assisted Language Learning.* New York, USA: Lawrence Erlbaum Associates.

Littlewood, W (1996) 'Autonomy': An anatomy and a framework. *System* 24/4: 427–435.

Mellor-Clark, S and Baker de Altamirano, Y (2005) *Campaign English for the Military 2 Student's Book.* Oxford: Macmillan.

Sharma, P and Barrett, B (2007) *Blended Learning.* Oxford: Macmillan.

Shaw, S and Igneri, N (2006) *Effectively Implementing a Blended Learning Approach.* Available online at http://wvuheducation.com/LinkClick.aspx?fileticket=7Hhk4Bw4lyg%3D&tabid=148

Sheldon, LE (1988) Evaluating ELT textbooks and materials. *ELT Journal* 42/4: 237–246.

Soars, L and Soars, J (2006) *New Headway: Elementary Third Edition: Students' Book.* Oxford: Oxford University Press.

Stracke, E (2007) A road to understanding: A qualitative study into why learners drop out of a blended language learning (BLL) environment. *ReCALL* 19/1: 57–78.

Toms, C (2004) *General English coursebooks and their place in an ESAP programme.* Available online at www.asian-efl-journal.com/04_ct.php

Williams, D (1983) Developing criteria for textbook evaluation. *ELT Journal* 37/3: 251–255.

Comments on Part 3

Brian Tomlinson

One of the obvious advantages of using a blended learning approach to designing English for Specific Purposes (ESP) courses is the affordance it gives for localising and even individualising the courses. Each course at a centre can benefit from a common store of language and activity input but can be tailor-made for specific clients, specific client courses and specific time allocations and, as a course develops it can be modified to allow individuals to work at their own pace and in relation to their own preferred learning styles, time available, needs, wants, problems and interests. At the same time each individual's output can be made available (with permission) for other students to benefit from and for different individuals with shared needs to collaborate in mutually beneficial projects. This sort of localisation and personalisation is what the courses reported in Part 3 achieved. It could possibly have been achieved face-to-face but to do so would have demanded great trainer skill, considerable investment in time and riches of resources beyond the means of most of the institutions concerned in the projects reported.

Another obvious advantage is that many ESP students on a course are busy working most of the week, are geographically dispersed, cannot always be released at the same time and do not have a lot of time available to work with other members of the course anyway. In such cases online modules can obviously help to overcome logistical problems as well as offering such pedagogical benefits as individualised feedback and focus plus the opportunity to recycle material and activities many times.

The courses reported in Part 3 varied considerably in the percentage of course time allocated to face-to-face approaches but all of them were agreed that a face-to-face component was needed partly because of the learners' prior learning experience and expectations, partly because the face-to-face mode is the best way of achieving a team and community spirit and partly, in some cases, because it was considered that instructors could best introduce, demonstrate and answer questions on new technologies if they were able to interact with the learners live. Most courses favoured starting with a face-to-face mode to establish understanding and co-operation but some actually use it as their prime mode throughout the course. This is another important reminder that the face-to-face mode should be treated as an important element of blended learning courses and should not be considered as a necessary but undesirable adjunct to the superior approaches offered by new technologies. This needs to be remembered, especially by course designers who are in danger of being seduced by technologies they enjoy using themselves, and by administrators who mistakenly think that online delivery of courses is always much more cost effective than face-to-face delivery.

Part 4 – English as a Foreign Language/ General English

17

A thinking-based blended learning course in an upper-secondary school in Latvia

Alexander Sokol, Edgar Lasevich, Renata Jonina and Marija Dobrovolska-Stoian

Course background

The course described in this study was offered to students aged 16–19, who study English as a second foreign language in an upper-secondary school located in the centre of Riga, Latvia. They have three 40-minute lessons a week. Many of them take a graduation exam in English, and are interested in General English. Groups are normally heterogeneous, from ten to 15 people and the levels range from A2 to B2. The study covers the period from September 2008 to December 2009. The blended approach was adopted for the following reasons:

- To provide learners with extra opportunities for learning (in addition to the official three academic hours generally viewed as insufficient in the local context).

- To improve motivation by integrating the use of ICT into the learning process (the use of ICT increased motivation as it was not widely spread at that time and students generally regarded its use in the lessons as a way of making learning more connected with the real world).

- To develop skills for autonomous learning and at the same time reduce the number of tasks performed by the teacher through delegating them to the online modules. This would allow the teacher to spend more time on individual support of each learner as technology would provide learners with feedback based on their typical mistakes.

Description of the blend

Online modules

The e-learning module of the blend was developed in the framework of an international project, New Learners in the New Europe (2005–08), supported by the European Commission (*New Learners in the New Europe, 2008*). The aim of the project was to develop modules for online learning that allow for an integrated development of language and thinking skills of learners. The learning environment was created specifically for the **purposes** of the project and it comprises three main modules:

- the planning module, where the decisions are made about what is going to be learned and how it will be done

- the creative grammar module, where learners develop and test their own models of grammar
- the text module, where learners develop their language and thinking skills through various text-based communicative tasks.

The modules are presented to learners through simple tutorials that demonstrate the structure of learning and the philosophy behind it (Staluns and Sokol, 2008). The language learning methodology underlying the modules originates from the 'Thinking Approach' to language teaching and learning (Sokol, 2008; Sokol et al., 2008). The approach is aimed at helping learners develop their thinking skills and dispositions in the process of learning a language, thus making the learning process more effective, as learners are dealing with both language and thinking syllabi in an integrated way. The design of the modules is underpinned by the thinking syllabus, e.g. focus on planning and evaluation of own learning, open ended tasks to texts, learner development of grammar rules, etc.

Learners can connect to the modules at any time. All their work is saved in the learner portfolios, which perform both formative and summative roles. The former is achieved as a result of the feedback obtained both from the system and the teacher, while the latter becomes possible when the learner has selected some of his/her learning outcomes for sharing with the wider community for assessment. Although the work with the modules is asynchronous, teachers can monitor both the process and the results of each learner through accessing their portfolios and leaving comments.

Due to mainly technological reasons, the creative grammar module was the one used most widely during the period the study reports. Therefore, it is this module that will be dealt with in this publication. Structurally it comprises seven parts, each aimed at a specific function, as illustrated in the table below.

Part	Name	Function
1	Define present knowledge	Help learners see how much they already know in a given theme and help make a decision about the necessity of further learning.
2	Clarify structures	Help learners come up with a list of structures used in a given theme.
3	Formulate learning goals	Help learners analyse examples of using structures found in Part 2 (Bank 1) and formulate the learning goal(s) connected with further work with the system of grammar tasks.
4	Develop a draft model	Help learners develop a draft model connected with goals formulated in Part 3.
5	Test and improve the model	Help learners transform their preliminary grammar model to a working model that is sufficient to cope with the goals formulated in Part 3.
6	Put the model into practice	Provide learners with contexts for language production practice based on their working models.
7	Evaluate and plan further learning	Help learners analyse the process and products of their work with the system of tasks offered in Parts 1–6 and as a result develop plans for further learning.

In each of the above parts, the learner works with one of the systems of tasks dealing with a certain communicative function, for example speaking about the past, expressing modality, describing objects, etc. One system includes about 35 tasks (Sokol et al., 2002–09).

The novelty of the online modules is reflected in the following underlying principles:

- no grammar explanations are offered to learners
- tasks ask for new knowledge
- learners build their own grammar models
- learner models are tested and improved instead of being evaluated as right or wrong
- learner banks are major tools for learning
- learners define learning goals and finalise content
- each learner works at his/her own pace.

Blend: online and face-to-face time

Despite the trend to include less grammar in General English courses, in Latvia it traditionally receives a lot of attention. Although we do not have any research evidence to support this, practically any local educator knows that both teachers and learners want to deal with grammar as part of their courses. The approach to grammar within the Thinking Approach, where learners develop and test their own grammar rules, normally requires more time than a more traditional approach. Given only three academic hours of classroom time for English, allocation of even one third of this to grammar was seen as unaffordable luxury. Thus, a decision was made to allocate one academic hour per fortnight to face-to-face work on grammar. The rest students had to do independently through work with the online modules. On average, students spent about two months on one system of grammar tasks. The table below gives an overview of how the work was normally organised.

Week	Time (mins)	Content	Part of the system	Medium
1	15	Entry test	1	Online
	10	Results overview	1	Classroom
2	60–90	Work on the discovery of structures	2	Online
	20	Overview: major problems, questions, technical support	2	Classroom
3	15	Formulation of aims	3	Online
	60	Work on concept questions tasks	4	Online
	20	Overview: major issues, hints	4	Classroom
	40	Development of models	4	Online
	20	Support session	4	Classroom
4	60–120	Testing the model	5	Online

Week	Time (mins)	Content	Part of the system	Medium
5	60	Work with banks of mistakes	5	Online
	20	Support session	5	Classroom
	30	Development of the improved model	5	Online
6	60	Testing of the improved model	5	Online
	30	Further work with the bank of mistakes	5	Online
	40	Presentation of models and their discussion	5	Classroom
7	40	Implementation of the model	6	Online
	40	Putting models to practice + discussion of remaining questions	6	Online and classroom
8	15	Final test	7	Online
	20	Analysis of results	7	Classroom
	30	Reflection and plan for further work	7	Online
	20	The teacher's reflection and advice for further work	7	Classroom

The time indicators above should be treated with caution. Normally more time should be allocated when students work with their first system, as in addition to new content, they are getting used to new technology and often a new approach to learning in which they are expected to 'build' their understanding instead of being given information to remember. In the beginning, one lesson was spent on introducing the online modules to learners and explaining the rationale for this work. Learners generally accepted the idea that classroom time can be used more effectively if it is allocated to those things that are impossible or very difficult to do without the teacher. Most grammar work does not fall under this category and thus can be dealt with online. The ease of doing was the main factor behind the rationale used for the division between classroom and online activities. It should be noted though, that in the beginning, more time was spent in the classroom to familiarise learners with some task types and the way of thinking expected on their part, especially in parts where own-grammar models had to be developed and tested.

It should also be stressed that work with grammar described in this study constituted only a part of the General English course offered to learners (about 20 per cent if both classroom and individual learning time are considered).

Methodology and skills developed

As seen from the description above, the approach to learning grammar is very different from the traditional present-practise-produce (PPP) models typical of most online resources. In the proposed approach, learners start with a hypothesis about the use of the structures, test it through collecting a bank of mistakes and then improve the initial hypothesis. The model is presented in Figure 1.

Figure 1: Cycle of working with grammar in online modules

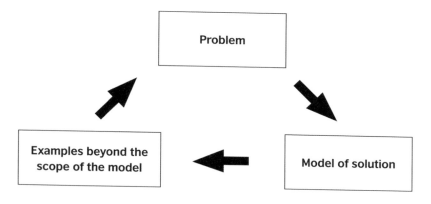

Production happens all the time from the initial testing of the hypothesis/model. In addition to specific grammar-related skills, this approach is intended to help learners develop the following skills:

- *Self-assessment* (when taking the initial decision on the need for dealing with this or that system of tasks and in the process of work being involved in the evaluation of own models and their application).

- *Noticing* (when discovering the structures used to express this or that communicative function).

- *Goal setting* (when deciding which aspects of the problem to focus on).

- *Building models* (when developing the model of solution through constructing their own grammar rule).

- *Description via parameters and values* (when presenting their own model/rule in the form understandable to the computer).

- *Finding applicability limits of models* (when testing their own model/rule and finding where it does not work).

- *Generalisation* (when formulating their own model/rule in such a way as to apply it in various contexts).

- *Specification* (when deciding on the application of a model/rule in a particular context).

It should also be noted that despite seeming to work on grammar only, learners were developing all the language skills:

- *Reading* (when collecting banks of examples at the stage of discovering structures, for example learners were asked to read a text of their choice and find examples of the author expressing this or that communicative function, such as referring to the future).

- *Writing* (in tasks and during online discussions, for example Skype chat sessions).
- *Speaking and listening* (during overview lessons in the classroom).

Actual examples of materials used would be rather lengthy to include here, therefore we encourage the reader to consult the online version (Sokol et al., 2002–09). However, we are presenting some of the models/rules developed by learners to give a better idea about what they were doing. Please note that these are not students of linguistics, they are secondary school students, many of whom are not interested in language as an object of study.

Examples of students' models on Speaking about Past 1 (Sokol, 2006)

Model by MS, Form 11

Structure	Model
Did	Continuousness: NO Finalisation: NO
Was doing	Continuousness: YES Finalisation: NO
Had done	Continuousness: NO Finalisation: YES

Model by JK, Form 12

Structure	Model
Did	Time: PAST Continuance: NO End of action: finished action
Was doing	Time: PAST Continuance: YES End of action: unfinished action
Had done	Time: PAST Continuance: NO End of action: finished action

Model by JP, Form 10

Structure	Model
Did	Definiteness of the moment: NO Completeness: NO When? past/before past/specific past: PAST
Was doing	Definiteness of the moment: YES Completeness: NO When? past/before past/specific past: SPECIFIC PAST
Had done	Definiteness of the moment: YES Completeness: YES When? past/before past/specific past: BEFORE PAST

Please note that the examples above are actual models of learners as they existed during the time of working with a particular system of tasks. Some models or their parts may appear incorrect from the conventional point of view. This, however, did not necessarily affect the quality of the learning process of this or that student, as the model was tested and often improved at a later stage. Moreover, it is surprising how useful this or that 'incorrect' model may turn out to be in the student's hands.

Students' feedback and further planned adaptations

Students' feedback concerned two aspects: the proposed approach to learning grammar and the mode for implementing it. The feedback was collected through various channels: anonymous online questionnaires, ongoing learner reflections (Learner reflections 2004–10), entries in the assessment portfolios and interviews. The main points are summarised below:

■ It is difficult for learners to accept working with grammar online if they previously dealt with it in the classroom. The situation is completely different when a group is introduced to the blended course from the very beginning.

■ Difficult aspects are even more difficult when working online.

■ Work online requires much more concentration than the same work in the classroom.

■ Learners' complaints about the technology do not really depend on the quality of the technological solutions offered to them.

■ Technical problems lead to a high level of frustration (in comparison to the classroom).

■ Online modules are a good way to have everything about grammar organised and kept in one place.

■ Developing and testing their own models leads to deeper understanding of how grammar works.

■ Various aspects of learning grammar are remembered much better when developed by learners.

- The online modules are never perfect – they can be improved all the time. It is reasonable to evaluate not how perfect they are but to what extent they help in reaching the learning objectives.

The following further adaptations of the online modules are envisaged:

- make it possible for learners to start working with the system from various parts (some learners already know structures and have draft models)
- reduce the time necessary for performing a task, thus decreasing the required level of concentration
- make it possible for learners to benefit from collaboration with other learners through discussing things with them/doing tasks related to their work
- increase the system effect of the site by improving connections between various systems, for example it should be possible for learners to use parts of the models developed for one system when working on the other
- introduce additional tasks that help learners understand that they are improving (measuring by tests only is not enough).

Lessons learned and advice

The lessons learned as a result of work with the blend are presented through the contradictions we faced. If a successful solution was found, it is presented here as well.

Contradiction 1
The design of the online modules required high concentration from the learners. At the same time, their concentration was low as most of them do 101 things when working online (we found this to be a general trend among the learners irrespective of how engaging the task was).

Solution 1
Not solved during the period described.

Conceptual solution: each task offered to learners requires low concentration as it can be done fairly quickly, however, all tasks together require high concentration.

Recommendation 1
Each task in the course should be short enough to ensure that learners can cope with it without being distracted in the process.

Contradiction 2
Tasks offered to learners should be easy enough so as not to discourage them and they should be difficult enough to ensure that there is room for the development of thinking.

Solution 2
Tasks are difficult when learners work alone and they are easy when they work as a group during the classroom sessions.

Recommendation 2

Ensure that the online tasks are challenging enough to provide enough room for thinking even to stronger learners. Use the classroom time to provide for an appropriate level of scaffolding for each learner if the technology fails to do it.

Contradiction 3

Scaffolding sessions should be organised at different periods of time for each learner to ensure that he/she has done all the assignments beforehand, and they should be organised at the same time for all learners given the constraints of the syllabus.

Solution 3

Timely submission of assignments online positively affects the total assessment.

A few days before the deadline, the teacher takes part in a synchronous meeting with learners where they can ask questions. This worked as a motivating factor for many learners to plan work with the online module before the meeting to have a chance to ask questions. Skype chat sessions with the group were used for this purpose.

Recommendation 3

Ensure that everything you want the learners to do is integrated in the system of assessment.

Get learners to want to do things by the deadline. The best way of achieving this is to give them something they feel they need when doing the task. The teacher's help may often be enough for motivating learners.

Contradiction 4

Tasks given to learners have to be different to ensure that they do not cheat when doing them and they have to be the same to make the implementation easier, both in terms of technological solutions and the teacher's labour.

Solution 4

This problem was resolved at the design stage by:

- Making the tasks open enough to ensure a variety of correct answers (thus, the same answer by several learners always signalled cheating. As the time of dealing with the task was recorded for each learner, only the answer of the first person was accepted by the teacher).

- Giving learners a choice of tasks in each part, thus reducing the possibility of the same tasks being performed by various learners.

Recommendation 4

Make sure that the tasks are open (allow for a variety of correct answers) and learners are able to choose tasks for themselves.

In addition to the above problems, one should be aware of the so-called 'mindset issues'. In our particular case these dealt with learners' preconceptions about learning ('I want answers', 'I don't like to get stuck', etc.) and attitude to technology ('I don't like to talk to the computer'). These are very important challenges for the teacher, as they may negatively affect the atmosphere of the learning process.

One should not expect these problems to be solved in a few days. They normally take an extended period of time. Helping learners achieve something and getting them to reflect on what has happened, and how, can be an important step in changing learners' responses. The technology will not always be successful in dealing with 'personal' issues, however, the teacher can always dedicate more time to addressing these issues in the classroom. The resource of face-to-face communication provided by blended courses is an important asset and both teachers and learners should definitely benefit from it.

Conclusions

Some researchers point out that there is a lack of sophisticated tools for online learning (Bonk, 2004: 2–3). The online modules used for the blended course described in this study definitely offer a rich learning experience addressing both the challenge of complexity and effective support for the learner (Kirkley and Kirkley, 2006). Our experience shows that offering the modules as part of the blended course significantly increased the motivation of learners in comparison to the distant use adopted earlier. We also succeeded in increasing the total time spent on learning and in helping the learners to take a step towards more autonomy when learning a language. In addition, the blended course created learning contexts for both the teacher and the learners that did not exist either during the online or classroom learning, thus creating useful systemic effects that became possible only as a result of integration of the two components. At the same time, the blended course brought about new challenges both to the teacher and the learners. Being ready to face these challenges and develop effective solutions appears to be one of the key requirements for a successful blended learning experience. The learner who is enjoying the process of constructing knowledge as a result of a rich problem-solving experience and the teacher who shares this kind of learning philosophy will be the ones benefiting most from the course described in this study.

References

Bonk, C (2004) The perfect e-storm: emerging technology, enormous learner demand, enhanced pedagogy, and erased budgets. Part 2: Storms #3 and #4. *The Observatory on Higher Education, 2004*. Available online at www.publicationshare.com/part2.pdf

Kirkley, SE and Kirkley, JR (2006) 'Expanding the boundaries of blended learning: transforming learning with mixed and virtual reality technologies', in Bonk, C and Graham, C (eds) *Handbook of Blended Learning: Global Perspectives, Local Designs*. San Francisco, CA: Pfeiffer Publishing.

Learner reflections (2004–10). Available online at www.thinking-approach.org/forum/index.php?c=11

New Learners in the New Europe (2008) *Online modules for the integrated development of language and thinking skills*. Available online at www.thinking-approach.eu

Sokol, A (2008) *Development of Inventive Thinking in Language Education.* Unpublished PhD Thesis, University of Latvia and the University of Strasbourg.

Sokol, A, Khomenko, N, Sonntag, M and Oget, D (2008) The development of inventive thinking skills in the upper secondary language classroom. *Thinking Skills and Creativity* 3/1: 34−46.

Sokol, A, Lasevich, E Dobrovolska, M and Buchinska, I (2002–09) *Systems of grammar tasks.* Available online at www.thinking-approach.org/index.php?id=19

Sokol, A (2006) *Speaking about Past 1 – a System of Grammar Tasks.* Available online at http://en.thinking-approach.eu/Materials/Material.aspx?mid=2

Staluns, M and Sokol, A (2008) *Tutorials for learners working with www.thinking-approach.eu.* Available online at: http://en.thinking-approach.eu/Tutorials/Default.aspx

18

A blended learning approach to soft skill training at Al Azhar University, Cairo

Liz Fleet

Introduction

This study focused on a group of students at Al Azhar English Training Centre (AAETC). AAETC was opened in 2008 in partnership with the British Council in Cairo. It provides English language provision to 350 students and teacher training to 25 Egyptian teachers. As part of this, the Centre encourages teachers and students to use technology to participate in English communication, independent learning and flexible study access. This has involved creating a site called New Generation (NG). Through the wiki, students have interacted informally with those inside and outside the university by taking part in topical forums, using the chat facility and sharing resources. Besides this, AAETC is providing flexible curriculum learning opportunities by developing study-focused content for specific classes. As part of this, a voluntary-access soft skills blend was recently established on NG and a case study conducted.

Background to the study

The project was conducted between October and December 2011 with 26 post-graduate academic English soft skills students. They were all male, between the ages of 22 and 24 and had previously studied English during Islamic Studies degree courses. The research involved integrating face-to-face presentation and lecture listening training with online delivery and the aim was to potentially do this with other courses later in the school year if the project was a success.

The blend was designed to increase postgraduate English input by adding to class provision. Doing so was considered beneficial because of their immediate job and course-seeking needs and the fact they had less face-to-face provision than undergraduate students. With many aspiring to study overseas, where courses typically contain blended learning elements (Tobin, 2011), it was vital to give them exposure to this style of education to further equip them for master's and PhD courses abroad. As they were by nature somewhat teacher-dependent, integrating classroom activities with online study aimed to foster more independent and collaborative learning by encouraging the students to review lesson content, collectively interact with follow-up material and prepare for future lessons. It was hoped that having the extra online exposure would help improve classroom performance because of the revision and interaction opportunities that it presented.

Moreover, as a result of increased political tension in Egypt, and the resultant disruption to classes and learning, there was a general advantage in enabling the students to participate in flexible online collaborative learning. This meant that if students were unable to attend classes, having material online would enable them to study independently and help maintain motivation in between face-to-face lessons. Therefore, rather than falling behind and losing momentum, they could return to classes having made progress.

The course

The optional blend combined 53 hours of soft skills classroom learning with online provision and was separated into two parts. The first worked in conjunction with a Presentations course of nine lessons and the second a Lecture Listening course of eight classes. After each class, students were advised to spend between 30 minutes and an hour on the web-based resources. At the start of each lesson, students were encouraged to share what they had discussed and learned online, or any learning difficulties they had experienced with the material. This was to consolidate the web-based study, encourage participation and establish a link between the two parts of the blend.

Every class focused on a particular element of presentations, such as introductions, signalling and concluding. The web-based resources were structured in the same way, following a consistent format to enable the students to access and interact with them simply (Niles, 2008). After each class, a clearly-labelled page was added, containing lesson materials and supplementary resources, such as YouTube clips and links to presentations advice. This was done so that absent students could easily obtain missed material and to allow further independent study.

Within each lesson page was a discussion activity that the students were encouraged to participate in. This allowed them to digest content, ask follow up-questions and collaboratively extend their knowledge. As Singer and Stoicescu (2010: 1531) say, 'the online forum is a very important piece of the blend. It supports the students to go deeper into the understanding of a concept that was presented in face-to-face'.

At the end of the course, presentations were filmed and uploaded, enabling students to re-watch themselves, learn from each other and comment on one another's work. According to students, being able to do this increased their confidence and blended learning motivation.

The Lecture Listening course followed a similar format on NG with each themed lesson focusing on a comprehension and note-taking skill and the online materials linking to this. Nonetheless, images were added to the text to increase aesthetic appeal. This was as a result of informal feedback after the Presentations course, saying the material 'didn't look interesting'. Another difference was related to copyright. As the 'Lecture Ready' coursebook and audio were used, it was impossible to upload these. Nevertheless, supplementary resources were added, which included lesson-related talks from YouTube. For example, a TED talk on consumerism was used for the first lesson theme of spending. Participants were encouraged to watch the clips, take notes, utilise the listening strategies from the face-to-face input and answer questions that had been written for each clip. Ideally, students would have attended actual lectures in English; however, this was not practical in Egypt. Furthermore, as it was difficult to find university lectures that related to the coursebook on YouTube, other talks were included that did connect.

The YouTube links and classroom audio were used to complement each other. The class work enabled students to develop their note-taking skills collectively and pay particular attention to transition signals and keywords to help with understanding. The physical presence of the teacher helped to support and encourage students before and in between activities. Furthermore, students were prompted to assist each other by sharing what they had understood from the audio. From a teacher's perspective, they appeared more confident with this face-to-face interaction and were encouraged by receiving instant feedback on their answers. Nevertheless, the online element added to this provision for different reasons. Firstly, the videos provided flexible revision opportunities with students being able to stream or download them in their own time. They allowed the learners to focus on their own needs as they could individually replay sections of the video or revise skills from particular lessons. In addition, they added authenticity to the course because while the classroom recordings gave students valuable listening practice, they were non-visual and presented little opportunity to understand from body language. Actual live lectures would have been the ideal provision but as this was impossible, the video-tasks were perceived to be more visually realistic than the classroom tasks. As Richards (2005: 6) says, such authenticity is advisable in any listening activity.

With respect to methodology, a learner-centred blend was designed that would encourage autonomous self-motivated personalised collective learning. As Arnold and Ryan (2003) say, if teachers '...are less shackled by the need to provide students with access to knowledge, their skills in pedagogy can be directed towards higher level thinking abilities, and developing a climate of positive, enthusiastic learning contexts in which rigorous intellectual work can flourish'.

The role of the teacher was therefore that of facilitator. In terms of the classroom work, this involved encouraging students to work more autonomously by adopting effective strategies and promoting collaborative discussion. The expectation was that learners would primarily rely on themselves and each other and the teacher would be present to elicit and help motivate when necessary. With respect to the online work, the teacher posted initial questions and provided learning material but participated in a more removed way to encourage students to take greater charge of their own learning. When interaction fell, messages were posted to initiate more involvement. Despite this, communication was encouraged rather than forced because of the desire to promote self-motivated learning. As evidence indicates, learner involvement in wikis tends to be more meaningful when they themselves choose to interact (Azizinezhad and Hashemi, 2011: 869).

Lessons learned

The following information was obtained through teacher reflection, student feedback from post-course questionnaires and informal comments throughout the project.

In general, the students remarked that they valued the blend, with 72 per cent regarding it as 'good' or 'very good'. Although they all regarded the face-to-face work as an essential part of their learning, there were various written comments about the online component providing greater flexibility. For example two asserted that it was 'useful' having access to materials, especially if they had missed classes. Others noted that they appreciated the discussion facility because this provided question and communication opportunities with one remarking that it helped make the content 'more interesting' and 'easy to remember'. Moreover, there were favourable comments in relation to independent learning; for example, one student said that he valued the supplementary Lecture Listening material because it gave him 'practice and confidence'. Nevertheless, he did say that links to real academic lectures would have matched the purpose of the course more.

With respect to participation, although learners worked collectively in the classroom and were motivated to re-watch and discuss their presentations online, web-based collaborative interaction was somewhat isolated rather than free-flowing. Feedback helps explain this, with six saying they had limited time to participate and one stating that he had expected tasks to be more teacher-led. On reflection, as Egyptians are accustomed to teacher-directed questioning (Dahawy and Kamal, 2009: 2), more involvement may have enhanced student activity. Moreover, two commented that greater hands-on support, such as help with signing up and locating pages, would have encouraged communication.

Besides this, from a teacher's perspective, those who worked actively online were generally motivated, vocal and confident in class. It is difficult to know whether this was as a result of the web-based work or due to these particular learners naturally being stronger. Nonetheless, there was a noticeable improvement in the classroom performance of three students after they became more technologically involved. In addition, there were two students who were particularly quiet in class but less so online. This indicates that the web-based part of the blend may have suited their learning styles more than the face-to-face aspect.

Despite this, based on informal comments, students regarded the online material as a course extension rather than an integral part. This expectation may be a fundamental reason why collective online interaction was not extensive. Although there had been logical reasons for making participation voluntary, had online interaction been compulsory, greater participation would have undoubtedly occurred. Although not based on intrinsic motivation, this would have increased student exposure to this style of collective learning and thus been a stepping stone to future self-motivated involvement in such a blend.

Conclusions and recommendations

As a result of this project, the following recommendations can be made. Firstly, blended learning presents many benefits such as flexibility, provision for different learning styles, increased collaborative opportunities and greater independent study potential. Nevertheless, with Egyptian learners, the face-to-face part of a blend is crucial in motivating students to participate in any web-based element. Without this, in view of their educational background, it is likely that many will feel isolated and unenthusiastic. There should therefore be a definite topic and skills link between class-based and online work, which learners need to be made aware of. For instance, learners will benefit linguistically and motivationally from pre-discussing internet tasks in class and feeding back on what they have learned online. Likewise, they are more likely to participate on wikis if the content is related to class input. This is because their primary focus is currently on lessons and not digital learning.

With respect to online material, attractive, relevant and personalised content motivates; therefore, it is beneficial to use images with text and to upload student class work to encourage discussion. Besides this, any web-based activities should not only complement classroom aims but also add value by compensating for the limitations of the classroom. For instance, including YouTube clips is beneficial because they are visual and allow students to replay content and work at their own pace.

In terms of technical support, it is preferable to have introductory face-to-face computer sessions to aid sign up, navigation and communication. If students have limited online learning experience, it is advisable to scaffold their participation by initially making involvement a course necessity and providing guided tasks. As confidence increases, they are likely to become more independently motivated to contribute in a less structured manner. Nevertheless, according to our study, more directed encouragement will help at first.

References

Arnold, R and Ryan, M (2003) *The Transformative Capacity of New Learning.* Melbourne: Australian Council of Deans of Education.

Azizinezhad M and Hashemi, M (2011) The use of blogs in teaching and learning translation. *Procedia – Social and Behavioral Sciences* 28: 867–871.

Dahawy, K and Kamel, S (2009) Using blended learning techniques in knowledge dissemination: lessons learnt from the case of the American University in Cairo. *The Electronic Journal on Information Systems in Developing Countries* 33. Available online at www.ejisdc.org/ojs2/index.php/ejisdc/article/view/558

Niles, R (2008) News websites need sharper focus, consistent design to attract audience, advertisers. *The Online Journalism Review.* Available online at www.ojr.org/p1534/

Richards, JC (2005) *Tactics for listening.* Oxford: Oxford University Press.

Singer, FM and Stoicescu, D (2010) Using a blended learning tool to strengthen teaching competences. *Procedia Computer Science* 3: 1527–1531.

Tobin, L (2011) *Get a Degree by Blended Learning.* Available online at www.guardian.co.uk/education/2011/apr/19/distance-blended-learning-degrees?INTCMP=SRCH

19

Students' CALLing: Blended language learning for students

Hatice Bilgin

Introduction

The expansion of online environments into language classrooms is now welcomed, in order to provide a potentially better teaching and learning experience. Osguthorpe and Graham (2003) indicate that as the face-to-face and online learning environments have been combined, the inherent strengths and weaknesses associated with both have been recognised. This combination of online environments with face-to-face learning is called blended learning. The aim in blended learning is to combine the benefits of these two environments in a harmonious way. The combination of a face-to-face instruction environment with an online environment within the same course allows not only capitalising on the advantages of each but also catering for diverse learning styles and the needs of different students. Allan (2007: 8) suggests that blended learning 'appears to offer the opportunity to combine the best of a number of worlds in constructing a program that fits the particular needs in terms of time, space and technologies of a particular group of students or end-users'.

Considering the great potential of blended learning, a study aiming at exploring the effects of a blended language learning (BLL) environment on the achievement and opinions of Turkish university preparatory students studying English as a Foreign Language (EFL) was conducted in Istanbul Technical University School of Foreign Languages. In this study, the 'blend' consisted of the completion of required materials and students' independent self-study phases at a computer with an online learning management system (LMS) called Macmillan English Campus (MEC), and conventional face-to-face classroom learning. Two upper-intermediate level preparatory classes were assigned as experimental and control groups. The students in the experimental class used MEC as part of their courses and self-study, as well as following the required materials of the preparatory programme. The control class followed only the required materials in a face-to-face environment. The students in both classes were given a pre-test, progress-test and post-test. The students in the experimental class were given a student questionnaire followed by a focus group interview in order to investigate their opinions on the blend.

This study was carried out in the autumn term of the 2009–10 academic year at Istanbul Technical University (ITU), where the one-year preparatory English programme is compulsory for all undergraduate students who do not meet the English language proficiency requirements. The participants of this study were from two of the upper-intermediate level classes in ITU School of Foreign Languages. In each class, there were 36 English as a Foreign Language Turkish preparatory students who had 18 hours of compulsory instruction per week, six hours of which was a 'Basic English' course focusing on teaching grammar, and 12 hours of which was an 'Integrated Skills' course, which was made up of six hours of reading, four hours of writing, and two hours of listening instruction per week.

The study

MEC is an online LMS designed for BLL, offering supplementary online practice at home or in class. In this study, there were four courses students had access to in MEC. These courses were 'General English Level 5', 'CEFR B2' and 'Academic English with IELTS'. The resources were language exercises, vocabulary activities, listening activities, pronunciation activities, exam preparation exercises, language tests and grammar reference units. The interaction types in these resources were gap-fill type-in, gap-fill drag and drop, rearranging words, phrases or sentences, multiple choice where students select one choice from a list of two or more options, true/false choices, checklists where students can select more than one choice from a longer list of options, highlighting words in a sentence or text, deleting words from a sentence or text, and matching words, phrases or sentences.

The interaction types in these resources did not enable any social interaction between students and teachers or among students. The system lacked features enabling social interaction, such as chat and discussion boards in which students could share their ideas and help each other online. There was only a messaging feature that enabled teacher–student interaction. The teacher could send messages to the whole class or individual students, and students could send messages to the teacher on MEC. However, students could not send messages to each other, and could not collaborate with each other when studying on MEC. Therefore, the class preferred email and their class group on Facebook when collaborating instead of using the message feature of MEC. Student interaction and collaboration were important in this course, to foster autonomy and learning.

In this study, the students in the experimental group were assigned resources by the teachers from the available courses weekly. While students continued to receive face-to-face instruction, they had a chance to study online within a controlled learning environment via this online LMS providing online support materials. The aim of the weekly assignments was to practise and revise the skills and points covered in the face-to-face lessons. The resources covered in MEC were considered as supplementary to the course materials used in class and matched with the syllabus of the upper-intermediate programme in a recursive manner.

Apart from the assigned resources, students were also free to work on any other resources available in MEC in addition to the assigned resources whenever they wanted. They could search the database of MEC for any materials that they needed or wanted to study. They could read news items which are published weekly, play games or work on different kinds of exam practice resources. In short, they could use MEC for self-study as well.

The students were taken to the computer laboratory for one hour bi-weekly after the study began. In the lab sessions, students were supposed to work on the assigned resources and ask for help with the technical problems they faced in using MEC. The lab sessions were useful in helping students solve technical problems and encouraging them to use MEC. At the beginning of the study, most of the problems students had involved how to use certain features of MEC. Later in these sessions, student focused on using the resources they wanted.

One of the aims of blending in this study was to compensate for learner differences and needs in experience with content, realising that some students had prior experience with the material and, thus, might not have to review the material as much as others. On the other hand, a student could receive additional information and training through extra online learning programmes while still attending in-class training with other students. Students who needed more practice could have that opportunity without taking face-to-face class time away from those who might not need the extra practice. This created a more learner-centered environment by addressing varying learning styles or needs.

Another goal of blending over using any single learning delivery mode was to have two major modes and environments, online and face-to-face delivery, in shaping the learning process. In this study, learners had a larger space to learn and teachers to teach more effectively. They were not confined to class boundaries any more. While teachers could help students any time by sending extra resources, students could access the materials at any time of day and review them as needed, which provided them with increased flexibility. In-class teaching on its own requires learners to participate in lessons at a fixed time, which limits the access. However, learning does not occur only in class. In this study, apart from the class instruction, learners could reach learning materials and teachers via MEC outside the class.

Results, implications and conclusion

The study aimed to explore the effects of an online LMS called MEC on Turkish EFL preparatory students' achievement and opinions in ITU School of Foreign Languages. The data for achievement was collected through the pre-test, progress test, and post-test. In all of these tests, students were tested on listening, grammar, vocabulary and reading. These tests were administered to both classes on the same day and at the same time. The listening sections of the tests were in the form of note-taking. The students were given note-taking sheets to take notes before the exam booklets were distributed. Students answered the listening questions based on their notes. Grammar was tested with multiple choice cloze tests except for the pre-test in which it was tested with discrete multiple choice items. As for the reading sections, students read a text and answered questions based on it. In the vocabulary section, students chose the correct word from a list of words to fill in the blanks in given sentences.

In order to find out any pre-existing difference in achievement, the pre-test scores were compared and revealed no statistical difference between the experimental class and the control class ($t(58) = 1.984$, $p = .052$). Later, the scores of the pre-test, progress test and post test were analysed to find out whether MEC had an effect on the achievement of students. The analysis of the test results indicated that the experimental class outperformed the control class ($F(2, 116) = 4.002$, $p= .021$). This, of course, could be attributable to the power of the online materials but it could also be a consequence of the extra learning time this class were given, their extra exposure to English or of a match between the tasks in the tests and those in the online materials.

The results of the student questionnaire revealed that nearly all of the students considered that MEC helped them improve their English. However, most of them did not want to have an online component in their conventional learning. The analysis of the interviews revealed that the compulsory use of the online materials, the design of the programme and lack of print materials were important reasons for students' discontent.

Blending face-to-face teaching with an online programme as supplementary can be used to improve the achievement of students studying English as a Foreign Language (Al-Jarf, 2004; Al-Jarf, 2005; Bañados, 2006; Pazio, 2010). Teachers can assign complementary resources to students to improve their learning and engage them with English outside the class. Incorporating online tools such as an online LMS and authentic materials like articles and podcasts in class can foster student learning. However, the interview results indicated that students valued print materials over purely online resources in their learning, which suggested that students might prefer to have paper materials over purely online ones when studying. It seems that as we mostly assume that students of our time are technology oriented, we might mistakenly take it for granted that they will appreciate online materials readily. Stracke (2007) suggests that there is a need to carefully plan a blended course, providing students with comprehensive teacher and document guidance. Therefore, when we are designing a blended course, we should fine-tune the balance between the online materials and paper-based materials.

If students use an online programme for the first time, it will take some time for them to get used to it. The way students are used to studying should be taken into consideration. In a report on the Hybrid Course Project at the University of Wisconsin, Aycock, Garnham, and Kaleta (2002) indicate that 'students don't grasp the blend readily'. They also indicate that many of the students don't perceive time spent in lectures as 'work', but they see time spent online as 'work', even if it is time they would have spent in class in a traditional course. In this study, the compulsory use of the online programme was one of the reasons for student discontent. It seems that although students today are very technology oriented in their daily lives, they may not be as eager in their learning.

This study offers some insights into blended language learning by showing a group of Turkish university upper-intermediate level EFL students' engagement in a particular online commercial LMS as part of their courses. The results indicate that teaching English blending face-to-face teaching with an online LMS can be beneficial over solely in-class teaching, by providing an extensive range of authentic materials as well as a more learner-centred medium of instruction, which can complement classroom-based activities.

When considering blended learning, there is, of course, no single perfect blend because it is grounded on the notion of flexibility. Allan (2007) maintains that there is no prescription for designing effective blended learning programmes. However, the planning and design of effective blended learning practices can be challenging and demanding. To what extent to use technology and when to integrate are important questions in BLL. The most important aim in designing a BLL course is to find the most effective and efficient combination of the two modes of learning for the individual learning subjects, contexts and objectives (Neumeier, 2005).

References

Al-Jarf, RS (2004) The effects of web-based learning on struggling EFL college writers. *Foreign Language Annals* 37/1: 46–56.

Al-Jarf, RS (2005) The effects of online grammar instruction on low proficiency EFL college students' achievement. *The Asian EFL Journal Quarterly* 7/4: 166–190.

Allan, B (2007) *Blended Learning: Tools for Teaching and Training.* London: Facet Publishing.

Aycock, A, Garnham, C and Kaleta, R (2002) Lessons learned from the hybrid course project. *Teaching with Technology Today* 8/6. Available online at www.uwsa.edu/ttt/articles/garnham2.htm

Bañados, E (2006) A blended-learning pedagogical model for teaching and learning EFL successfully through an online interactive multimedia environment. *CALICO Journal* 23/3: 533–550.

Neumeier, P (2005) A closer look at blended learning: parameters for designing a blended learning environment for language teaching and learning. *ReCALL* 17/2: 163–178.

Osguthorpe, RT and Graham, CR (2003) Blended learning environments, definitions and directions. *The Quarterly Review of Distance Education* 4/3: 227–233.

Pazio, M (2010) Blended learning and its potential in expanding vocabulary knowledge: A case study. *Teaching English with Technology* 10/1: 3–30.

Stracke, E (2007) A road to understanding: A qualitative study into why learners drop out of a blended language learning (BLL) environment. *ReCALL* 19/1: 57–78.

20

Lessons in blended learning: Implementing an online learning platform in the adult education sector

Astrid Krake

The setting

In many classrooms, the days when a printed coursebook was the learners' only aid are quickly vanishing, and teachers and administrators alike are faced with questions of how to integrate different materials into their classrooms. This is true not only for language schools with predominantly younger learners: adult education institutions such as the German 'Volkshochschulen', with their reputation for adhering to more traditional approaches, are increasingly looking for ways to incorporate online resources into their teaching.

The Munich Volkshochschule (MVHS), the biggest German institution of its kind, caters for the needs of approximately 4,000 learners of English per term. Their learning backgrounds are as manifold as their reasons for learning English: while some wish to increase their employability by improving their language skills, others are motivated by more personal reasons such as a relative whose partner speaks only English or the wish to be able to communicate when on holiday. The MVHS course offering reflects these different needs: learners can choose between General English at A1 to C2 levels of the Common European Framework for Languages, Business English as well as Cambridge exam preparation, with General English amounting to approximately 65 per cent of the courses offered. The needs to cater for in this section are the most extensive. Therefore, learners of General English can opt for:

- Intensive courses (10 hours/week, one level in 5–6 weeks).
- Twice-a-week offers (6–8 hours/week, one level in one term).
- Fast-track courses (once a week, three hours, one level in two terms).
- 'Traditional' courses (once a week, 90 minutes, one level in three to four terms).

Assuming that learners who need to progress quickly opt for more intensively-paced learning, and knowing that professional commitments, business trips, illness or other reasons can prevent them from coming to class, MVHS sought ways to keep the attrition rate low and to become more attractive to new target groups, among them younger learners accustomed to being surrounded by technology in their everyday lives.

Introducing Macmillan English Campus

One way of meeting the changing needs of learners was to shift some of the learning to a different medium and opt for an approach that includes technology. In this context, additional features had to:

- be available 24/7
- be easy to access and straightforward to use
- provide opportunities for interaction between learners and teachers
- cover a range of skills
- offer opportunities for review
- provide plenty of enriching activities of good quality without overburdening the teachers.

Therefore, a blended learning solution, i.e. 'a language course which combines a face-to-face (F2F) classroom component with an appropriate use of technology' (Sharma and Barrett, 2007: 7) seemed worth considering. The combination of synchronous and asynchronous learning was one way towards making language learning more flexible.

Contextual limitations

Unlike most language schools, Volkshochschulen offer their courses at a number of locations spread across the city, thereby facilitating access. Most courses are held on school premises, i.e. in classrooms originally laid out for classes of 25–35 pupils aged 11–19. Teachers are allowed to use the blackboard/whiteboard in the classroom and temporarily change the seating arrangement. Classrooms are equipped with CD players, but the schools' IT firewalls prevent internet access even via the teacher's notebook.

Volkshochschulen have some buildings of their own which they can use for teaching, but a rather low proportion of courses are held there. These tend to be courses that require special equipment, such as arts and crafts, music, or computing classes. This does not leave much space for language teaching on the premises.

Moreover, Volkshochschule teachers work on a freelance basis, i.e. they are paid by the teaching hour. Asking them to work on an online component for their courses, to devise quality material and update it regularly, and to supervise the platform as well as their learners would be demanding too much, and would ultimately lead to questions of remuneration. What would happen if someone prepares a component for a course that ends up being cancelled? How do you remunerate the hours spent creating an online component? Furthermore, content used by a number of classes has to be developed and updated regularly, and its quality has to be checked as well. How do you deal with issues such as quality control and copyright in these circumstances?

At first glance these conditions appeared to argue against introducing a technology strand to the classroom. In order to make multimedia teaching feasible, the institution had to find a way around the cost of creating materials. At the same time, it had to ensure that teachers would be working with easy-to-use devices without spending inordinate time preparing materials, assigning tasks and marking them.

Given the context, the solution lay not in an open-source platform such as Moodle, but rather in acquiring ready-made content of high quality to eliminate development time and cost. Macmillan English Campus (MEC) was the logical step in that direction.

MEC is an internet-based, interactive learning environment that comprises material for both adult and teenage courses, and covers General as well as Business English. Users can choose between ready-made courses that complement one of the Macmillan coursebook series, opt for a course built according to the guidelines of the Common European Framework for Languages, or use the material available to build their own course. The flexibility of the platform and the variety and quality of material it provides makes MEC suitable for practically every need. In addition, to set courses users have access to news articles, tests, web quests, a grammar reference section, games, the Macmillan English Dictionary Online, and materials to prepare for Cambridge exams and the TOEFL test, an alternative to Cambridge examinations often needed when applying to work or study in the United States. Teachers as well as learners are users of the virtual learning platform (VLE), and can log on wherever they have internet access. New content is constantly created, and the company is responsible for the quality of the material. The institution pays for the number of user IDs needed per month. It has to issue all users with a password, upload them onto the VLE, and allocate them to their courses. All in all, MEC does not create a lot of additional work at institutional level.

Set up

In spring 2007 MEC was introduced to course types that are designed for quick progress: intensive, twice-a-week, and fast-track courses at levels A2–C1, representing a total of 28 classes. The circumstances outlined above limit blends to two usage scenarios in which MEC is deployed as:

1. A tool complementing the face-to-face sessions and thus used predominantly outside the classroom.

2. An integral part of the course used both inside and outside the language classroom.

Both scenarios commence with an introductory session in the language laboratory or an IT room on the second day of the course. The teacher introduces the class to MEC, helps with logging onto the site and provides learners with an overview of its features. The group tries out some activities, creates an entry in the word list, is introduced to the dictionary, and spends the remaining teaching time working on some exercises – both individually and in groups. Depending on the level of the group, this session can provide learners with a very detailed overview or focus on more advanced features of MEC, thus providing learners with the kind of support that meets their needs.

In both scenarios, the ratio of content delivered face-to-face and online is 70:30. The number of face-to-face teaching hours has remained identical, thus the overall time learners spend learning the language has increased. (See, for example, Hockly and Clandfield [2010: 11]. They suggest starting by putting 10–20 per cent of the course content online. Since the MVHS courses do not lose teaching time we opted for slightly more than 20 per cent, thus replacing the average time spent on revision and homework.)

After this introductory phase, scenario 1 courses use MEC as a complement to face-to-face sessions with a focus on consolidating or reviewing language. The teacher uses the messaging system to assign homework and checks the learners' progress before the next lesson. This enables him/her to plan subsequent lessons to target the learners' needs more closely: if a specific topic causes little difficulty to learners at home, the next face-to-face lesson will not have to begin with a detailed review of it. If, however, learners are struggling with a given task, lesson plans for the next face-to-face session will take this into consideration. The number of hours spent online is higher during school holidays when classes do not meet face-to-face. Thus MEC provides for continuation and review during non-teaching times.

Since scenario 2 courses take place in the institution's own buildings, they use MEC both inside and outside the classroom. Usage outside the classroom is the same as described above. Inside the classroom, 90 minutes per week are spent working with MEC, either as a class activity projected onto the wall or as individual tasks in the language lab. Whereas whole-class activities introduce new topics or provide an opportunity for review, individual work mainly serves as consolidation.

In both scenarios the teacher acts as intermediary, previewing the content of each unit of the online course and selecting the activities most suited to his/her learners' needs. When the messaging system is used to alert learners to homework, learners are more likely to log on regularly; MEC thus becomes an integral part of their language learning.

Lessons learned

All in all, user feedback from teachers as well as learners is positive. Questionnaires students filled in at the end of the first term of using MEC, along with feedback retrieved from teachers, illustrate that implementing a blended learning approach as illustrated above was a step in the right direction. Of the 336 questionnaires sent out to course participants, 42 per cent (141) were sent back. Teacher feedback was even higher: 18 of 25 teachers (72 per cent) replied to an email questionnaire asking for detailed feedback.

Teachers mention the following:

- MEC gives access to quality resources and tools (95 per cent).
- MEC makes lessons more interesting (70 per cent).
- Teachers can tailor the syllabus to suit their students' needs (82 per cent).
- MEC helps keep track of students' progress (79 per cent).

In July 2011, teachers and participants were interviewed for a Macmillan Case Study used for marketing purposes. The following statements of teachers and learners have been taken from this case study. When asked about the advantages of using MEC in the classroom, Dana, a teacher of intensive classes, says: 'It's definitely more interesting. You know, sometimes you forget about the chore of having to learn a language or teach a lesson because you work with something new and you focus on it. I think this is the same for the students: when they play a game they forget about learning structures.'

Learners appreciate:

- Independent access (89 per cent).
- 24/7 access to engaging L2 exercises (95 per cent).
- Automatic marking, encourages them to re-do exercises (78 per cent).
- Extra practice (95 per cent).
- Playing language games (32 per cent).
- Listening and pronunciation activities (73 per cent).

When asked their opinion, an elementary level learner in an intensive class that uses MEC during the lessons said: 'I can make the very good exercises, and after the exercises are coming all these answers and I can correct my own answers and think about what I make wrong.'

Another elementary level student pointed out: 'It's very important for me to do some English exercises at home and to know if I have done it right or false. So for someone that say me 'You have maybe 80 or 90 per cent right' is important for me.'

Students like listening, grammar and pronunciation exercises and emphasise the fact that MEC is 'modern and very useful'. Their opinions underline the results of recent studies in the field of language learning review. 'The overall finding of the meta-analysis is that classes with online learning (whether taught completely online or blended) on average produce stronger student learning outcomes than do classes with solely face-to-face instruction' (US Department of Education, Office of Planning, Evaluation, and Policy Development (2009: 18).

The crucial factors in the successful implementation of a VLE – sufficient training for teachers and participants, administrative and pedagogical support, integration into the syllabus – have proved advantageous for the successful implementation of MEC (see also Bax, 2003: 26).

Because of the ability of students to self-pace and keep in touch with the class even when away on business, the chances for learners in blended learning classrooms of completing their course are higher.

Although overall acceptance is high, there is a slight difference between learners of the two scenarios. The degree of acceptance of MEC as an integral part of their learning process is slightly higher with learners in intensive courses than with those attending scenario 1 courses. The outcome shows that it would be beneficial for more face-to-face sessions to incorporate MEC. As a result, MVHS has relocated as many courses as possible into its own buildings to take advantage of multimedia equipment there and continues to do so whenever an opportunity arises.

Mapping learners' language and computing skills over time has been enlightening and has helped tailor introductions to the needs of individual groups. The same applies to training new teachers to use MEC in the classroom. At the beginning the focus was on a detailed description of the site; today training pinpoints specific features such as the dictionary. Training for teachers is no longer provided predominantly by MVHS. After the initial in-house training session MVHS refers its teachers to the online clinics MEC offers regularly and to the MEC teachers' blog. Learners and teachers alike have become more independent users over the past years.

MEC offers ample opportunities for usage inside the classroom. It is the institution's aim to provide MEC courses with classrooms equipped with a projector and a notebook as well as with internet access. Nevertheless, despite introducing MEC to its course offerings, MVHS does not intend to offer courses that rely solely on MEC. Pure distance learning in a language-learning context is not the institution's aim because the social aspect of learning within a group setting would be lost. Volkshochschulen have a duty towards society, their goal is to render a service to the inhabitants of their city and to make learning accessible to any adult learner regardless of age, sex, and learning background. Therefore, environmental and social aspects which stimulate learning such as interacting with other people and discovering the importance of peer support for successful learning are essential to fulfilling this goal, and a mere online course is not adequate in the context of Volkshochschulen.

However, Volkshochschulen cannot ignore trends in language learning and the society they are situated in. In order to attract people to learning they need to keep an open mind and to constantly seek to improve the service offered by choosing learning tools relevant to their target group, no matter whether it is a new coursebook series or a VLE. Incorporating MEC in the way described above has proved to be a good compromise and does not take away face-to-face teaching time. In addition, it is another step towards the ideal of autonomous learners being responsible for their own progress and taking the necessary steps to meet their needs. Combining the advantages of face-to-face learning with VLE opportunities such as MEC has proved a step in the right direction for this particular learning context.

References

Bax, S (2003) Call – Past, Present and Future. *System* 31: 13–28.

Hockly, N and Clandfield, L (2010) *Teaching Online: Tools and Techniques, Options and Opportunities*. Peaslake: Delta Publishing.

Sharma, P and Barret, B (2007) *Blended Learning: Using Technology in and Beyond the Language Classroom*. Oxford: Macmillan Education.

US Department of Education, Office of Planning, Evaluation, and Policy Development (2009) *Evaluation of Evidence-Based Practices in Online Learning: A Meta-Analysis and Review of Online Learning Studies*. Washington, DC.

Comments on Part 4

Brian Tomlinson

There is no doubt that General English courses in schools and tertiary institutions are unable to devote enough classroom time to facilitate the effective acquisition of a second language (Barker, 2011). General English learners typically do not get enough exposure to the language in use and they do not get enough opportunities to communicate nor to make discoveries about the language for themselves. As a result, only those learners with the motivation and opportunities to seek language experience outside the classroom manage to actually acquire communicative competence in the target language. Blended learning courses, as pointed out in the chapters in Part 4, are one solution to this problem, especially if they follow up work done face-to-face in order to provide online opportunities for exposure, discovery and use.

Another benefit pointed out in the chapters in Part 4, as well as in many other chapters in other parts of the book, is the potential which blended learning offers for independent learning. The online components can not only provide each learner with the possibility of recycling at their own speed and in their own time what they have already experienced, but can also offer extra opportunities for further learning both from course-specific materials and from materials from other web sources. In addition, such experiences can help the General English student to become less dependent on teachers and more self-reliant both during the course and in subsequent language learning experiences. Many contributors to the book stress though, that such independent experience can be enhanced by face-to-face preparation and follow up in class guided by a teacher.

Preparation for future courses is another potential benefit for General English students in relation to future academic or professional courses, which are becoming increasingly likely to be delivered using a blended learning approach. Most contributors to this book agree that unfamiliarity with blended learning can initially hold learners back and that the more familiar with, and enthusiastic about, blended learning the learners are at the beginning of a course the more likely they are to maximise their benefit from it. Therefore, if students have done a blended learning General English course, they are more likely to gain from a subsequent English for Academic Purposes (EAP) or English for Specific Purposes (ESP) course which uses a blended learning approach. This is a powerful argument but I would not like to see it used as the main reason for imposing blended learning in situations where it is inappropriate. I am thinking, for example, of poorly resourced secondary schools from which most students are unlikely to progress to tertiary or professional courses in English, and which are struggling to provide basic library resources. Even more inappropriate would be to impose blended learning on primary school learners of English because it is modern, fashionable and a preparation for future courses. Such learners are in no hurry to acquire English and they need to have social fun whilst learning it (Ghosn 2013; Rixon, 2013). I have seen seven-year olds enjoying playing with English, developing social skills and gaining positive attitudes towards English in classrooms without electricity in Vanuatu. I have also seen seven-year olds in resource-rich regions such as Hong Kong and Singapore sitting staring blankly at computer screens whilst working through tedious drills because their teachers have been told to use a blended learning approach in which a fixed amount of the course has to be delivered electronically.

What matters most when making a decision to use a blended learning approach is its contextual appropriacy and the likelihood that it will be more beneficial for the learners than a purely face-to-face or purely online course. What matters most also when deciding how many and which components to deliver online in a blended learning course is the likelihood of benefits for the learner. Fortunately all the contributors to the chapters in Part 4 (and to the other chapters in the book) appreciate these priorities and made such principled decisions in designing their courses. They obviously had in mind such pragmatic considerations as widening participation, increased retention, saving time and eventually saving money but their priority was to provide value to the learner in relation to the short- and long-term learning objectives of their courses. Perhaps the courses which achieved these objectives best were those which were able to provide the learners with informed choices. The ideal is the choice of whether or not to join a blended learning course plus the choices within a blended learning course of which components to do online and which to do face-to-face. Learners need information and sample experience before making such choices and maybe this should be the starting point for all blended learning courses.

References

Barker, D (2011) 'The role of unstructured learner interaction in the study of a foreign language', in Menon, S and Lourdunathan, J (eds) *Readings on ELT Materials IV*. Petaling Jaya: Pearson Longman, 50–71.

Ghosn, I (2013) 'Language learning for young learners', in Tomlinson, B (ed) *Applied Linguistics and Materials Development*. London: Bloomsbury, 61–74.

Rixon, S (2013) 'Materials for young learners', in Tomlinson, B (ed) *Developing Materials for Language Teaching*. Second edition. London: Bloomsbury.

Conclusion

Claire Whittaker

Conclusion

In this chapter a list of blended learning design-related questions will be presented for course designers to consider when developing their courses. The questions have arisen from the advice on blended learning course design that is presented in the literature and from the experiences of the authors in this publication, including my own. The questions will be presented under four headings (context; course design; learners, teachers and tutors; and evaluating and developing the blend), with examples drawn from the case studies providing suggested answers or guidance for each.

A principled approach to blended learning course design

The Introduction to this book concluded by stressing the importance of getting the blend 'right', whilst at the same time acknowledging that 'determining the right blend isn't easy or to be taken lightly' (Hofmann, 2001: 3). Despite these words of warning the literature provides us with a limited amount of advice on how to blend and simply suggests that we approach it in a principled way (Neumeier, 2005; Levy and Stockwell, 2006; Sharma, 2006; Mayes and de Freitas, 2007) because if we do not 'a course ... may be seen as an "eclectic" blending together of course components and can end up as rather a mish-mash' Sharma and Barrett (2007: 8). Therefore, to ensure that this does not happen and to achieve a principled approach to design in relation to English Language Teaching (ELT), Sharma and Barrett (2007) suggest that course designers follow four guiding principles (outlined in the Introduction). Also Dudeney and Hockly (2007) propose a list of questions under five headings (delivery mode; task design and materials; learners; teacher/tutors; assessment and evaluation), which acts as a checklist of key considerations, but does not suggest answers or provide examples from blends.

Although helpful to a degree, when I was redesigning the Bosnia and Herzegovina blend (Chapter 16) I did not find this advice detailed enough to guide me and moreover I was frustrated by the lack of descriptions of blends in ELT contexts. It was rather belatedly in the redesign process that I discovered Neumeier's (2005) framework of parameters, which originated from the design of a 33-hour job application course in a German university (see Table 1). The aim of this short course (73 per cent of which was taught online) was to teach the students how to apply for a job in English and the course's primary focus was on writing (CVs and covering letters) and to a lesser degree speaking (interviews). Neumeier (2005: 176) hoped this framework could act as the starting point for designing a blended learning environment for language teaching and learning, and that it would 'help course designers and practitioners to move closer to answering the initial question of which combination provides the optimal basis for language learning and teaching given the particular conditions at hand.'

Table 1: Neumeier's (2005) framework

Parameter	Individual descriptors
1. Mode (typically face-to-face and CALL)	• Focus on mode • Distribution of modes • Choice of modes
2. Model of integration	• Sequencing of individual modes • Level of integration
3. Distribution of learning content and objectives and assignment of purpose	• Parallel or isolated
4. Language teaching methods	• Use of teaching methods in each of the modes employed
5. Involvement of learning subjects (students, tutors and teachers)	• Interactional patterns: individual vs collaborative language learning activity • Variety of teacher and learner roles • Level of autonomy
6. Location	• Classroom, home, outdoors, computer room, institutional settings

Other authors recommend that course designers approach the design process in stages. Beetham and Sharpe (2007: 7), for example suggest a four-step process:

- Investigation – who are my users and what do they need? What principles and theories are relevant?
- Application – how should these principles be applied in this case?
- Representation or modelling – what solution will best meet users' needs?
- Iteration – how useful is it in practice? What changes are needed?

Another example is provided by Jones (2007) cited in Gruba and Hinkelman (2012: 30) who suggests that designers consider 'an educational programme as a three-part structure that operates on a micro, meso and macro level', within which the designer has different considerations at each level.

Faced with this range of differing advice on how to approach blended learning course design, which is not always as accessible, comprehensive or practical as it could be, it is challenging for a designer to know where to begin. With this in mind I will draw on the advice given in the literature, largely though not exclusively from Neumeier's (2005) framework, and supplement it with supporting evidence from the case studies in this book. In recognition of Beetham and Sharpe's (2007) stages I will organise it under four headings:

1. **Context**

2. **Course design**

3. **Learners, teachers and tutors**

4. **Evaluating and developing the blend.**

Under each of the above headings will be a series of questions that mirror the approach that Dudeney and Hockly (2007) took when considering the design of online learning courses. However, where it differs is that suggested answers and examples will be provided to the questions with information drawn from the case studies.

1. Context

The reasons for employing a blended approach are context dependent and therefore will differ from setting to setting, as will the eventual course design. Despite these differences, before embarking on a design or redesign process it is important to carefully consider the teaching and learning context, to identify the reasons for adopting a blended approach and to determine what the limiting factors to the design will be.

What are the reasons for blending?
In the Introduction the reasons stated in the literature for employing a blended learning approach in the corporate and academic sectors were outlined. With reference to higher education Graham et al., cited in Stracke (2007a: 59), condensed the lists down to three main ones: improved pedagogy, increased access/flexibility and increased cost effectiveness. In relation to ELT, Sharma and Barrett (2007) reiterate these reasons whilst adding convenience, and being able to work in your own time and at your own pace to the list. Also in relation to ELT, Hockly (2011) repeats flexibility as a reason for blending and adds a further two, namely learner expectations and Ministry of Education (or similar) directives.

So how do the reasons given in the case studies in this book, where they are explicitly stated, compare with those given in the literature by Graham et al. in Stracke (2007a), Sharma and Barrett (2007) and Hockly (2011)? Interestingly there is a high degree of agreement, in particular with regard to increased access/flexibility and improved pedagogy.

Table 2: Reasons for employing a blended approach

Reasons given in the literature for blending	Supporting statements from the case studies
Improved pedagogy	The main driver of change therefore to incorporating technology in our practice is pedagogic (Aborisade, Chapter 2)
Increased access/flexibility	Blended learning offered flexibility in the learning environment, which was crucial to our context (Pardo-Gonzalez, Chapter 4)
Increased cost effectiveness	Cost effective because the learners, military personnel, could be trained at their place of work (Whittaker, Chapter 16)
Convenience, working in your own time, at your own pace	Due to the size of China... participants had to travel anything up to 12 hours by train or bus to get to the face-to-face training (Bo and O'Hare, Chapter 7)
Learner expectations	One way of meeting the changing needs of learners was to shift some of the learning to a different medium and opt for an approach that includes technology (Krake, Chapter 20)

Reasons given in the literature for blending	Supporting statements from the case studies
Ministry of Education (or similar) directives	It was a vertical decision from the administration, but was favourably received by EFL instructors (Pardo-Gonzalez, Chapter 4)

In addition to these reasons, the authors provide the following rationale for incorporating technology into their courses: motivation, autonomy, collaboration, market reach and experiential learning (see Table 3). What is noteworthy is that the majority of the reasons given indicate that a blended approach is adopted for practical or financial reasons rather than pedagogic or because it is considered to be more effective than traditional face-to face teaching. Maybe the underlying assumption is that it is more effective, or as effective, but this is not articulated.

Table 3: Additional reasons for employing a blended approach

Additional reasons for blending	Supporting statements from the case studies
Motivation	Improve motivation by integrating the use of ICT into the learning process; develop skills for autonomous learning... (Sokol et al., Chapter 17)
Autonomy	... to foster more independent and collaborative learning... Fleet (Chapter 18)
Collaboration	To make the course more interactive and provide more opportunities for collaboration (Eydelman, Chapter 3)
Market reach	A blended model increases the market reach of the course, by appealing to teachers who may be concerned about embarking on a fully online training course (Dudeney and Hockly, Chapter 6)
Experiential learning	Participants will have the opportunity to experience the kinds of methods, approaches and problems that their students will encounter and this should help to give them deeper insights into the process and systems that should help to support the students they construct their own courses for (Peachey, Chapter 5)

In the Bosnia and Herzegovina blend that I describe in Chapter 16 there were four reasons (or drivers for change as we termed them) for redesigning our original blend:

1. a change in goal direction

2. the need for the long-term sustainability of the course (particularly in terms of cost)

3. user feedback (teachers and learners) on the shortcomings of the original blend

4. personal beliefs on how to design a blended learning course that would provide an optimal learning experience in our context.

These reasons influenced all the decisions that we took and helped ensure that the final blend was suitable for and therefore worked in our context. This supports Shaw and Igneri's (2006: 3) belief that there is '...no single optimal mix. What configuration is best can only be determined relative to whatever goals and constraints are presented in a given situation'.

What are the limiting factors?

Although not directly referred to in the case studies there are indications that this question was considered, especially when it came to choosing software. For example, Eydelman (Chapter 3) was constrained by costs; as there was no budget for software the choice was limited to what was free. In my context sustainability was a key consideration so the design had to reflect this and the courses had to be cost-effective to run and maintain once the financial support from stakeholders had been removed. This had an impact on the materials we chose and the number of computers that we purchased. There was also no internet connection in our language centres, which significantly limited the software that was available to us.

2. Course design

The second stage in the design process can commence once you have familiarised yourself with your context, determined what your reasons for blending are and identified the limiting factors. Armed with this information and having determined that a blended approach is appropriate for your context the design stage can begin and the next set of questions can be addressed.

What are you going to blend?

The definitions of blended learning in ELT given in the introductory chapter all refer to a combination of two modes, face-to-face and technology – computer assisted language learning (CALL), or online. These two modes were incorporated in all the blends described, with the authors choosing a variety of software for the online component, with Moodle being the most popular choice (see Table 4). The decision on what software to use was often influenced by the level of institutional infrastructure and support, so for example Gilbert (Chapter 1) chose Moodle because it was the University's official Course Management System and Pardo-Gonzalez (Chapter 4) chose Wimba because 'it suited our needs and allowed us to further develop the English program without becoming programmers or engineers.'

Table 4: Software choices for the technology mode

Software	Author and Chapter
Moodle	Gilbert (Chapter 1); Aborisade (Chapter 2); Peachey (Chapter 5); Dudeney and Hockly (Chapter 6); Bo and O'Hare (Chapter 7); Hirst and Godfrey (Chapter 9)
PBWorks	Eydelman (Chapter 3); Ingham (Chapter 15)
Wimba	Pardo-Gonzalez (Chapter 4)
A VLE e.g. Moodle or Blackboard	White et al. (Chapter 8)
Pearson Fronter	Douglas and Paton (Chapter 10)
Mobile phones	Kern (Chapter 11)
Posterous	Kern (Chapter 11)
Flash	Beagle and Davies (Chapter 12)
Email	Keedwell (Chapter 13); Russell (Chapter 14)
Screencasts	Russell (Chapter 14)
Reward CD-ROMs	Whittaker (Chapter 16)

Software	Author and Chapter
New Learners in the New Europe framework	Sokol et al. (Chapter 17)
Macmillan English Campus	Bilgin (Chapter 19); Krake (Chapter 20)
Internet	Gilbert (Chapter 1); Pardo-Gonzalez (Chapter 4)
Creating a site called New Generation (wiki)	Fleet (Chapter 18)

No reference is made to the possibility of a third mode, self-study, which played a significant role in the blend I describe in Chapter 16. We were fortunate enough to have well-equipped and resourced self-study rooms with numerous books, graded readers, language CDs and videos, etc., from the original blend so this mode remained an integral part of the design of the resultant blend. Therefore I would consider self-study as a potential third mode to the design of any blend.

What is the lead mode going to be?

In 16 of the 20 blends described in this publication, the face-to-face mode was the lead mode, which I find unsurprising as I believe that an existing face-to-face course is most commonly the starting point for developing a blend. The four blends that did not comply to this apparent norm are Peachey (Chapter 5) whose blend starts with eight weeks/80 hours of tutor-moderated online delivery; Dudeney and Hockly (Chapter 6) with a one-week online orientation period (although they state that the course 'officially starts with the face-to-face component') so I might have taken a liberty here suggesting it started with the online mode; Douglas and Paton (Chapter 10) and Beagle and Davies (Chapter 12), whose courses are both predominantly online with very little in the way of a face-to-face mode.

Which mode will set the pace?

Being able to work at your own pace is given as one of the reasons for blending, but at the same time on certain courses I believe the pace needs to be set in order to cover the syllabus in the allocated time. In the Bosnia and Herzegovina blend the lead mode was the face-to-face mode and this regulated the pacing of the course by ensuring that all the learners covered the core material at the same time in class before the follow-up extension activities that they could then complete at their own pace on the computers or in self-study.

How much time will the learners spend on each mode?

Most of the authors state the amount of time that was spent on the face-to-face mode, yet are less explicit about the time spent on the online mode. This could be because the learners determine how much time they dedicate to that mode, and/or because in some instances this mode is optional (Ingham, Chapter 15; Fleet, Chapter 18). The most information is provided by Peachey (Chapter 5), Dudeney and Hockly (Chapter 6) and White et al. (Chapter 8) as their blends are delivered in 'blocks' (my terminology) where one mode of delivery appears to be used for each block, rather than both modes being used simultaneously for teaching and learning purposes (see Table 5).

Table 5: Time spent on each mode

	Block One	Block Two	Block Three
Peachey, Chapter 5	Eight-week 80-hour tutor-moderated course delivered online using the Moodle LMS	Two-week 60-hour face-to-face workshop delivered at Bell Teacher Campus	Three-month 160-hour self-study element (optional)
Dudeney and Hockly, Chapter 6	One-week online orientation period in the course Moodle platform	50 hours face-to-face over two weeks	70 hours of the course are taken online in a VLE called Moodle
White et al., Chapter 8	Two weeks face-to-face	Six-months online tuition and assessment	One-week online simulation

When redesigning the blend in Bosnia and Herzegovina, a considerable amount of time was spent determining the distribution of modes especially given the intensity of the courses (12 weeks x 23 hours per week). As the learners saw the classroom sessions as the most productive part of the course, time spent on the face-to-face mode needed to outweigh or at least balance the amount of time spent on the other two modes (computer and self-study). At lower levels I believed that students needed more time in class than those at higher levels where the students should have developed a greater level of autonomy by completing the lower level courses (most worked their way through the levels) and therefore be able to cope with more time in the self-study and the computer modes. So at elementary level 61 per cent of the learners' time was spent in class, 19.5 per cent in self-study and on the computers whereas at upper-intermediate level 50 per cent of the learners' time was spent in class, 25 per cent in self-study and on the computers.

What will the pedagogic purpose of the modes be?
With reference to choice of mode (Neumeier, 2005), thought had clearly been given to determining what each mode would be used to teach. Typically the face-to-face mode was used to introduce the language or topic and the online mode was used to either extend the students working hours (Aborisade, Chapter 2); or aid and reinforce classroom instruction (Pardo-Gonzalez, Chapter 4); or to serve as the supplementary part to the face-to-face training (Bo and O'Hare, Chapter 7); or to check understanding (Hirst and Godfrey, Chapter 9); or for practice (Kern, Chapter 11); or to practise and revise the skills and points covered in the face-to-face lesson (Bilgin, Chapter 19); or to consolidate or review language (Krake, Chapter 20).

Neumeier (2005: 171) introduces the terms 'parallel' or 'isolated'. Parallel incorporation means that 'both modes are used for teaching and learning'. In practical terms this means that the language item may be presented in class and then practised using CALL, or vice versa. Isolated incorporation means that only one mode would be used, for example writing sessions could be restricted to the face-to-face mode. One consideration at this stage must surely be if 'the method of delivery is suited to the content' (Dudeney and Hockly, 2007: 140) and the example they give is that the use of email would be an inappropriate way to teach and practise pronunciation.

Keedwell's (Chapter 13) blend on soft skills training, report-writing and giving presentations, is a good example of isolated incorporation. In this design Keedwell acknowledges that 'the real-life differences between oral briefings and written reports suggested a face-to-face briefings course and an online writing course'. The design of Peachey (Chapter 5) and Dudeney and Hockly's (Chapter 6) blends also appear to reflect isolated incorporation. However, the majority of the blends seem to adopt a parallel approach, typically with the face-to-face mode presenting material and the online mode providing supplementary extension activities.

How will the modes be arranged in the timetable?
At its simplest the face-to-face sessions can be alternated with the computer sessions in the timetable. The way the modes in the Bosnia and Herzegovina blend were arranged is shown in Table 6. As the face-to-face element was the lead mode it started the cycle in the timetable that was then followed by the computer session and then the self-study session.

Table 6: Timetable for intermediate and upper-intermediate courses in Bosnia and Herzegovina

	Monday – Thursday	Friday
90 minutes	Class	Class
45 minutes	Computer	Computer
45 minutes	Self-study	Self-study
60 minutes	Class	
30 minutes	Computer	
30 minutes	Self-study	

What is the optimal length of time for each session?
When putting the timetable together we also considered the optimal length of time for each session, based on our beliefs as to what the maximum amount of productive time that could be spent on the computer or during self-study was. This also varied according to the learners' level and at elementary and pre-intermediate levels the classroom sessions were limited to an hour and computer and self-study to 30 minutes.

How many sessions will the timetable include?
Consideration was also given during the redesign process that I was involved in to the optimal number of sessions per mode per day on our intensive courses. As you can see in Table 6 at the higher levels there were six sessions per day, two in each mode, and this was a reduction from eight that were in the original blend. My rationale for reducing the number of sessions was to reduce the amount of movement, both physical and mental, between the modes and to 'streamline' the course design by reducing its complexity.

How much choice will the learners be given in the blend?
Neumeier (2005) suggests that the modes within a blend can either be 'optional' or 'obligatory'. More often than not the face-to-face mode is obligatory, as are synchronous online sessions, but other sub-modes of CALL can be presented

as being optional, which allows the student a degree of flexibility and autonomy. A number of the authors considered this in the design of their blends, for example, Ingham (Chapter 15) states, 'The face-to-face aspects of the course were compulsory …. In contrast, contributing to wiki was optional as it was experimental.' Hirst and Godfrey (Chapter 9) also incorporated optional tasks into their blend to '[promote] participant interaction and self-responsibility'.

However, difficulties were encountered in a couple of designs from either making the modes compulsory or optional. Bilgin (Chapter 19) found that 'the compulsory use of the online program was one of the reasons for student discontent'. Whilst the optional component of using web-based resources in Fleet's (Chapter 18) blend failed because '… students regarded the online material as a course extension rather than an integral part. This expectation may be a fundamental reason why collective online interaction was not extensive. Although there had been logical reasons for making participation voluntary, had online interaction been compulsory, greater participation would have undoubtedly occurred'.

How will the modes complement each other?
One of the reasons that students leave blended learning courses according to Stracke (2007a: 57) is due to 'a perceived lack of support and connection/ complementarity between the f2f and computer-assisted components of the "blend"….' This is also one of Sharma and Barrett's guiding principles for blended learning course design: 'use technology to complement and enhance F2F teaching' (2007: 13–14). In the blend I redesigned this was one of my guiding principles and to achieve it we linked the content of the three modes to a relatively high degree either by grammar, vocabulary or topic. For example, the REWARD (Greenall, 2002) software that was used in the computer mode was grammatically linked to the General English coursebooks *Headway* (Soars and Soars, 2006) and *Going for Gold* (Acklam and Crace, 2003) that were used in the face-to-face mode. This complementarity aspect was also widely referred to in the case studies, with Fleet (Chapter 18) stating 'There should therefore be a definite topic and skills link between class-based and online work, which learners need to be made aware of.'

What methodology will the blend employ?
According to Levy, cited in Neumeier (2005: 172), CALL methodology is 'predominantly expressed through the design of the computer programme' and this can result in it being somewhat limited and repetitive. In the face-to-face mode, however, it is the teacher who determines the methodology and the choices open to them are far greater. The methodology of each of the modes should therefore be considered, with variety being the aim when designing a blended learning course so as to appeal to as many learning styles as possible. Reference is made in the case studies to a wide range of learning theories (such as behaviourism, connectivism and constructivism), and language teaching approaches and methods (see Table 7).

Table 7: Learning theories, language teaching methods and approaches

Learning theories and language teaching approaches and methods	Author/Chapter
A student-centred, experiential learning approach to instruction framed the design	Gilbert, Chapter 1
Project-based learning approach	Gilbert, Chapter 1
...a combination of process and product approaches with some elements of genre approach to writing	Eydelman, Chapter 3
Different aspects of peer-editing pedagogy	Eydelman, Chapter 3
Student/learner centred approach	Gilbert, Chapter 1; Ingham, Chapter 15; Fleet, Chapter 18; Pardo-Gonzalez, Chapter 4; Eydelman, Chapter 3; Douglas and Paton, Chapter 10; Bilgin, Chapter 19
Situative perspective of learning	Kern, Chapter 11; Beagle and Davies, Chapter 12
Face-to-face component uses a communicative training approach	Dudeney and Hockly, Chapter 6; Whittaker, Chapter 16
Skill theory view of learning	Bo and O'Hare, Chapter 7
Thinking approach to language teaching and learning	Sokol et al., Chapter 17
A task-based approach	Russell, Chapter 14
A 'flipped' approach	Peachey, Chapter 5
A form of 'loop input', a style of experiential teacher training process that involves an alignment of the process and content of learning	Peachey, Chapter 5
Reflective learning	Bo and O'Hare, Chapter 7
Independent, self-paced study	Beagle and Davies, Chapter 12
Behaviourist approach	Whittaker, Chapter 16
Problem-based approach	Whittaker, Chapter 16
Constructivist/constructivism	Gilbert, Chapter 1; Whittaker, Chapter 16
Socio-constructivism/ socio-constructivist approach	Hirst and Godfrey, Chapter 9; Douglas and Paton, Chapter 10; Ingham, Chapter 15
Connectivist/connectivism	Peachey, Chapter 5
Transmission approach	Bo and O'Hare, Chapter 7

Where will the course take place?
Blended learning means that learning is no longer restricted to the classroom and can take place in a wide range of locations at times that are convenient to the learner. However, Neumeier (2005) believes that familiarity with a learning environment, or the ability to become familiar with it, is vital for learning to take place. It is therefore advisable when determining locations to view them from the student's perspective and maybe to 'anchor' one of the modes to a location to generate a feeling of stability. Initially this seems like a less valuable consideration although I can relate to the idea that you need to be familiar with an environment for learning to take place, as there are always places where I simply cannot study as I do not associate them with that activity.

We were fortunate in Bosnia and Herzegovina to be able to provide intensive English courses where all three modes took place in one location, i.e. the classroom was next door to the computer room that was next door to the self-study room, so learners simply rotated between the three. Anchoring all the modes to one location is atypical though and in the vast majority of the case studies the face-to-face mode took place in a classroom, whereas the online element took place wherever the learner chose to study, which presumably was at home although this was only clearly stated in four case studies (Eydelman, Chapter 3; Pardo-Gonzalez, Chapter 4, Kern, Chapter 11, Krake, Chapter 20). In some instances of course the online work had to be carried out at home due to a lack of facilities at the school, university etc., although six authors do mention having access to a language laboratory (Eydelman, Chapter 3; Gilbert, Chapter 1; Pardo-Gonzalez, Chapter 4; Whittaker, Chapter 16; Bilgin, Chapter 19 and Krake, Chapter 20).

How do I design for a 'suite of courses'?
Most of the blends described in this publication refer to short courses and indeed Neumeier's (2005) framework arose from a 33-hour course. However, a large number of the learners who attended our courses in Bosnia and Herzegovina worked their way through the levels, often from elementary upwards to upper-intermediate, which is typical in many language schools I believe. With this in mind the content and design of the Bosnia and Herzegovina blend altered to realise the learners increased abilities as language learners, to cater for their needs, to maintain their interest and to fulfil our aims (Whittaker, Chapter 16). Despite these changes to the content and design of the blend there was still a high degree of 'horizontal integration' where there is 'some continuity in learning tools across programs and courses as [this] is clearly advantageous from the student's point of view' (Levy and Stockwell, 2006: 30). This continuity manifested itself in the structure of the timetable, the use of a coursebook in class, CD-ROMs in the computer session and the types of tasks in the self-study mode.

3. Learners and teachers/tutors

As the learners, teachers and tutors play such a key role in any blend I believe they warrant their own section. It is important to note that the teachers and tutors may need as much support in the move towards a blended approach as their learners. It may be the case that the teachers and tutors lack the computer skills their learners possess, and that this can be a daunting prospect for many and may act as a barrier to change.

Who will be involved in the design process?
The instructors and teachers were involved in every stage of the redesign process in Bosnia and Herzegovina (Chapter 16) as I felt it was vital to have their input in the decision-making process to create a sense of ownership. Moreover, they attended training sessions when necessary to prepare them for the changes in advance, for example familiarising them with new coursebooks before they were introduced. This ensured to a large extent that we had buy-in from them as ultimately as the end users they would be responsible for the success and the longevity of the blend.

What will the interactional patterns be?

Individual, pair and group work are all standard forms of communication in the face-to-face mode of most courses, and they can also be found in the computer mode too. Neumeier (2005) identifies 11 interactional patterns for the CALL mode, which are grouped under three headings:

- interaction **through** computers/networks (synchronous/asynchronous) e.g. student to student, teacher/tutor to student
- interaction **with** computers networks, e.g. student and teacher/tutor to computer
- interaction **at** computers/networks e.g. student and student in collaboration at the computer.

It is easy for a blended learning course designer to underestimate the number of interactional patterns that working with technology presents, and I will be the first to acknowledge that in the Bosnia and Herzegovina blend I did. One of the mistakes I made during the redesign process was to remove the need for students to share computers and therefore work together by providing them with one computer each. What I believed to be an improvement to the design removed the need for students to work collaboratively, which to quote Beatty 'is among the most useful ways in which learners acquire language at the computer' (2003: 99). Keedwell (Chapter 13) also recognised a design flaw in relation to interaction patterns in his blend: 'I had initially visualised the course as a two-way dialogue between trainer and trainee and neglected the critical element of peer interaction.'

Other authors recognised different interaction patterns in their design, with Eydelman (Chapter 3) saying '...the design of this course allows for a variety of interaction patterns from those initiated by the teacher to those initiated by the student(s).' However, it was the third interaction pattern 'at the computer' that was most commonly referred to in the case studies with the key word being 'collaboration'. With the exception of four authors the rest referred to collaboration in their case studies in a number of different ways, such as:

- a key consideration in task design (White et al., Chapter 8)
- a way to encourage participation (Ingham, Chapter 15)
- a way to foster a socio-constructivist approach (Douglas and Paton, Chapter 10)
- a way for students to learn from each other and improve their answers (Ingham, Chapter 15; Hirst and Godfrey, Chapter 9).

What will the learners and teachers/tutors roles be?

Within any learning environment teachers and learners alike adopt different roles at different times, which the use of technology further affects. This leads Neumeier (2005) to speculate that with the introduction of CALL the learners are exposed to a wider variety of roles than if the course were simply face-to-face. For teachers/tutors it also means differing roles between the modes, i.e. classroom teacher and online tutor.

The change in roles was recognised in a number of the case studies, with Aborisade (Chapter 2) summing it up by stating 'We have learned that teacher roles are changing, as learners' engagement is enhanced by the creation of new learning environments and as they take more decisions in the process.' This change in role was also questioned and the challenges the new roles presented recognised: 'As student participation increased and the wiki evolved as a result, I began to question the nature and extent of my online involvement. The challenge was to balance my presence on the site with the learner's contributions and decide how much I was going to correct or ignore mistakes and to advise on content.' Ingham (Chapter 15).

Likening the teacher's role to that of a facilitator was the most common comparison (White et al., Chapter 8; Peachey, Chapter 5; Fleet, Chapter 18; Whittaker, Chapter 16). However, references were also made to the teacher acting as an intermediary (Krake, Chapter 20) and as a mediator in discussions (White et al., Chapter 8). Peachey (Chapter 5) outlines three roles that differ according to the mode, that of a moderator in the initial online element; facilitator as well as technical support in the face-to-face element; and in the third, online element of the course, a more traditional role.

The change in the teacher/tutors role can mean that it becomes very time-consuming 'as many participants feel that an online tutor is available 24/7 and they do not have the limitations of "class time" to restrict their access to their tutor' Peachey (Chapter 5). An increase in the teacher's workload was also noted by Aborisade (Chapter 2), Dudeney and Hockly (Chapter 6) and Hirst and Godfrey (Chapter 9).

Changes to the learners' role were also recognised in the case studies, although less was written on this subject. What was acknowledged was that a blended course leads to a shift towards a more learner-centred approach (Eydelman, Chapter 3; Pardo-Gonzalez, Chapter 4) in which learners play a more active role as they have to take more decisions (Aborisade, Chapter 2). This does not suit all the learners though and can result in disappointment as Russell (Chapter 14) noted 'In v5 we hoped that the learners would lead and instigate conversations about the feedback given, and to talk about issues more than they had previously in direct email contact with their tutors. However, the communication between participants was not as voluminous as had been hoped, and the tendency for quite static, trainer – participant – trainer moves continued.' Overall, as Ingham (Chapter 15) recognised, a blended learning course and the type of activities it entails leads to a shift in the balance of power as 'any user can view and edit the contributions of others so peers as well as the teacher can correct mistakes or give feedback.'

What level of autonomy will be expected from learners?
Level of autonomy is a particularly important aspect of blended courses because their design means that students have to take on different degrees of responsibility in the different modes. In line with this, they will 'have to know when to take action and when [to] hand over responsibility' along with being 'able to handle different degrees of responsibility over the process and content of learning' (Neumeier, 2005: 175).

There were different expectations from the blends regarding autonomy. Gilbert (Chapter 1) expected her course 'to help learners gain autonomous strategies for evaluating the credibility of online information'; Bilgin (Chapter 19) believed that 'Student interaction and collaboration... would foster autonomy and learning';

Whittaker (Chapter 16) believed that the 'self-study mode promoted a type of autonomous learning where the primary objective was that learners were "engaged in self-directed work" (Littlewood 1996: 433)'; Sokol et al. (Chapter 17) adopted a blended approach to 'develop skills for autonomous learning' and Peachey (Chapter 5) believed that the tasks they used '[helped] to develop and support participants' autonomous learning through video based instruction in the use of technology.'

It is necessary to add a note of caution because as Benson (2001), cited in Stracke (2007b: 101), states in relation to CALL and autonomous learning 'there is no necessary relationship between self-instruction and the development of autonomy.' Studies by Stracke (2007b) and Corder and Waller (2007) into the use of CALL software packages for teaching and learning and student autonomy in universities conclude that CALL does not automatically result in autonomous learning. They also conclude by stressing the importance of the role the teacher plays in the process of fostering autonomy.

How will learners be supported in the transition to a blended approach?
Based on my experience I believe that careful consideration needs to be given to the type of learner and the teaching and learning environment that they are familiar with when determining the degree of autonomy expected from them in blends. In Bosnia and Herzegovina the military officers had experienced a predominantly teacher-centred, transmission approach to education, so expecting a high degree of autonomy from the outset on our courses would have been inappropriate. In recognition of this, the learners were guided through the computer and self-study sessions with easy-to-follow study paths that essentially told them what to study when. Other authors in this publication also recognise the need for such scaffolding (Gilbert, Chapter 1; Dudeney and Hockly, Chapter 6; Douglas and Paton, Chapter 10; Ingham, Chapter 15; Sokol et al., Chapter 17; Fleet, Chapter 18). Fleet (Chapter 18) sums this up by saying, 'If students have limited online learning experience, it is advisable to scaffold their participation by initially making involvement a course necessity and providing guided tasks.'

What is repeatedly mentioned in the case studies is the importance of an introductory session at the beginning of the course primarily to familiarise the learners with the blended approach and the type of tasks that they will encounter. Keedwell (Chapter 13) sums this up by stating that 'B-learning is still an unfamiliar concept to many: the course described here included an introductory f2f session to B-learning in which principles were explained and discussed and this I think is essential.'

How will the teachers/tutors be supported in the transition to a blended approach?
The authors of the case studies appear to not only be the course designers, but also the teachers/tutors too, which implies an interest in technology and experience in using, or at least a willingness to use it for teaching and learning purposes. Russell (Chapter 14) noted that 'the teachers who worked on this project were the ones who were most able to grasp this use of IT, and could see how this could support language learning', but this was not always the case and Pardo-Gonzalez (Chapter 4) refers to tutors with no experience of using technology at all. Moreover, even those

with a willingness to use technology did not always change their teaching styles and White et al. (Chapter 8) recognised a 'diversity of experience of blended learning pedagogy, expectations and commitment' amongst trainers. Training and support for teachers/tutors is therefore as crucial as it is for learners and needs to be considered in the design process.

What will the ratio of learners to teachers/tutors be?
Dudeney and Hockly (2007: 141) include this question in their list for online course designers, possibly to account for the increase in the teacher/tutor workload that has been mentioned. In Chapter 6 they address this question and inform us that a tutor is assigned 6–10 participants and no more to accommodate the increased workload and the additional one-to-one support. The value of asking this question during the design stage is highlighted in Aborisade's case study (Chapter 2) in which 'teachers are unable to respond to all questions and posts because of large numbers'.

4. Evaluating and developing the blend

Once the course has been designed and is underway it will need to be evaluated as according to Beetham and Sharpe (2007: 8) 'effective designs will evolve only through cycles of practice, evaluation and reflection'.

How will the blend be evaluated?
There are a number of areas of a blend that can be evaluated such as the choice of software and materials, the balance of time spend in each mode, the learners and teachers/tutors' attitudes towards the blend, and its effectiveness in terms of teaching and learning. Evaluations were referred to in the case studies, for example Aborisade (Chapter 2) used a questionnaire to collect feedback on six aspects of the course; Fleet (Chapter 8) collected information 'through teacher reflection, student feedback from post-course questionnaires and informal comments throughout the project' and Bilgin (Chapter 19) explored the effects of Macmillan English Campus on her students' achievement. The designer will therefore need to determine what aspects of the blend to evaluate, at what stage of the course and how, and in my experience this will often be an ongoing process.

How will the blend evolve?
The redesign process that I undertook in Bosnia and Herzegovina took three years because it employed an iterative approach to the redesign process in that small changes were made, implemented, then evaluated before moving onto the next one. Pardo-Gonzalez (Chapter 4) also views blended learning courses design as a constant process and advises designers that it 'needs to be seen as an ongoing and gradual process in which the course evolves. It is not a final product.' This can be a lengthy process as Sharpe and Oliver (2007: 49) state that 'as many as three of four iterations of course design, development and implementation may be needed to complete the transition from traditional to blended e-learning course'. Russell's description of the evolution of his blend in Chapter 14 from V1 in 2004 to V5 in 2010 clearly demonstrates this iterative approach and gives some indication as to what a lengthy process it can be.

Summary

This chapter draws on the literature on blended learning course design in ELT and on the authors' experiences as course designers to provide a list of user-friendly design-related questions under the four headings (context; course design; learners, teachers and tutors; and evaluating and developing the blend) along with suggested answers and examples for other designers to consider (see Appendix 1). The questions are not presented as a definitive list to blended learning course designers, but rather as a guide that will help them determine what blend would be most effective in their particular contexts.

There were very few references to the literature on blended learning course design in the case studies, which leads me to conclude that the authors learned mainly by experience and that their blends evolved over time to become more appropriate and effective for their learners. This being said, it is worth noting that collectively the case studies provided suggested answers and examples for every question that arose from the literature. This would seem to affirm the usefulness and validity of the advice that it provides.

Conclusion

In the preface I described my frustration as a blended learning course designer at the lack of advice on the principles and practicalities of blended learning course design (above lesson level), and lack of descriptions or studies of blends in ELT contexts. I believe that this publication goes some way to addressing those concerns as not only does it provide detailed descriptions of blends from a number of contexts, but it also outlines the lessons the authors learned whilst designing them and offers constructive advice. To quote Sharpe and Oliver (2007: 41) 'the process of course design is complicated and often remains a private, tacit process'. It is hoped that this publication goes some way to countering this.

References

Acklam, R and Crace, A (2003) *Going for Gold Intermediate Coursebook*. Harlow: Pearson Longman.

Beatty, K (2003) *Teaching & Researching Computer-Assisted Language Learning*. Harlow: Pearson Education.

Beetham, H and Sharpe, R (2007) 'An introduction to rethinking pedagogy for a digital age', in Beetham, H and Sharpe, R (eds) *Rethinking Pedagogy for a Digital Age*. Abingdon, Oxon: Routledge, 1–10.

Corder, D and Waller, G (2007) 'Using a CALL package as a platform to develop effective language learning strategies and facilitate autonomous learning', in Miller, L (ed) *Autonomy in the Classroom 9*. Dublin: Authentik Language Learning Resources Ltd., 7–26.

Dudeney, G and Hockly, N (2007) *How to... Teach English with Technology.* Harlow: Pearson Education Limited.

Greenall, S (2002) *Reward CD-ROM.* Oxford: MacMillan Education.

Gruba, P and Hinkelman, D (2012) *Blended Technologies in Second Language Classrooms.* Basingstoke: Palgrave Macmillan.

Hockly, N (2011) Five things you always wanted to know about blended learning (but were afraid to ask). *English Teaching Professional* 75: 58.

Hofmann, J (2001) *Blended Learning Case Study.* Available online at www.pttmedia.com/newmedia_knowhow/KnowHow_Design/Instructional%20Design/iLive/Blended%20Learning%20Case%20Study.htm

Levy, M and Stockwell, G (2006) *CALL Dimensions. Options and Issues in Computer-Assisted Language Learning.* New York, USA: Lawrence Erlbaum Associates.

Littlewood, W (1996) Autonomy: An anatomy and a framework. *System* 24/4: 427–435.

Mayes, T and de Freitas, S (2007) 'Learning and e-learning: the role of theory', in Beetham, H and Sharpe, R (ed) *Rethinking Pedagogy for a Digital Age.* Abingdon, Oxon: Routledge, 13–25.

Neumeier, P (2005) A closer look at blended learning – parameters for designing a blended learning environment for language teaching and learning. *ReCALL* 17/2: 163–178.

Sharma, P (2006) Technical support. *EL Gazette*, 315, March, 17.

Sharma, P and Barrett, B (2007) *Blended Learning.* Oxford: Macmillan.

Sharpe, R and Oliver, M (2007) 'Designing courses for e-learning', in Beetham, H and Sharpe, R (ed). *Rethinking Pedagogy for a Digital Age.* Abingdon, Oxon: Routledge, 41–51.

Shaw, S and Igneri, N (2006) *Effectively Implementing a Blended Learning Approach.* Available online at http://wvuheducation.com/LinkClick.aspx?fileticket=7Hhk4Bw4Iyg%3D&tabid=148

Soars, L and Soars, J (2006) *New Headway: Elementary Third Edition: Students' Book.* Oxford: Oxford University Press.

Stracke, E (2007a) A road to understanding: A qualitative study into why learners drop out of a blended language learning (BLL) environment. *ReCALL*,19/1: 57–78.

Stracke, E (2007b) 'Conflicting voices: blended learning in a German university foreign language classroom', in Miller, L (ed). *Autonomy in the Classroom 9.* Dublin: Authentik Language Learning Resources Ltd., 85–103.

Appendix 1 – Questions for blended learning course designers

1. Context

What are the reasons for blending?

What are the limiting factors?

2. Course design

What are you going to blend?

What is the lead mode going to be?

Which mode will set the pace?

How much time will the learners spend on each mode?

What will the pedagogic purpose of the modes be?

How will the modes be arranged in the timetable?

What is the optimal length of time for each session?

How many sessions will the timetable include?

How much choice will the learners be given in the blend?

How will the modes complement each other?

What methodology will the blend employ?

Where will the course take place?

How do I design for a 'suite of courses'?

3. Learners and teachers/tutors

Who will be involved in the design process?

What will the interactional patterns be?

What will the learners and teachers/tutors roles be?

What level of autonomy will be expected from learners?

How will learners be supported in the transition to a blended approach?

How will the teachers/tutors be supported in the transition to a blended approach?

What will the ratio of learners to teachers/tutors be?

4. Evaluating and developing the blend

How will the blend be evaluated?

How will the blend evolve?

Contributors

Contributors

Peter Aborisade lectures in English for Academic Purposes (EAP) at the Federal University of Technology Akure (FUTA), Nigeria. He specialises in English and Communication, with over 28 years of teaching experience across educational levels. In 2007 he received the Commonwealth Academic Fellowship and visited the University of Sussex, UK as Senior Research Fellow, where he took up the challenge of integrating technology into the language teaching curriculum. His current area of research and practice is the integration of learning technologies into the curriculum; he is heading a Blended Learning Group working on using Moodle as a university-wide VLE platform. FUTA is one of few universities in Nigeria delivering courses via a VLE. He has presented recently in the area of blended learning, at Durham University, UK (April, 2007), E-Learning Africa, Dakar, Senegal (2009), Lusaka, Zambia (2010), Cardiff, UK (April, 2009), University of Toronto, Canada (July, 2009), iPED Coventry, UK (2010) and SOLSTICE Edge Hill, UK (2012).

Lynda Beagle is currently Deputy Director at RMIT English Worldwide (REW) in Melbourne. She has worked in the field of English Language Teaching for more than 25 years. Her roles have included English language teacher, CELTA teacher trainer, Academic Manager and Director of Studies. She has an MA in Applied Linguistics and a Graduate Certificate in Flexible Learning. She has been using technology in language teaching since the 1990s and is now interested in how internet-based technologies can be used to enhance second language acquisition.

Hatice Bilgin graduated from Bogazici University in 2005. She has been teaching English to Turkish university preparatory programme students since then. She completed her MA in Bogazici University Foreign Language Education Department in 2010. She was a Fulbright foreign language teaching assistant at Portland State University in the 2011–12 academic year. She taught Turkish as a foreign language there. She is interested in the use of technology in language learning and teaching. She conducted a research project on the effects of different online programmes on student achievement and opinions in Istanbul Technical University School of Foreign Languages in the 2009–10 academic year.

Xu Bo has an MA degree in French linguistics and has been working as project lead since July 2010, for 'Communicative Assessment – Development of Testing Skills' in China. She has been actively involved in co-ordination with the British Council's Global Product Team, the UK trainers and Chinese partners for content revision and project management. From an academic perspective, her main contribution to this project is to build stronger links to the local teaching and testing context.

Graeme Davies has worked in the English Language Teaching field for more than 15 years and was Curriculum Unit Aviation Co-ordinator at RMIT English Worldwide (REW) until he retired in 2012. Graeme joined REW's Aviation Curriculum Writing Team in 2006 when the International Civil Aviation Organisation (ICAO) introduced language proficiency requirements for aviation personnel. He was involved in the writing of print-based General English teaching materials to meet this new industry requirement. His subsequent experience in writing computer-delivered aviation language proficiency tests brought an understanding of the learning and teaching requirements of online delivery. Graeme has successfully integrated this knowledge into REW's Beyond Level 4 blended learning products.

Jacqueline Douglas has been an English language teacher since 1997, working in the UK, Turkey, Spain and Bolivia. She is also an experienced teacher trainer and has delivered courses in the UK, China, Thailand, Bolivia, Peru and Saudi Arabia. She has worked as a CELTA tutor for eight years, delivering courses at International House, London. Additionally she is a CELTA Assessor. Among various in-house materials development projects at IH London, Jacqueline helped to write the Cambridge CELTA Online. She also taught demonstration lessons for the online input and worked as Teaching Practice Tutor on the Pilot Course in 2011. She has recently completed an MA with Norwich Institute of Language Education, focusing on Learner Autonomy and Materials Development.

Gavin Dudeney is Director of Technology of The Consultants-E, an online teacher training and development consultancy. He has been involved in English as a Foreign Language (EFL) teaching and teacher training since 1989, and has (co-)authored a number of methodology books on ICT in English Language Teaching (ELT) including *The Internet & The Language Classroom, How to Teach English with Technology*, and most recently *Digital Literacies* (2013). He is currently working on a book about mobile learning, with Nicky Hockly.

Natalya Eydelman has been teaching English for about 20 years but still finds teaching exciting and challenging. Throughout her career she has taught a variety of courses, with academic writing and ICT for ELT Methods courses among her favourites. For several years now she has been teaching them as blends. She has taught a number of INSET courses devoted to the use of technology in the classroom in face-to-face and blended modes. Natalya has also worked as a moderator of an online course ICT in ELT for the British Council. In 2010 she completed a course of study in the master's programme in TESOL and ICT at the University of Leeds on a Hornby Trust Scholarship. Her thesis is devoted to the study of affordances and limitations of asynchronous tools such as blogs and wikis for peer-editing. She has presented the results of her research at a number of national and international conferences, including IATEFL (2010–12). Presentations included *Peer commentary made better* (2012), *Peer-editing using MS Word, blogs, and wikis: how to make the most of them?* (2011), and *Using Writing Portfolios in Academic Writing Courses* (2010).

Liz Fleet is a teacher trainer and English teacher. At the time of this case study, she worked for the British Council as an Assistant Programme Manager at Al Azhar English Training Centre in Cairo. She currently works at Liaoning University in China. She specialises in ICT integration and has a master's degree in Digital Technologies Communication and Education. She has wide experience of using online learning platforms in ELT and has designed various wiki-blended courses, in relation to general and academic English.

Jody Gilbert taught in post-secondary contexts in China for two years, and has taught EAP in Canada for 12 years. He has special interests in content-based instruction, reading instruction, and web-based tools for enhanced language learning, and uses the Moodle VLE to support blended course projects including collaborative vocabulary journals, project-based collaborative reports, and pre-arrival courses for short-term university exchange groups. Jody currently works as a Programme Co-ordinator at Bow Valley College in Calgary, Canada. Contact: jgilbert@bowvalleycollege.ca.

Tom Godfrey has worked as an EFL teacher and teacher trainer in a variety of countries. He is Director of International Training Institute (ITI), which is a centre for teacher training and development and an ELT consultancy in Istanbul. He currently runs teacher-training courses leading to the Cambridge ESOL qualifications. He is an ELT consultant specialising in Curriculum Design and Teacher Education. He completed his EdD at Exeter University, UK. He is the founder of Speech Bubbles, which is a theatre company that performs to raise money for charities that support education and children in Turkey.

Stephen Heap is a Director of Studies at the Institute of Continuing and TESOL Education at the University of Queensland, and has been the Brisbane co-ordinator of the International Diploma in Language Teaching Management since 2001. He has an MA from the University of Birmingham as well as the IDLTM, and has carried out a variety of teaching, teacher training, management and TESOL consultancy-related work from Britain to Brunei, Malta to Malaysia, and from Nigeria to North Korea.

Sally Hirst works as Director of DELTA training at ITI, Istanbul. She has taught language in a variety of contexts and specialises in Business English. She has trained on CELTA, ICELT and DELTA courses. She tutors online for the Distance DELTA. She has an MSc in TESOL from Aston University, UK.

Andy Hockley is a freelance educational management consultant and teacher trainer based in deepest Transylvania. After 15 years of teaching English worldwide, he moved into management and worked as an educational project manager at the School for International Training (USA), including participating in the curriculum working party that developed the International Diploma in Language Teaching Management (IDLTM). He has been co-ordinating and training on the IDLTM since its inception in 2001. He is co-author, with Ron White, of *From Teacher to Manager* (CUP, 2008).

Nicky Hockly is Director of Pedagogy of The Consultants-E, an online teacher training and development consultancy. She has been involved in EFL teaching and teacher training since 1987, and has co-authored a number of methodology books on ICT in ELT including *How to Teach English with Technology, Teaching Online* and most recently *Digital Literacies* (2013). She has published an e-book, *Webinars: A Cookbook for Educators* (the-round.com), and is currently working on a book about mobile learning with Gavin Dudeney. She maintains a professional blog, E-moderation Station, at www.emoderationskills.com.

Louise Ingham has taught English to Speakers of Other Languages since 2004 in the further education sector in the UK. Courses have included all levels of Cambridge Skills for Life and Cambridge main suite exams. Additionally, she has designed and delivered ESOL courses without traditional exams to meet specific local needs. Her interest in blended learning came about through participation in a TESOL MA at the University of Manchester. She was using existing free web-based resources in her teaching and had some experience of Moodle. However, the Manchester TESOL MA involved experiential learning using Blackboard, wiki and Moodle, and introduced her to ELT literature and the possibilities of educational technologies from the perspective of learners and teachers. The 'Blended Learning Course Design' and 'Teaching and Learning Online' modules were particularly influential.

Andy Keedwell has been working as an English language teacher, trainer, trainer-trainer and manager since 1986, and has worked in a variety of locations including East Africa, the South Caucasus, the Middle East and South East Asia. He has been involved specifically with blended and online learning in Sudan, Armenia and Ethiopia. He is currently Head of Training at the British Council in Afghanistan and is particularly interested in facilitating skills sharing amongst teachers, enabling teachers to train others and English for the world of work.

Nergiz Kern is a teacher with a Diploma in English Language Teaching to Adults. She has taught academic, general, business and technical English in different countries for 13 years. Nergiz also has considerable experience in teaching and teacher education in online 3D virtual worlds. Currently, she is in the final stages of an MA in Educational Technology and TESOL at the University of Manchester and teaches academic English in Turkey and the UK. Her interests are integrating technology meaningfully in language and teacher education, developing and teaching English for specific purposes (ESP) courses, creating multimedia materials, blended learning, teacher education, and learner and teacher autonomy.

Astrid Krake has been involved in aspects of English Language Teaching for 20 years. After working as an editor for a publishing company she was the Head of English at the Munich Volkshochschule (2002–11). In 2004 she also became Head of Languages at the same institution. She recently accepted the position of Head of the Language Centre at the University of Bamberg/Germany. In addition to her contracted positions Astrid has been a teacher of English as a Foreign Language at a number of adult education institutions. She is interested in finding opportunities to enhance the language-learning experience by means of technology.

Keith O'Hare has a CELTA and Trinity TESOL diploma and has been working in the world of ELT as trainer and consultant for over 15 years. He presently works in the British Council in China as head of English Teacher Training programmes and is responsible for setting up partnerships with provincial governments with a view to designing and delivering teacher training projects in China. He is one of the leaders on the quality control of the Communicative Assessment project.

Juanita Pardo-González (BA Hons in Modern Languages, Universidad de los Andes) is an Assistant Professor in the Departamento de Lenguajes y Estudios Socioculturales at Universidad de los Andes. She has undertaken research studies at Lancaster University on Corpus Linguistics. She is a Hornby Scholar and has an MA in ELT and Multimedia from Warwick University (2005). Her current research interests are related to pronunciation, conscious language learning, and technology in teaching. She is interested in incorporating language and technology into her teaching. She is designing a blended course for instructors to help them incorporate blended learning into the teaching of other foreign languages in her Department.

Colin Paton has been working in the e-learning field since 1998. He started his career as an EFL teacher and teacher trainer in the early 1990s and spent 15 years working in Latin America. In 1998 he founded one of the first online language schools (Cultura Inglesa Online) and subsequently developed a number of online and blended teacher training courses for teachers in Latin America. Since returning to the UK in 2005, Colin worked at the Social Care Institute for Excellence designing and leading national fully online and blended programmes for nurses and social care professionals. He also helped found the first online television channel for social care professionals. Since April 2011 he has been Head of eLearning at International House London, responsible for all online and blended programmes including the CELTA Online.

Nik Peachey is a leading technology consultant writer and trainer. He is also associate trainer for Bell and Visiting Lecturer – Media and Technology – at the University of Westminster. He has been involved in ELT for more than 20 years and over the past ten has specialised in the use of technology for teacher development. He has worked on a wide range of projects for educational organisations including the British Council in the UK, Morocco and Venezuela, the Open University, Cambridge ESOL, Oxford House TEFL and IATEFL. He publishes a number of free blogs including Nik's Learning technology blog http://nikpeachey.blogspot.com/ and has published a free e-book *Web 2.0 Tools for Teachers*. www.scribd.com/doc/19576895/Web-20-Tools-for-Teachers which has been accessed more than 100,000 times.

George Pickering is an educational coach, trainer and consultant, who has delivered talks and consultancies in over 60 different countries. He is a tutor on the International Diploma in Language Teaching Management and is the academic director of the English UK Diploma in English Language Teaching Management. George has coached senior managers in a range of international and educational contexts. He is an inspector of language schools for the British Council in the UK (Accreditation UK). George is a trustee of IATEFL.

Edward Russell (MA TESOL and Teacher Education) is now a teacher trainer working for the British Council Teacher Development Centre in Singapore. Originally from England, he has been working for ten years in the field of TESOL and has been overseas in a variety of places for most of the last eight. He is interested in giving feedback, skilled helping, psychology and applications of technology in language education. For his MA dissertation he studied his period of transition from teacher to teacher trainer, while in Palestine. He hopes to work as an educator, of sorts, on all continents in his lifetime.

Alexander Sokol, PhD, is principal developer of the Thinking Approach (TA) to language teaching and learning, a teacher educator and a course designer. Alexander taught English at a secondary level for 13 years, including teaching blended courses. His co-writers for this paper are Edgar Lasevich, Renata Jonina and Marija Dobrovolska-Stoian. All of the authors of this paper are collaborating on developing learning tools, materials and curricula for an integrated development of language and thinking skills of learners. The approach is being used in more than ten European countries and the materials are available in various languages. The team is also involved in developing teacher education programmes on teaching thinking and bringing the culture of thinking in work of various organisations. Detailed information on all these projects can be found at www.ta-group.eu

Brian Tomlinson is a Visiting Professor at Leeds Metropolitan University and a TESOL Professor at Anaheim University. He has worked as a teacher, teacher trainer, curriculum developer, football coach and university academic in Indonesia, Japan, Nigeria, Oman, Singapore, UK, Vanuatu and Zambia and has given presentations in over 60 countries. In 1993 he founded MATSDA (the international Materials Development Association) and he is now President of the association. His many publications include *Discover English* (with Rod Bolitho); *Openings; Materials Development in Language Teaching; Developing Materials for Language Teaching; Research for Materials Development in Language Learning* (with Hitomi Masuhara) and *Applied Linguistics and Materials Development*.

Ron White is former Director of the Centre for Applied Language Studies, the University of Reading, UK, Ron White has 30 years' experience of teaching and managing in Britain, the Pacific and Japan. He has worked as a consultant for Cambridge ESOL, and was involved in the initial development of the TKT (Teaching Knowledge Test) and in the revision of the DELTA. He is co-author of *From Teacher to Manager*, and has been a trainer on the International Diploma in Language Teaching Management since its inception.

Claire Whittaker is the Head of Learning and Teaching at Bell and is based in Cambridge. For a number of years she worked overseas with the British Council as a teacher, teacher trainer and project manager in Bosnia and Herzegovina, Poland, Tajikistan, Ukraine and Uzbekistan. She has also consulted on ELT projects in Kazakhstan, Kyrgyzstan, Serbia and Nigeria. She is a member of the British Council's English Language Advisory Group and holds a Doctor of Education (EdD) in Teaching English to Speakers of Other Languages from the University of Exeter.